MUSIC EXPRESS

MUSIC EXPRESS

THE RISE, FALL & RESURRECTION OF CANADA'S MUSIC MAGAZINE

BY KEITH SHARP

FOREWORD BY ALAN FREW OF GLASS TIGER

DUNDURN

TORONTO

Editor: Michael Melgaard
Design: Courtney Horner
Printer: Webcom

Library and Archives Canada Cataloguing in Publication

Sharp, Keith, author
     Music express : the rise, fall & resurrection of Canada's music magazine / author, Keith Sharp ; foreword by Alan Frew.

Issued in print and electronic formats.
ISBN 978-1-4597-2194-4

     1. Music express (Willowdale, Ont.). 2. Music--Periodicals--History. 3. Musical criticism--Canada--History. I. Title.

ML3484.S532 2014   782.42164   C2013-908374-X
                                              C2013-908375-8

1   2   3   4   5   18   17   16   15   14

 Conseil des Arts   Canada Council
du Canada   for the Arts
 Canada
 ONTARIO ARTS COUNCIL
CONSEIL DES ARTS DE L'ONTARIO

We acknowledge the support of the **Canada Council for the Arts** and the **Ontario Arts Council** for our publishing program. We also acknowledge the financial support of the **Government of Canada** through the **Canada Book Fund** and **Livres Canada Books**, and the **Government of Ontario** through the **Ontario Book Publishing Tax Credit** and the **Ontario Media Development Corporation**.

Care has been taken to trace the ownership of copyright material used in this book. The author and the publisher welcome any information enabling them to rectify any references or credits in subsequent editions.

J. Kirk Howard, President

The publisher is not responsible for websites or their content unless they are owned by the publisher.

Printed and bound in Canada.

Cover design by Agency 71 Inc., www.agency71.com

Visit us at
Dundurn.com | @dundurnpress
Facebook.com/dundurnpress | Pinterest.com/Dundurnpress

Dundurn   Gazelle Book Services Limited   Dundurn
3 Church Street, Suite 500   White Cross Mills   2250 Military Road
Toronto, Ontario, Canada   High Town, Lancaster, England   Tonawanda, NY
M5E 1M2   LA1 4XS   U.S.A. 14150

This book is dedicated to the memory of my beloved parents,
Richard and Lily Sharp, who both passed away recently.
My mom died July 4, 2009, and my dad passed away September 12, 2012.

Both were energetic people who enjoyed a great love for life.
Both were accomplished ballroom dancers who married young and
loved the contemporary music of their day — Elvis Presley,
Frankie Laine, Johnnie Ray … and yes, The Beatles.

They would have been proud of this book
and of my achievement in completing this project.

TABLE OF CONTENTS

FOREWORD

BY ALAN FREW (GLASS TIGER)

I was recently purging the contents of my office when I came across several items that one might label "memorabilia." Now of course in this day and age, memorabilia has become synonymous with items that tend to have great "collectable" and/or monetary value. Particularly to those who are so inclined to wheel and deal in such things.

Mostly of great interest and value seem to be items that had previously belonged to the rich and famous of Hollywood, politics, sports, and, of course, rock 'n' roll. For instance, someone at this very moment may own a droplet of Keith Richards's blood from his now famous "Swiss Transfusions" of the seventies; or perhaps it's one of Elton John's many toupees from a time just prior to the miracle of "follicle reassignment;" maybe, in fact, it's something much simpler — like the peas and carrots that Slash threw up backstage in Helsinki just prior to the Guns N' Roses concert being cancelled due to the fact that Axl wasn't in Helsinki!

The value of memorabilia, however, may have little or nothing to do with its monetary status, qualifying in fact merely as a souvenir, memento, or a treasured little keepsake. The objects only real significance is the psychological connection the possessor has with it as a symbol of his or her past experience. This, ladies and gentlemen, was precisely the type of memorabilia I found that day in my office.

So you may ask, What did you discover?

No, it wasn't the pink (I'll never admit it) T-shirt from Glass Tiger's old "Someday" video of 1987. Nor was it the enormous white plastic sunglasses from the horrible American "Don't Forget Me (When I'm

Gone)" reshoot video of a previously horrible Canadian version by the same name. No, it wasn't either of those.

It was in fact a copy of the very first *Music Express* magazine that I or Glass Tiger ever appeared in. That, ladies and gents, is indeed a symbol of past experience and I will never part with it. When I hold it and take a look through its pages, I get the exact same feelings I get when I hear an old friend playing on the radio. Like say, "Maggie Mae," "Every Breath You Take," "Simply the Best," or, yes, even "Don't Forget Me (When I'm Gone)." I see the sights, I still hear the sounds, I smell the aromas, and I savour the tastes of great music and of great times.

No magazine symbolized those times greater than *Music Express*. Yes indeed, if the music symbolized an old friend, then by the same token, *Music Express* symbolized "family."

A great big musical family!

Now, for the record, I'd like to be able to say, "I remember it well." However, what I need to say is, "I remember it well, but not as well as Keith."

I heard once that music is the true international language of the world. In his book, Keith has also given it a name, a place, a time, and a date.

Alan Frew
April 2012

MUSIC EXPRESS:
THE RISE AND FALL OF
A CANDIAN MUSIC ICON

I boarded an Air Canada flight out of Toronto in May 2004. My destination: the Music West Conference in Vancouver. It was my annual trek to attend that gathering of nightclub showcases and music industry conferences, modelled on more successful events like SXSW in Austin, Texas, and Toronto's own NXNE festival.

To be honest, I don't know why I bothered going. Few new bands or artists ever get discovered at these things, and attendance from out-of-town industry delegates had dropped off drastically in recent years. The few conferences that were actually staged usually featured guest speakers who didn't believe their own verbiage. Still, it was a good chance to touch base with key West Coast industry types, like top managers Bruce Allen and Sam Feldman, and musician mates like The Payola$ singer Paul Hyde and Trooper front man Ra McGuire (who could usually be found hanging around the clubs), while also executing store checks for my magazine, *Access*.

Settling into my aisle seat for the four-hour flight, I was joined by a young man who slid across me and slumped into the window seat. He introduced himself as Zack Werner, a Toronto-based entertainment lawyer representing female vocalist Esthero. He was also heading out to the festival to press flesh with industry contacts. Werner would later become one of four judges on *Canadian Idol*, but on that day, Zack was more interested in me.

I introduced myself as Keith Sharp, publisher of *Access*, and mentioned that I had been editor-in-chief of *Music Express*, Canada's leading music magazine from the time of its Calgary birth in 1976 to its unfortunate demise in 1993. It was that snippet of information that triggered a reaction from him. "*Music Express*! I loved that magazine, I grew up reading it. Really loved those regional sections."

What followed was an incessant conversation in which we talked about our favourite Canadian artists and records, the state of the domestic industry, and, in particular, the international success achieved by *Music Express* during a heady three-and-a-half-year period (1986–90) when *ME* was the official in-store magazine of the Minneapolis-based Musicland/Sam Goody chain, as well being distributed all over Great Britain and Australia, courtesy of Gordon and Gotch, a multi-national magazine distribution company.

As Zack deplaned, he looked at me and said, "You know, Keith, you should write a book about that stuff."

Zack Werner wasn't the first person to suggest I write a book about those *Music Express* years. Doug Wong, a good friend and survivor of my early Calgary days, who started his career as a record-studio owner and owner of such independent record labels as Mootown Records, was forever pestering me about documenting my past. He even gave me a box full of old copies of the mag. "There's history in this box," he said, noting my disbelief at his comments.

The reality is that I never felt a book about a Canadian music magazine was that interesting. As a Manchester England–born sports journalist who progressed into music-magazine publishing, I had always been a fan of British and American music magazines, and had tried to mirror those publications with *Music Express*. Yet I never really believed your average Canadian music fan would find a book about Canadian music from a magazine's standpoint that interesting. Yes, I have read books about The Guess Who, Trooper, Neil Young, Celine Dion, and even Greg Godovitz's *Trouble With My Amp* (one of the better efforts), but I felt you had to be a hard-core fan to actually want to read those books.

Then there was the additional handicap of my not having kept many records from a period that goes back all the way to October 1976. When *Music Express* was dissolved into a new magazine called *Impact* in September 1993 (and I was subsequently fired by the new owner), all the files, and even the one remaining copy of the debut issue of *Alberta Music Express,* were destroyed.

Without this information, writing a book about *Music Express* didn't seem feasible. And who had the time? I had restarted my magazine publishing career with *Access* (launched June 1994) and, immersing every waking minute in this operation, I never felt I had the time (or the inclination) to chronicle past events.

Yet over the years since my meeting with Zack, I have found myself reflecting on past memories with old colleagues and members of the bands I interviewed (many still performing), and jotting down dates, names, and contacts. Rereading the back issues had me marvelling at some of the achievements our tiny staff did manage, and I decided that, yes, there may indeed be some historical interest in the domestic and international music scene of the 1970s and 1980s as told through the eyes of *Music Express.*

The magazine was originally launched as a one-off in Calgary, Alberta (October 1976), by a twenty-three-year-old sportswriter from the *Calgary Herald. Alberta Music Express* expanded, first as a tabloid chronicling Western Canada's music confederacy, and then, after I joined forces with Conny "The Dragon Lady" Kunz in 1978, we moved to Toronto in February 1980 to establish *Music Express* as "The Pulse of Canadian Music."

What followed was thirteen more years of promoting the Canadian music scene from our Toronto base, publishing a magazine that featured star performers, aided in the creation of new artists, and eventually expanded to the United States, the United Kingdom, and Australia. Our zenith was the 1.3-million-copy print run of our October/November 1987 issue (with the late Michael Jackson on the cover), a domestic print record for a Canadian magazine that still stands to this day.

And, of course, there was the decline. Losing our distribution agreement with Musicland/Sam Goody in 1990, struggling on with alternative U.S. circulation, and being taken over by new ownership in 1992. Then, having the magazine's name changed to *Soundcan,* then *Impact,* before I was fired in early 1993 — but I bounced back to launch a new magazine, *Access,* which celebrated its one-hundredth issue anniversary as a bi-monthly in September/October 2009.

Over the course of this book, I will reminisce about the fun and excitement of touring the world with major (and not so major) artists, I'll go behind the scenes of a then-vibrant music scene, and introduce you to the industry's major characters and stars — while avoiding as many lawsuits as possible!

In all cases, I have strived to record correct dates and names. But if I happen to be off by a month or two or forget the odd name, I ask for your forgiveness.

Trust you enjoy the trip.

Keith Sharp
Toronto
October 20, 2013

1

ANKLE DEEP
IN COW MANURE!

Truth is, the launch of *Alberta Music Express* (as *Music Express* was originally titled) was purely an act of revenge against my then employers, the *Calgary Herald*.

Rolling into the summer of 1976, starting a music magazine was the last thought on my mind. Having joined the *Herald*'s sports department at the age on nineteen in March 1972, straight out of Cambrian College, North Bay (now called Canadore), I was happily settling into a career as a junior sportswriter on a six-man staff, of which the next youngest member was forty-two years old. This meant that while the other five members all had their established beats (the Calgary Stampeders (CFL), Calgary Centennials (Junior A Hockey), varsity sports, golf, baseball), I was assigned a whole range of minor sports, from high-school games to Junior A Tier Two hockey. I was also given all the British sports (soccer, rugby, cricket), which reflected my English heritage.

In my four short years with the paper I had covered the 1975 Calgary Grey Cup Final (Montreal 9, Edmonton 8) — at minus fifteen degrees it seemed like the coldest final ever! — spent two weeks in Czechoslovakia with the Calgary Spurs Midget Hockey team in 1976, and established a reputation as a young writer willing to hustle for a story. But in the summer of 1976, I took the first steps that would eventually lead me to toss all of this away.

One of the beats that went with the territory of being a rookie writer was the Calgary Stampede. You are no doubt aware that the Stampede is a famous rodeo and entertainment festival staged in Calgary during the first ten days of each July. To tourists and professional rodeo athletes alike, the Stampede is a spectacle of rodeo events: chuckwagon races, parades, pancake breakfasts, and major rock stars performing each evening at the Stampede Grandstand. Being such a major news event, the *Herald* sports department was obliged to provide extensive coverage — which meant yours truly got stuck with this gig four years running.

Trust me, there is nothing more gruelling than trudging through cow and horse crap for ten straight days, then interviewing some cowboy about his performance on a bull or a stallion, only to hear that his score had just been beat by someone else, thus rendering the interview irrelevant. By the time 1975 came around, I was looking for a new challenge — which, surprisingly, came from the *Herald's* entertainment department.

Now you need to know that the resident music critic at the *Herald* at the time of my arrival was a chap called Eugene Chadbourne. Eugene was a talented jazz-fusion guitarist, but he totally hated pop music and felt that actually interviewing musicians was beneath him, which made him an odd choice for the job as the *Herald's* music reviewer!

Chatting with Eugene during lunch breaks in the *Herald* cafeteria, I was able to score a few free LPs off him to review in the weekend entertainment section. My first break into music reporting came when Shelly Siegel, owner of Vancouver-based Mushroom Records, called Chadbourne to ask if he was interested in interviewing the label's debut band Heart, who were opening for ZZ Top at The Corral.

This was March 1975. Chadbourne (as usual) passed on the interview, but did suggest I tackle it. I jumped at the chance to meet Shelly and the Wilson sisters, Anne and Nancy, at the Crowne Plaza Hotel (now called the Marriot). It was my first ever music interview and Heart had an amazing story to tell. Band member Mike Fisher had dodged the draft, moving from Seattle to Vancouver, and Anne Wilson chased after him. They were joined by Roger Fisher and Anne's sister Nancy, the group that would form the nucleus of Heart. I was particularly impressed that Siegel funded the band out of his own pocket. I found the Wilsons to be very engaging (and both stunningly attractive), and their debut LP, *Dreamboat Annie*, would go on to be a classic rock album. And, shock of all shocks, the *Herald* actually ran a positive music feature in its pages — an unusual occurrence at the time.

When I was asked to review a concert by English band Strawbs (with Calgarian Gaye Delorme opening) soon after, the local record industry started taking note. What was this? Another positive review in the *Herald*? What the hell was going on? Suddenly the *Herald* switchboard was receiving calls from record companies asking for Keith Sharp — and were surprised to have their calls directed to the sports department.

Entertainment editor Pat Tivy wasn't too thrilled about these calls. As the 1976 Stampede approached, a call came through from Mel Shaw, the manager of Calgary-based rock band The Stampeders, suggesting the *Herald* run a major feature on his band. The request was passed on to me, and I jumped at the chance. Here was my opportunity to tackle an interesting story idea while avoiding that dreaded rodeo routine.

So there I was, a couple of days before the band's Thursday concert, hanging out with Stampeders Rich Dodson, Ronnie King, and Kim Berly at their Calgary rehearsals, getting the full lowdown on their rags-to-riches story. I banged off what was supposed to be a major, two-page feature scheduled to run in the Saturday entertainment-magazine insert, two days after the band's scheduled performance. But there was a problem!

Brian Brennan had taken over the music beat from Chadbourne, and he wrote a review of the Thursday night concert that totally trashed the band. Now imagine Bruce Springsteen performing in New Jersey and being ripped apart by the local press. It was a hometown gig! It just doesn't happen. But it did in Calgary! Based on the severity of the review, Tivy decided it wouldn't look right to trash The Stampeders in one edition and then rave about them in the next issue. He decided to pull my feature out of the Saturday edition.

I wasn't in the office that morning, but when I dropped by in the afternoon to pick up my copy of the paper, I could see by the faces in the entertainment department something was wrong, even before I realized my feature was missing from the magazine.

Hal Walker, my sports editor, got to me first. He explained the entertainment editor's rationale and asked me not to be too upset. Upset! I went bloody ballistic! Even worse, the entertainment department asked me to call Mel Shaw and explain their logic in pulling the piece. Despite having seen the hatchet job Brennan had done on The Stampeders' concert performance, Shaw was quite gracious; he knew it wasn't my fault. But I wasn't willing to drop the matter.

Now the *Calgary Herald* was the western bureau head office of a national news gathering source called the Canadian Press, and as a member of this service, the *Herald* was obliged to contribute content. So I took my Stampeders story over to the local bureau chief of the CP and asked her to service the entire country with my feature.

Two weeks later she came back to me and reported that my story had run in fourteen major Canadian newspapers. The only Canadian paper that didn't run the story was the *Calgary Herald*! At that moment, without any pre-planning or forethought, I decided I was going to print that Stampeders' story in a Calgary newspaper. Even if I had to publish it myself!

2

A MUSIC
MAG IS BORN

To say there was no pre-planning involved would be an understatement. I never thought of *Alberta Music Express* as being an ongoing entity. I had a very nice, well-paying job covering sports at the *Calgary Herald,* and any music enterprise was intended to be purely a sideline operation. Still, I received enough encouragement to think launching a music magazine could be a viable hobby.

The Canadian music scene in 1976 was ripe for eruption. Newly introduced Canadian Radio-television Telecommunications Commission (CRTC) regulations meant radio stations had to play at least 30 percent Canadian content. Branch offices of American record companies were launching in Toronto and Montreal, with secondary offices stretching out to all the major provinces. Canadian independent record labels were sprouting up all over the country and encouraged domestic artists to head into the studios.

From July until October 1976 I interviewed everyone who travelled through Alberta, with an eye toward generating content for my first issue. I talked to Randy Bachman, Trooper, Olivia Newton-John, The Bay City Rollers, Al Martino, The Statler Brothers, and Bobby Bare, and I even travelled to Edmonton to catch The Who. A live shot of Roger Daltrey on stage with the band's innovative laser beams from that show was featured on our debut cover. The photograph was taken by Ian Mark, who had found out about the impending launch of *AME* via Sheldon Wiebe, a mutual friend of ours who ran the Opus 69 record shop in Calgary. Ian proved to be invaluable for my early issues, shooting some sensational shots of The Who, Queen, KISS, and others, as well as photographing me interviewing them.

I was supposed to get an interview with either Roger Daltrey or Pete Townshend for that debut issue, with the chat to be conducted at the brand new Edmonton Plaza Hotel after the gig. The show itself was spectacular, especially with all the laser effects, but when I went backstage it was obvious trouble was brewing. Drummer Keith Moon had gone berserk in the dressing room. He had embedded a bunch of chairs upside down into the ceiling tiles and was running around with no pants on, literally "mooning" everyone in sight.

Back at the hotel, he destroyed his suite, resulting in the hotel banning all rock bands from the facility in the immediate future. Suffice to say, the rest of the band were in no mood to talk, so we had to settle for some great live shots taken by Mark and a concert review.

Alberta Music Express was launched the first week of October 1976 without much fanfare. Joe Thompson, local manager for the Kelly's record store chain, who had been frustrated in his efforts to promote local music, had agreed to bag-stuff copies of the mag in his stores as a giveaway to his customers. This guaranteed circulation in Calgary, Edmonton, Lethbridge, Red Deer, and Medicine Hat. The first issue went out with the Daltrey cover and my feature on The Stampeders finally available for the hometown audience.

Alberta Music Express was designed like the British music tabloids — in fact, I derived the name from the famous British *New Musical Express* — with a few key stories on the front, the obligatory album and concert reviews, and a section for local concert listings. For that first issue, CKXL DJ Tommy Tompkins contributed a column plus an interview with Graham Nash, the *Edmonton Journal's* Joe Sornberger featured an Edmonton column and interviewed Nazareth, while Mike Rogers supplied a Lethbridge column (I guess we couldn't find anyone in Red Deer or Medicine Hat!). But the rest of the book was written by yours truly under the guise of a number of false by-lines.

I had no investment cash on hand for my new venture, and had no thought beyond that first issue. I was quite shocked when I had to pay the printers up front; I maxed out my credit card to fund that first issue. I printed about ten thousand copies, and according to Thompson the mag was eagerly snatched up at Kelly's. I did the rounds and dropped off copies at all the local record company offices where the book was enthusiastically received.

All the local industry reps gave *Alberta Music Express* a strong endorsement. They also encouraged me to send copies to music reps in Toronto and Montreal, and supplied me with the names of contacts. Shortly after *AME* debuted, I received a phone call from Terry Magee at Columbia Records in Toronto. "Hey, Keith received your first issue of *AME*. Good stuff. When's the next one coming out?"

"Next one? Jeez, you mean I have to do this again?" said I, having not even considered printing a second issue.

Shortly after, I received a call from Lou Blair at the Calgary's Refinery nightclub saying he wanted to meet to discuss a potential investment in the magazine. The Refinery was *the* focal point for our supposed music confederacy in Calgary. It was a meeting place for key industry figures who provided encouragement for me to push forward with the magazine. There was booking agent Greg Thomas, who brought in a slew of developing local and West Coast bands (Streetheart, Trooper, Harlequin, The Pumps) to play the venue; David Horodezky, the principal Alberta concert promoter for larger acts; Bryan Tucker, Western Canada manager for Columbia Records, a major supporter of local talent; and Don Boas, manager of local group Fosterchild.

I showed up for the meeting to discuss my future plans and was introduced to Blair's accountant, a Dutch lady called Conny Kunz, who sat in on the sessions. He asked for financial details, passed the information to Kunz, and said he'd get back to me. As I got up to leave, Conny gave me a nod, indicating she wanted to continue the conversation.

We went next door to this Mexican restaurant (Primos), and over a plate of tacos Conny advised me she didn't think Blair was serious about investing and that I should be looking at other options. She also hinted that her services might be one of those options.

Although the magazine was still without funding, I kept tapping into my credit card and utilized funds from my *Calgary Herald* paycheque to keep *AME* alive. If I needed incentive to continue the book, I found it when Dave Horodezky's Brimstone Productions announced they were bringing Queen back to town (for two nights, March 16–17, 1977) on their Day at The Races tour, with Thin Lizzy opening. I gathered up my photographer and went for both nights. It was at the second night's show that I found out my continued association with the *Herald* was not without its perils.

The paper had been negative about the first night's show, and although the reviewer, Brian Brennan, had reluctantly complimented Queen, he absolutely shredded Thin Lizzy. Backstage before the second show, I was chatting with the promoter and somehow my connection with the *Herald* was mentioned. Next thing I know, Thin Lizzy vocalist Phil Lynott is behind me and throttling me with his bare hands. "So you work for the fooking *Calgary Herald*, you fookin' bastard," he screamed.

"Sports department," gasped I, on the verge of turning blue and passing out.

"Oh sorry mate, I thought you were that fookin' Brian Brennan," said Lynott, apologizing profusely.

"No worries," said I, and he took me back to meet the band where we, of course, talked football and I plugged my magazine.

Ian Mark had brought along a stack of live shots he had taken of Queen on the first night. We handed them over to the band's tour manager and he disappeared inside the dressing room. A few minutes later, he re-emerged and said the band was impressed with the shots and wanted to meet us. Next thing I know, Ian and I are sitting next to Freddie Mercury, Brian May, Roger Taylor, and John Deacon, and they are raving about the photos. If I had any doubts I was in the wrong business, meeting Queen sealed my fate.

Despite my excitement, the future of *AME* was in doubt after I received news from Conny that Blair had passed on any financial investment. I got the word May 1, the day CJAY-FM was launched as Calgary's hot new radio station. I attended the event convinced *AME* was past tense. For the record, Blair acknowledged he decided to decline investing in *AME* (he was also launching a booking agency with Dean Cross and Tim Contini at the time). However, he booked the back cover of the magazine for his Refinery club as a show of support, so maybe there was hope after all. After the event, I was further cheered by a phone call from Terry Magee at Columbia in Toronto; Heart was headlining a major concert in Seattle and he invited me to catch the show and interview the band for the cover of my next issue.

Convinced now there would be a next issue, I somehow wrangled the time off from the *Herald* and flew out to Seattle. I met Terry at the airport and spent an amazing warm May afternoon at the Seattle football stadium (in the shadows of the famous Space Needle). With an all-access pass, I utilized the event to interview the opening acts. Foreigner was making their U.S. debut by launching their self-titled album, and I also chatted with Stephen Bishop and the initial seven-piece Prism lineup (starring drummer Rodney Higgs a.k.a. Bryan Adams's song writing partner Jim Vallance, and future top producer Bruce Fairbairn).

Heart was amazing live and after the concert the whole band gathered backstage for interviews with a number of journalists, including Tom Harrison from the *Georgia Straight* and the *Toronto Sun*'s Wilder Penfield III. Dee Lippingwell took some stunning shots of the band silhouetted against the fading light. I flew back from Seattle determined more than ever to make *Alberta Music Express* successful, yet still keep my hands clean at the *Herald*.

I executed a series of major interviews during the summer and fall of 1977, the most memorable being with KISS. I have always found KISS (especially Gene Simmons) to be accessible for interviews, going back to that first interview in the summer of 1977. The band was executing a major tour of Western Canada, with the colourful Cheap Trick opening. I got help from PolyGram's Ken Graydon, who secured the interview, and I travelled to Lethbridge to catch the band open the city's brand new Sportsplex Arena on July 28. There are no words to describe vintage KISS. Their live show was simply unbeatable. The pyrotechnics, Simmons blowing flames and spitting blood, Peter Criss's hydraulic drum kit shaped like a dragon's head that spewed flames during their climactic encore. It was all incredible.

On July 31, the day of the first Calgary gig, I went to the Calgary Inn, and knocked on the door of the band's road manager. "Oh you'll find Gene in the coffee shop," said he, pointing down the hallway. As I walked toward the coffee shop it dawned on me: I didn't know what Gene Simmons looked like! It wasn't a problem though. One table was occupied by two elderly ladies drinking afternoon tea, and the other by a tall guy dressed in black leather with a silver dollar sign on his boots. Er! I think that's him.

Simmons proved to be a colourful and informative interview. He told me of the band's early gigs in Calgary at SAIT (Southern Alberta Institute of Technology) when their Kabuki makeup was greeted with heckles and derision, and how they created their KISS army after the success of their *Alive* album. The interview went so well he invited me back the band's hotel rooms where he insisted I also talk to drummer Peter Criss and guitarist Ace Frehley. I was surprised Criss, sans makeup, looked quite old with his greying hair, but he gave me a great insight into how a hard-rock band was able to top the charts with a ballad, "Beth." Frehley, sans makeup, boasted the sharp high cheekboned features of a Native American and wasn't particularly coherent. Overall, though, it was quite a revealing look at such a superstar unit.

3

CANADA ROCKS!

The late 1970s was the perfect time for my fledgling magazine to find its legs. Within Canada, the music industry was exploding. New albums and new bands were arriving daily and growth was evident right across the country. Toronto led the way with the likes of hard rock bands like Rush, Triumph, Max Webster, Goddo, and Moxy, the versatility of Lighthouse, plus the True North folk scene powered by Bruce Cockburn, Dan Hill, and Murray McLauchlan. Not to mention the still influential veterans Gordon Lightfoot and Anne Murray.

Montreal had Mahogany Rush, April Wine, Gino Vannelli, Michel Pagliaro, Walter Zwol, Patsy Gallant, and a new French Canadian movement around Beau Dommage, Harmonium, and Sudbury Ontario's Cano. Ottawa claimed Five Man Electrical Band and The Cooper Brothers. Even the East Coast boasted a distinctive blues scene with Sam Moon, Matt Minglewood, and Dutch Mason leaving their mark, along with Oakley, Molly Olliver, Figgy Duff, and The Wonderful Grand Band.

Out West, the Vancouver-based management tandem of Bruce Allen and Sam Feldman broke ground with Bachman-Turner Overdrive, Prism, and Trooper, and soon Bryan Adams and Loverboy would be added to Allen's stable of acts. The Poppy Family's Susan and Terry Jacks, Stonebolt, Chilliwack, Valdy, Bim, The Hometown Band, Powder Blues, and Doug & the Slugs also made their mark, while Nick Gilder's Sweeney Todd dominated the charts with No. 1 single "Roxy Roller," and Vancouver's Mushroom label spawned Seattle immigrants Heart and former Montreal native Jerry Doucette.

"Trooper was coming up as the Canadian music scene was beginning to find its legs," reflected the band's lead vocalist, Ra McGuire. "The international music industry was flourishing and a lot of that power, money, and energy was filtering into Canada. As we went from record to record, we could feel not just our own career growing, but the entire Canadian industry was taking shape."

Alberta boasted Hammersmith, a band formerly managed by Bruce Allen; Fosterchild, signed with Columbia Records; and Edmonton's One Horse Blue launched on Wes Dakus's Vera Cruz label. Burton Cummings still ruled the Prairies, and the region also spawned Streetheart, Queen City Kids, Crowcuss, Kick Axe, and Harlequin. All these acts recorded albums and most received encouragement from local radio airplay and retail sales awareness.

What really powered Canada's domestic music movement in the mid-seventies were Toronto concert promoters Michael Cohl and Bill Ballard's Concert Productions International (CPI), which linked up with Montreal's Donald Tarelton's DKD Productions and Norm Perry's Perryscope Productions in Vancouver to create a national touring circuit.

Taking top Canadian bands like April Wine, Rush, Triumph, Chilliwack, Trooper, The Stampeders, and Lighthouse, this triumvirate of promoters executed coast-to-coast concert tours that hit all the small arenas as well as the larger venues like Vanocuver's Pacific Coliseum, Toronto's Maple Leaf Gardens, and Montreal's Forum. This personal exposure created a national fan base, developed radio airplay awareness, and stimulated record sales.

The beginnings of this alliance had taken place a few years earlier, at a time when Martin Onrot and John Brower were the chief Toronto-based concert promoters. A young Ottawa transplant, Michael Cohl, was trying his hand at concert promotion in Toronto, and after a few failed attempts, lucked out when he agreed to promote Pink Floyd at Maple Leaf Gardens when Onrot was only prepared to offer them Massey Hall. Cohl soon became a force in concert production. This was strengthened when he joined forces with Bill Ballard, the son of the owner of Maple Leaf Gardens, to form Concert Promotions International.

Ballard Senior had recognized that Maple Leaf Gardens was the largest concert facility in Canada, and by having his son join forces with Cohl he was able to turn a large profit on the building through an exclusive concert promotion agreement. After that, CPI became a powerhouse.

Their only real competition came from David Horodezky's Calgary-based Brimstone Productions, which controlled Alberta and the Prairies. Horodezky had developed loyal clients in Supertramp, Queen, Rod Stewart, and the Dire Straits, to name a few. "I didn't have much if anything to do with CPI/DKD and Perryscope," noted Horodezky. "I kept busy developing my own acts and we pretty well owned Alberta through to Winnipeg."

CPI/DKD's main Alberta contact was Ron Sakamoto, who ran his Gold & Gold Company from Lethbridge and acted as their main connection whilst avoiding a direct clash with Horodezky's Calgary-based operation. He emerged as a major national country music promoter, and owned the distinction of booking Shania Twain's first North American tour.

Chris Dobbin's Springfield Productions, also based in Calgary, attracted his share of concerts throughout Alberta and the Prairies, including concerts at Calgary's McMahon Stadium and Edmonton's Commonwealth Stadium for the Eagles and Boz Scaggs. With this infrastructure in place, Canada was becoming a priority for international acts, who often had domestic talent open for them.

In 1978 the Commonwealth games were to be held in Edmonton. The *Herald* assigned me to be the sports reporter for the event, and I knew continuing *AME* would be a challenge as the weeklong event and the month leading up to it would be the primary focus of my summer.

I was still being inundated by calls to cover bands. One such request was from Columbia. They wanted me to fly to Toronto to witness the debut of the label's new band Zon, who were launching their *Astral Projector* album. I didn't know anything about the band, but if a label was prepared to fly me to Toronto and put me up in the Westin Hotel (now the Hilton) for two nights, I reasoned they must be good.

At Zon's debut, their front man, Denton Young, was wearing a Peter Gabriel–type mask and the band noodled with these electronic arrangements. Not exactly the next coming of Led Zeppelin. Three songs in, some of the audience started to head for the buffet table. Obviously, things weren't going well for the band. As Zon concluded a seemingly abbreviated set they were met with a polite ripple of applause, but nothing that suggested a national media launch had been warranted.

The following afternoon, I met the band at Columbia Records and Young was obviously upset with their performance. "It was too early for us to do a show like that," he complained. "To play in front of an industry audience who don't know who we are was crazy. Probably did more damage than good." *Astral Projector* actually ended up doing okay. The band were nominated for a Most Promising Group of the Year Juno, and toured with Styx and Foreigner, before being dropped from the label after their follow-up, *Back Down To Earth,* failed to generate sufficient interest.

While in Toronto for the Zon gig, I got in touch with Greg Godovitz of the band Goddo, who I'd previously interviewed for *AME* (which earned me a thank you in the album credits). He invited me to their concert at the popular Knob Hill Tavern (located in suburban Scarborough) and said he would get his label, PolyGram, to arrange for me to interview him for the new album.

We had a pleasant chat about his roots in his first band, Fludd, and Goddo's struggles to be treated seriously by national radio. During lunch the PolyGram press agent handed him the wine list to order a bottle. Godovitz placed the order and the wine steward walked away. "Excuse me," said the press agent. "Can I see what he just ordered?" The wine steward noted Godovitz had just ordered a seventy-dollar bottle of wine. "I don't think so," said she. "I think we'll have the fifteen-dollar bottle." Godovitz and I became solid friends over the years and it is one of Canadian music's great mysteries why Goddo never broke out internationally. They were, and still are, one of this country's most entertaining live acts.

Back in Calgary I decided to take Conny Kunz up on her offer of a partnership. When I announced this to my wife Dawn, it was received with cold indifference. Dawn knew I had a secure job working at the *Herald*, and that any move to work full time with Conny would potentially jeopardize my future. At my end, I saw this as a chance to maintain the magazine while still putting time in at the *Herald*. I was drawn into an emotional tug-of-war. Dawn was dead set against me pursuing the book while Conny provided me with the emotional support to push forward. In the end, Conny won out!

Conny negotiated office space for us at Northern Lights and Sound, 455 Manitou Road, just off the Blackfoot Trail in the South East industrial area of the city. In return for her doing their book keeping, Northern, owned by Brent Rawlinson, offered us the office portion of the building. The warehouse portion contained one of the region's most comprehensive sound and lights systems that were used by touring bands.

Especially during the winter months, bands coming from Vancouver and touring east would not chance hauling their equipment across the treacherous Rogers Pass. Instead, they picked up their sound systems at Northern Lights, did their tour of Saskatchewan or whatever, and dropped off Northern's gear on the way back home. When the bands who rented the equipment returned it to the warehouse, they would often set up their gear and perform an impromptu midnight concert for the local industry. These concerts proved very popular.

One night Rawlinson informed us a band called Sweeney Todd were going to perform at the office. I was aware they had enjoyed great success with "Roxy Roller" off their first album in 1976, but lead singer Nick Gilder and guitarist Jim McCulloch had been signed by Chrysalis shortly afterwards. Without a singer, manager/producer Martin Shaer released two more versions of the hit with Clark Booth, and later Bryan Guy Adams, singing over the original bed track.

The band was touring on the strength of their second album, *If Wishes Were Horses,* when they rolled into Northern Lights. Conny and I showed up, more to protect our stuff than to see the band, and when we arrived at the office we noticed this young kid hovering around our space. Conny probably said something smartass like, "Isn't it past your bedtime young man?" He announced he was Bryan Guy Adams, singer with the band. To prove it, he pointed to a poster on the wall. Sure enough, there was this seventeen-year-old kid sporting a distinct page-boy haircut, photographed under a gas light with the rest of the band and a couple of tarty young ladies.

He told us he had written a couple of tracks on the new record and had been a huge Sweeney Todd fan before joining the group. He also gave us some background about being born in Kingston, Ontario, to British parents, and how he was now living with his mother and brother Bruce in Vancouver. I've got to say I was quite impressed with his set, and I remember calling our Vancouver writer Tom Harrison to tell him about Bryan. "Yes, I know about Bryan," reported Harrison. "I think he's gone back to school but I know he's writing songs for Prism. Kid's definitely got talent."

Conny proved to be a woman of many talents. Aside from keeping track of the books, she started to design the magazine. Sometimes she worked at our office, but the lack of space at this facility often meant she had to improvise in her kitchen at home, using a window screen as a graphics table. Copy was composed as a column strip with photos reduced on some huge camera wheel at the printers. Find a typo in the copy and you had to use a paper cutter and position a correct letter over the typo with surgical precision using hot wax. Inevitably, many of these corrections would slide off the final page, which then had to be photographed before being presented to the printers as final film. The whole process was prehistoric by current digital standards.

Back at my day job, I was into my sixth year at the *Herald*. Sports Editor Hal Walker had promised me better assignments; I supposedly had a choice of the local pro baseball team or the golf beat and the Western Canadian Hockey League junior Calgary Wranglers. But again, fate took its hand and conspired to shake things up.

Walker, who had been a great supporter of mine, retired in March of 1978 and shortly after died of a heart attack in Toronto. Replacing him was George Bilych, a senior writer who covered the Stampeders football team and, along with Larry Wood, also authored Canada's national curling magazine. I mention this because it was Bilych who began pressuring me about *AME* being a conflict of interest. If that was the case, what the hell was his national curling magazine all about?

Returning from my Commonwealth Games stint in Edmonton, I discovered drastic changes in the personnel at the *Herald* that negatively affected my position. Bilych, my new editor, had hired two of his Winnipeg buddies for the beats I had been promised and told me I was still considered to be the junior writer on the staff. He then promptly assigned me to a high school track meet. Bilych was also harassing me about my music magazine activities. That would be the last straw.

I started to look for options and a new opportunity quickly dropped in my lap. I had gotten to know Garth Vallely during his stint as general manager for the 1976 national midget champion Calgary Spurs hockey team, which I accompanied during their two-week tour of Czechoslovakia (as it was known then).

Vallely had been appointed general manager of the Western Hockey League junior Calgary Wranglers by their new owner, real estate magnate Jim Morley, and he was desperately looking for a director of public relations. Noting my sports background and knowing I was anxious to leave the *Herald*, he offered me a part-time post with the Wranglers that would allow me to continue working with *AME*. Trouble was the Wrangler season was about to launch and they needed an immediate response.

Six years at the *Herald* was about to go up in smoke. As a reassurance, I asked Vallely for a written contract that offered me at least three-quarters of what I was receiving at the *Herald*, a minimum two-year agreement, plus sufficient time off to work on my magazine. As hockey was seasonal, this would be an ideal scenario.

To cut a long story short, the whole episode was a disaster. Although I received payment from Morley, he made all sorts of excuses in delaying my contract. The team's on-ice performance was pathetic, and Morley wouldn't spend any money promoting the team. Then one day in early January 1979, I tuned into CFAC TV to learn from sportscaster Mike Adams that Wrangler owner Jim Morley had just fired General Manager Garth Vallely — and that director of public relations Keith Sharp was also let go. Nice of Morley to tell me!

By this point, I had left Dawn for Conny and was ensconced in her house on 16th Street SE in the Ogden area of Calgary. As my Wrangler public relations job proved to be a bust, and there was no hope of returning to the *Herald*, it was time for both of us to roll up our sleeves and pursue *AME* as a full-time venture.

4

1979:

A PIVOTAL YEAR

I t was at a meeting with the band Fosterchild that I first bumped into Paul Dean, lead guitarist for Streetheart. I had just conducted a phone interview with Streetheart's keyboardist, Daryl Guthiel, but I hadn't extracted much of an insight from him, so I welcomed the opportunity to do an in-person with Paul. He proved to be a very cordial and colourful subject. The band had just won a gold record for their debut LP, *Meanwhile Back in Paris,* and I was preparing to write a major profile on the band.

Dean was in Calgary to write songs for Streetheart's second album, and Lou Blair had provided Dean with practice space in Frank's automotive garage, located adjacent to The Refinery. "He [Dean] had this portable tape machine that he was working with but he was writing some really good stuff that was going to be material on the new album." Blair recalled. "I never rated Streetheart and I thought he could do better and jokingly asked when he was going to leave the band. He flew out to Winnipeg. Next thing I know, Paul is back on the phone. 'Where are you?' I asked. 'I'm back in Calgary,' he replied. 'Gary Stratychuck (the manager) and Kenny Shields (lead vocalist) just fired me.'"

Dean followed that call with one to me. "Hey Keith, I don't know what you are going to do with that interview but you should know I have just been kicked out of the band," said the obviously shaken Dean. Still, he attended Streetheart's headline concert at The Corral to receive his gold record for the band's debut.

In trying to cheer up Dean, I suggested he come with me to Studio City's annual talent showcase, in 1979 it was at the Southern Alberta Institute of Technology. At this weekend session, bands performed for prospective college and high-school bookers, and there were always a number of musicians hanging about looking for new gigs, so it seemed like the kind of place Dean could make some connections for a new band. Dean took my advice and showed up at the concert, along with Mike Rynowski, who had just returned from his one-album stint with Moxy. Dean and Reno, as Rynowski was about to start calling himself, obviously clicked, and as we chatted about other potential members, bassist Craig Blair, formerly of Hammersmith, was suggested. I also mentioned Doug Johnson, now playing keyboards for Fosterchild.

At this juncture, there are several different stories on how Loverboy formed. From my end, I definitely remembered suggesting Dean attend the Studio City function, and I know I mentioned Johnson's availability. Bernie Aubin, now owner of Classic Rock Canada booking agency out of Maple Ridge, B.C., remembered bumping into Dean and Reno at the Refinery nightclub. "I had just seen Streetheart in concert and I complimented him on the performance when he told me he had been ousted from the band. He also said he and Reno were looking at forming a new band and they were looking for a drummer," explained Aubin. "I was drumming for a band called 2000, so they dropped by to see me play at the Airliner Hotel and afterwards offered me a gig."

Aubin invited Reno and Dean to relocate to his Vancouver house where they formulated their new project. "Vern Wills, from Fosterchild, joined for a while on bass and they also tried Ab Bryant but that didn't work out. They also brought in Johnson who was an amazing keyboard player. We started to write songs and I had the original outline for 'The Kid is Hot Tonite' which got restructured, but I still earned a co-writer credit. We even got as far as recording some demo sessions at Bullfrog Studios and I remember Bruce Allen pulled up in his Excalibur to check us out."

Aubin eventually left Loverboy to join up with the Headpins. His replacement was former Streetheart drummer Matt Frenette, who had been in the original Headpins lineup. "I wasn't that upset at the time because Loverboy hadn't done anything yet and I switched positions to joined Brian McLeod and Ab Bryant in the Headpins with Darby Mills,"explained Aubin. "I would kick myself later but that's the way these things go."

With Dean, Reno, Frenette, and Johnson committed to the project, the final piece in the Loverboy jigsaw puzzle was a bass player. That search drew Reno and Dean to The Blindman Valley Festival, near Bentley, which I attended with them. The focus of their attention was Lisa Dal Bello's bassist, Scott Smith. "We knew he was exceptional and when we saw him on stage, that clinched it for us," noted Reno. With that, Loverboy became a band.

Almost immediately after Bentley, PolyGram's Ken Graydon asked me if I wanted to be a guest of the label at Canada's first Disco Awards event, to be staged in Vancouver on Saturday, June 16. The show was put on in conjunction with two major concerts at the Pacific Coliseum, Village People on the sixteenth and the Bee Gees the next day. PolyGram owned disco at that time, with the Bee Gees, Village People, Donna Summer, and even KISS (who got into the act with their "I Was Made For Loving You" on their *Dynasty* album). My itinerary was to attend the Disco Awards in the afternoon, catch the Village People that evening, attend a post-concert party at the Luv Affair, and, the following night, attend the Bee Gees concert followed by a private PolyGram party back at the hotel.

On the afternoon of the sixteenth, I walked into the Holiday Inn on Pender Street to attend the awards. I had literally just stepped into the hotel foyer when I was approached by a young man dressed in a sports jacket, wearing a bow tie, glasses, and sporting a trim haircut. "Good to see you could make it Mr. Sharp. Do you remember me? I'm Bryan Guy Adams." Wow! What a difference. The long page-boy cut was gone, he was dressed smartly, even business-like. I quickly found out Bryan was attending to promote his first solo single, "Let Me Take You Dancing," and was going to present an award to Cheryl and Robbie Rae for their "Que Sera Sera" track. The event itself was pretty forgettable, but I promised Bryan *Music Express* (as it was now called due to our expansion throughout Western Canada) would be there for his album debut. I also talked to Brian Chater, who had signed Adams to a publishing contract with A&M, and he was confident the label would be on board for any future activity.

The Village People that night were a sight to behold. They were pushing their *Go West* LP and had a massive hit with "In the Navy." I had a backstage pass, which was probably a mistake because by standing off to the side of the stage I could see the six Village People dance through their choreography, with a full band playing behind a screen, hidden from view.

Only the lead singer actually performed. These days lip-syncing is accepted, but in 1979 it was quite shocking to watch a band in a live concert actually mime their songs.

The next night was the Bee Gees, and they were on a roll with their *Spirits Having Flown* album and their "Tragedy" single, which was proving to be an ideal follow up to their *Saturday Night Fever* opus. Concert-wise, the brothers Gibb were amazing, slickly choreographed, great vocals, tons of hits, totally absorbing. But what happened in the band's dressing room after the concert wasn't so diplomatic. PolyGram Canada's marketing team all had VIP passes and, buzzed by the show, were looking forward to meeting the Bee Gees. But when they arrived backstage, they were told that only the label's president, Tim Harrold, could meet the band. They returned to their hotel obviously disappointed at the snub, and even Harrold admitted he had been given a perfunctory welcome and was quite disappointed at the reception he received. Back at the hotel, the attitude was, "Sod the Bee Gees." We had a great party anyway.

There was no getting away from the disco craze at that time. When a band like KISS releases disco-inspired songs like "I Was Made for Loving You," you knew rock music was in trouble. Fortunately, this proved to be a quickly passing phase, but while it lasted, disco music was a powerful force.

By midsummer, Conny and I decided that if we were to expand *Music Express* we would have to leave Calgary. We didn't believe we could make a go of it in Toronto, so we set out on a bit of a holiday/road trip to Vancouver to explore whether the West Coast should be out next destination. Industry response was positive; we found a potential office on Broadway, and were refreshed enough by the mini vacation to take stock of our options. I still wasn't 100 percent sure that west was the right move. Our quandary was that it was becoming obvious that the Alberta music scene was regressing, and Vancouver had so much more to offer by comparison — yet our Toronto contacts were also suggesting that to become really established as Canada's music magazine we needed to move east.

We put the moving conversation on hold to attend the Edmonton Summer Rock Cirkus being staged Saturday, August 26 at Commonwealth Stadium. The event was promoted by Martin Melhuish and Doug Pringle, and featured Heart, Peter Frampton, Streetheart, Eddie Money, the Dixon House Band, and Frank Ludwig's last performance with Trooper. Ludwig was moving on to join Randy Bachman's Ironhorse, the result of a song-writing dispute between Ludwig and band leaders Ra McGuire and Brian Smith, sparked by the success of the Ludwig song, "Round, Round We Go," and his ability to contribute future songs to the band.

Melhuish and Pringle were both based in Montreal, and at that time were airing a weekly four-hour syndicated radio show titled the *Pringle Program* (which aired on some fifty radio stations nationally). An acquaintance of Pringle's, Lucien Richard, had a client who wanted to stage a major concert at Montreal's Olympic Stadium, and was prepared to table a six-figure budget. "We had too much respect for Donald Tarelton [DKD Productions] to encroach on his territory," remembered Penzance, England, native Melhuish. "So Doug, who was in Edmonton working on the launch of AOR station K-97, decided a concert at Edmonton Commonwealth Stadium would be a great way to launch the station."

Conny and I drove up to Edmonton on the Friday, stayed at the Edmonton Plaza both nights, and, based on *Music Express* pre-promoting the concert, we obtained VIP backstage passes. The venue was excellent, the weather was warm and sunny with about 35,000 people in attendance, and we had a great time watching the bands and hanging out in the VIP lounge. We hung out with Streetheart after their solid early afternoon slot, and I made friends with Eddie Money, who was happy to meet with us. At one point he pointed a finger at Heart guitarist Howard Lesse, who was wearing a ridiculous pair of purple velour bell bottom trousers, and shouted at him, "Look at that rock star ponce wearing those pants." Leese's reaction was to scurry backstage.

Running security backstage was our old friend Garth "the Bear" Werschler. Werschler was Dave Horodezky's head of security at Brimstone. A great guy, but as his nicknamed suggested, a bear of a man who you would be advised not to tangle with. His signature move, especially at Calgary's Jubilee Auditorium was to hoist any would-be miscreant up off their feet and carry them head first through the swinging doors, usually leaving behind a significant dent!

Frampton, who had dominated the charts with his *Frampton Comes Alive* LP, performed a superb, low-key set. From the VIP lounge Conny and I watched the stage, and also saw MCA President Scott Richards present Trooper with their quad-platinum album for *Hot Shots* in the lounge. He later repeated this presentation on stage. I introduced myself to Richards. He said he was very aware of *Music Express* and invited me to drop by his office during my next trip to Toronto. We then moved closer to the stage to witness what I rate as one of Trooper's best-ever live performances. I think they only played about an hour, but their onstage energy was electrifying. I remember they did "Summertime Blues" and had the whole audience on their collective feet clapping and singing along. And then came the moment when Ludwig marked his imminent departure from Trooper by singing "Round, Round We Go" for the last time, and you could see people shedding tears. It really was a poignant moment. Trooper pulled so much energy and emotion out of the crowd that the fans seemed spent by the time Heart came out to close.

"We only got the gig after The Runaways cancelled," reflected McGuire, who also rated the gig as a career highlight. "Thanks to Frampton insisting on going on earlier, it was like he opened for us. Our short, high-energy set was a rock 'n' roll dream and we were presented with our quadruple *Hot Shots* record on stage. It was a great way to finish off our two and a half years working with Frank."

A major party ensued in the VIP lounge, with Trooper, Streetheart, and Eddie Money all involved. The Stampeders' Ronnie King (a native Hollander) launched into a Dutch-language conversation with Conny, and Ludwig asked Conny if she thought he had made a mistake by leaving Trooper for Randy Bachman's new (and ultimately short-lived) Ironhorse project. "Yes you've made a big mistake, you are a fucking idiot," snapped back Kunz, not one to mince words. Not the response Ludwig was looking for.

5

HEADING FOR
THE T DOT

As 1979 lurched to an end, Conny and I had a decision to make. We had definitely decided Calgary had reached its sell-by date music-wise, and we would need to relocate if *Music Express* was to have any chance of surviving. Vancouver seemed a natural venue for our relocation. Most of our industry contacts were based on the West Coast, and we still weren't 100 percent confident we could succeed with *Music Express* in Toronto.

So Vancouver it was going to be. To prepare for this move, I flew to Toronto that October to explain our plans to relocate to the West Coast to as many major labels as I could connect with. Accepting an offer to stay at Cam Carpenter's house in the Beaches (Cam being a Toronto record industry contact who was a strong supporter of *Music Express*), I scheduled a red-eye flight into Toronto that got me in about 6:00 a.m. Understanding I would be pretty jet-lagged from the trip, I scheduled only one meeting that day, a 9:00 a.m. rendezvous with Scott Richards at MCA (who I had met backstage at Rock Cirkus). He seemed to be quite positive when I suggested connecting with him first thing the morning of my arrival.

I got into Toronto early and headed to Richards's office for the meeting. Richards was a couple of hours late, but was apologetic for the delay. He confirmed we should be thinking about Vancouver as he wasn't particularly enthusiastic about the idea of us setting up shop in Toronto. "I'm not sure this industry can support a national music magazine," noted Richards. "We are not a big print business. Most of our monies go into co-op and radio. But if you think about coming here, good luck."

He must have felt bad about me spending the morning sitting in his reception because he handed me the carrot of booking a Tom Petty and the Heartbreakers' *Damn the Torpedoes* ad in my next issue. I emerged from that session feeling that a move to Vancouver was still our next logical step.

This opinion changed when I hooked up with Cam later that day. He had just started working with Larry McRae at Quality Records and was very enthusiastic about *Music Express* relocating to Toronto. He also passed along a nugget of information: Toronto's only existing consumer music magazine, Jim Watters's *New Music*, had just pulled the plug, seemingly due to industry indifference. That left *Music Express* as the only surviving consumer music mag in the country! Over the next couple of days I barnstormed the majors and met with various marketing contacts at EMI, Warner, A&M, Columbia, RCA, and Quality. With *New Music* now toast, there seemed to be a genuine interest in *Music Express* relocating to Toronto. I believe it was Terry Magee at Columbia who told me, "Hey, you're the only magazine left. You *have* to come to Toronto!"

When I arrived back in Calgary, Conny asked, "Okay, what's the word?"

I said, "The word is we're moving to Toronto." Surprisingly, Conny didn't require much convincing. I told her about *New Music,* and that since we were the only music mag in Canada, it made sense to relocate to Toronto, centre of Canada's music industry. Better to move now than have another magazine spring up and take our spot.

By January I was back in Toronto looking for suitable accommodation. I contacted a local real estate company and explained what kind of residence we were looking for. The second place the lady showed me was 209 Kingslake Road, a detached house located just southwest of the 404/Finch intersection, around the corner from Seneca College. The two storey house was ideal for a magazine operation. The basement was subdivided into office spaces, there was plenty of additional space on the main floor, and the second floor had three bedrooms. I took one look and said, "Right, this is the place." I made a quick call to Calgary, told Conny I had found an ideal location, and signed on the dotted line.

I targeted Triumph as the cover band for our debut Toronto issue, which was to come out in April. We had originally met Triumph during their Western Canadian tour in 1979. Their live show was impressive to say the least, and due to their extensive use of lights and pyrotechnics, I nicknamed them "Ontario Hydro." Learning they had a new album, *Progressions of Power*, was about to be released, we figured it would be appropriate to have one of Toronto's top rock acts on our debut national cover.

I think our first meeting with Rik Emmett (guitarist/vocalist), Gil Moore (drummer/vocalist), and Mike Levine (bassist), was at their managers' office (Neil Dixon and Steve Propas). Triumph were starting to break big in the U.S., but they maintained a specific mandate to develop their own live show and not just be an opening act for other big bands in the States.

"In Toronto, at that time, most bands were playing cover tunes and trying to fit their own songs into the set and it rarely worked," explained Emmett. "Mike and Gil had this vision that we would develop our own show and our own identity. At first we played high schools and small gigs but as Concert Productions International saw our development as a live act, we progressed to arena tours out West with Moxy and Trooper, and Donald K Donald sent us east with Teaze."

Triumph's live show was strong; they appeared on the Canada Jam bill on August 6, 1978, before 110,000 fans at Mosport Raceway, northeast of Toronto. Buoyed by the success of their 1978 second album, *Rock & Roll Machine*, which hit radio pay dirt with Moore's cover of Joe Walsh's "Rocky Mountain Way," Triumph also cracked the U.S. market when San Antonio Texas radio station KISS-FM started playing "Blinding Light Show," from the band's debut release.

"KISS-FM had been big supporters of Rush so when they heard about us, they started playing 'Blinding Light Show' late at night and the listeners loved it," explained Emmett. "Then Sammy Hagar had to pull out of one of their radio concert broadcasts so they invited us to fill in. We lugged all our gear down to San Antonio and the show went well (The Runaways opened). That proved to be a big break for us, not just with San Antonio but also other cities in the KISS-FM chain."

Toronto in 1980 was developing as one of North America's music hot spots, but there wasn't a plethora of live venues to utilize. Maple Leaf Gardens, Massey Hall, and the O'Keefe Centre were the primary soft-seat concert venues, while the city's new rock acts were drawn to the top rock club, The Gasworks on Yonge Street. Gary Topp and Gary Cormier promoted alternative acts in The Edge and Larry's Hideaway, and they had access to The Horseshoe until it switched to a country and blues format. Yet it was a dingy venue on Spadina Avenue, illuminated by a garish neon light in the shape of a palm tree, that served as the heartbeat of this city's live-entertainment scene.

Anyone who was anyone debuted at the El Mocambo. The Rolling Stones' infamous performance on March 4, 1977 (with April Wine as an opening act decoy), put the place on the music map. The likes of U2, Elvis Costello, Paul Young, Stevie Ray Vaughan, and Bon Jovi, along with Canadian up-and-comers like Bryan Adams and Corey Hart, all paid their dues at the El Mo.

Bryan Adams debuted at the El Mo to mark the Toronto launch of his first solo album. It was midweek in March 1980, and there was a small smattering of press and A&M Record reps on hand. Adams was decent enough. The material wasn't great and his pick-up band was forgettable. After the gig, I went upstairs to the small dressing room where Adams was chatting with manager Bruce Allen. I had first met Allen previously at the Refinery in Calgary where he and Bachman-Turner Overdrive's Robbie Bachman and Blair Thornton were ogling the Refinery's notoriously skimpily dressed waitresses. Since then, we had met Allen a few times in Vancouver, and he was a guest speaker at our music conference in Calgary. Allen had emerged as a dominant force in the Canadian music industry, taking charge of Adams, Loverboy, Prism, and Red Rider, to create a Vancouver-based powerhouse talent roster. Despite his legendary gruff exterior, I believe he genuinely supported *ME* and was appreciative of our interest in his clients.

Greeting me backstage, Allen kicked the rest of Adams's band out of the dressing room and asked for my honest opinion of the performance. I was forthright in stating I thought Adams was an engaging performer, that the songs weren't quite there, and that his band didn't cut it live. Adams instantly tore into Allen blaming him for assembling a second-rate band. I could still hear the argument raging as I descended the stairs into the street.

The following night, my new photographer, Kandice Abbott, and I checked in on Adams, who was playing at the Jarvis House. There were only about thirty largely disinterested patrons sucking on their draught beers when we got there, but Bryan acknowledged our presence and we sat through the rest of his set. Afterwards, he motioned Kandice and I upstairs and asked if we would have a beer with him. He and his band were alone; no management or record reps around. As I drank a beer and asked him how he was doing, I actually felt sorry for the poor kid!

Magazine-wise, our major features and cover stories were still focused on Canadian artists, I wrote a monthly column titled "Rockpiles," and we also featured editorials on movies and musical instruments. We were able to connect with our readers via our "Letters to the Editor" section, and the editorial that was creating the most interest was our "Regional Reports." Understanding most newspapers were still not adequately covering their local music scene, we set up a network of stringers to write about new talent and major events in each area. This allowed us to inform our readers about such bands as Saskatoon's Northern Pikes, Prince Edward Island's Haywire, and Edmonton's Models, months before they broke nationally.

Reaction and support from major record labels was spotty and inconsistent. The fact we were Canada's only national music magazine seemed to work against us. We struggled to position ourselves in their marketing plans. Capitol-EMI and Columbia were supportive, A&M were so-so, Warner Music was a struggle, and we couldn't get any interest from PolyGram or MCA. Our stumbling block at MCA was Scott Richards, who just didn't want to know about print. Fortunately, he was soon replaced by Ross Reynolds, who proved to be a great ally and was personally very supportive of our efforts.

Though initially a struggle, the move to Toronto would ultimately pay off, as the burgeoning Canadian scene was beginning to trigger the international exposure it always deserved.

6

FORGING A
NATIONAL IDENTITY

Advertising-wise, our lifeline was the indie labels that had major domestic records they would promote in our magazine. Most of the major record labels were not used to dealing with a national music magazine. Previously, most of the major's ad revenue had been spent on radio or on newspaper co-op ads with specific retail chains. To get one of the larger record labels to run a band-specific ad in the magazine, without a retail tie-in, became quite a challenge for us. We had more success with independent labels, who were more promotionally minded with their releases.

Canada's most influential domestic label was Anthem Records, home of Rush, Max Webster, Ian Thomas, Wireless, and Aerial. Originally operated by Ray Danniels and Vic Wilson, Anthem's first office was located at this funky Oak Ridges farmhouse. To be honest, I wasn't initially a big fan of Rush. In my *Calgary Herald* days, Eugene Chadbourne pitched me a copy of the band's second album, *Fly By Night*, and the first thing I noticed was an eight-minute song called "By-Tor and the Snow Dog." I thought, nah! I can't handle this.

Rush subsequently built quite a following with *2112* and *A Farewell to Kings*. PolyGram's Ken Graydon convinced me to check them out when they played The Corral in 1978, but even though the crowd support was enthusiastic, that strange looking bassist (Geddy Lee) with that high-pitched voice singing "Closer to the Heart" did nothing for me.

But, as I started to visit Anthem in Toronto, Danniels and sidekick Tom Berry played me Rush's latest demos, and I started to relate to their instrumental talents and complex lyricism. I remember Berry playing me a demo of "The Spirit of Radio" (from *Permanent Waves*) and feeling the same sense of anticipation and excitement that those new tracks would generate with the band's fans. I subsequently got to interview Lee, drummer Neil Peart, and guitarist Alex Lifeson, and became a fan as I found a new appreciation of their musical sensibility.

Attic Records, formed in 1974 by Al Mair and Tom Williams, proved to be Canada's most industrious domestic label with a major roster of Canadian talent. Fludd headlined a list that also included Triumph, Lee Aaron, Patsy Gallant, Hagood Hardy, Anvil, Downchild Blues Band, Teenage Head, The Diodes, and Haywire. If a form of music was happening, be it blues, punk, or heavy metal, Attic was in there. Mair, in particular, was receptive to *Music Express*. I had given Patsy Gallant one of our first covers, and we covered Teenage Head and Triumph early on in their careers. Al always wanted to play Monty Hall in negotiating ad rates, but he was one of the first label managers to actively support *ME*.

True North, run by the two Bernies (Finklestein and Fiedler), was a throwback to the late-sixties Yorkville era, and their major acts, Bruce Cockburn, Murray MacLauchlan, and Dan Hill, never fell into the rock star category that excited the masses, yet *Music Express* provided coverage for all three. The label was rewarded when Dan Hill's "Sometimes When We Touch" single became an international success. We were also on board when Finklestein went against rote by signing the controversial Rough Trade.

The revolving Sparkles disco atop of the Toronto's CN Tower served as the venue for the launch of another major indie label in the summer of 1980. Solid Gold Records, operated by Steve Propas, Ed Glinert, and Neil Dixon, debuted to the industry with the introduction of the band Toronto and their debut album, *Lookin for Trouble*. Fronted by Annie (Holly) Woods and featuring guitarists Brian Allen and Sheron Alton, keyboardist Scott Kreyer, bassist Nick Costello, and drummer Jimmy Fox, Toronto connected with their fiery Heart-like image fuelled by an impressive debut single, "Even the Score."

Proving the label's initial success wasn't a fluke, Solid Gold registered two consecutive platinum albums. Vancouver's Chilliwack racked up sales with their *Wanna Be A Star* album in 1981. The label had another success with Chilliwack spin-off-band the Headpins, launched by Brian (Too Loud)

McLeod and bassist Ab Bryant (with lead vocalist Darby Mills), when their 1982 debut, *Turn It Loud*, also hit platinum.

Solid Gold also released records by The Good Brothers and imported releases by British bands like Mama's Boys and Girlschool. Dixon, Propas, and Glinert were great to work with, both for advertising support and editorial content. It was always an adventure going to their office on Bloor West near Avenue Road. The SCTV office was one floor above them, so on more than one occasion I found myself squeezing into the elevator with John Candy or Joe Flaherty.

Outside of Toronto, Montreal's Aquarius Records was another early *Music Express* supporter. The label was formed by legendary promoter Donald K Donald Tarleton when he recognized Montreal needed its own major indie label. My first visit to Aquarius occurred when *Music Express* was still based in Calgary. I had dropped by their office, which was still in Old Montreal near the docks, and met Keith Brown and members of Teaze, who I had seen previously open for Aerosmith at Maple Leaf Gardens in 1979. Future trips to Montreal always included a visit to Aquarius; they understood the value of *Music Express,* and always promoted April Wine releases with ads and feature stories.

One band I never came to terms with in the Bruce Allen camp was Prism. Formed in 1976 by former Sunshyne trumpeter Bruce Fairbairn and drummer Jim Vallance, in partnership with Seeds of Time guitarist Lindsay Mitchell, the Prism band I witnessed at the Heart concert in Seattle in the mid-seventies was a seven-piece blues/rock outfit that boasted a horn section. By the time they recorded their self-titled debut in May 1977, Prism had been transformed into a five-man rock band with Ron Tabak handling lead vocals, Mitchell on guitar, Tom Lavin on bass, Vallance on drums, and John Hall on keyboards, with Fairbairn retiring behind the console to embark on a highly successful career as a record producer. Over the next four years, Prism tinkered with their lineup, replacing Vallance with Seeds of Time's Rocket Norton, and Norton's bassist band-mate Al Harlow replaced Tom Lavin, who focused on fronting his own Powder Blues Band. Record and radio success for albums like *See Forever Eyes* and *Armageddon* and singles like "Flyin'," "Spaceship Superstar," and "A Night to Remember," ensured a decent profile in arenas across Canada, but Prism never caught on in the States.

Prism's live shows were pretentious to say the least. I had seen the band play live several times during my stint in Calgary, and one aspect of their show always amused me. Now, it's a given most headline acts take an encore; it's built into their set list, normally saving their big single or current hit for the grand finale. Yet Prism took numerous encores — whether they were warranted or not. I distinctly remember a concert in Calgary, probably at The Corral. *Armageddon* was huge at the time. They performed their regular show with the obligatory smoke bombs and pyrotechnics, and received polite closing applause — yet they were back on stage for an encore before the clapping had even died down. So they do their encore (which was probably "Armageddon"), get another smattering of applause, and they run back on stage for a second encore — which was definitely not requested. Prism ran through another song, received even less applause than their previous song, and went off stage a third time. With the house lights down and no sign of the sound man leaving his board, it seemed Prism were coming back for a third encore when some wag in front of me stood up and screamed at the top of his voice: "Would everyone please shut the fuck up. Otherwise we'll be here all night." I thought his reaction was priceless — and Prism declined to take a third encore.

Bruce Allen knew there were serious limitations to Prism. Lead vocalist Ron Tabak had a stutter, which made him useless with the media, plus he didn't contribute any songwriting material and was supposedly in trouble with gambling debts. With Vallance in dispute with Mitchell over the band's musical direction, and with internal conflicts raging n the group, it didn't help Prism were looking for a new record company after GRT pulled the plug in 1979. But Allen, being Allen, pulled a fast one on Capitol, convincing the label that since *Armageddon* had been such a big seller, Prism should receive a major multi-record deal. Capitol agreed, with one caveat: Allen had to take over management of Red Rider to keep them away from the sweaty grasp of Anthem Record's Ray Danniels.

Allen's ensuing decision to move Red Rider out to Vancouver was not a successful one. Red Rider was not a Bruce Allen, bic-flicking live act like Loverboy or Bryan Adams. They were more like Pink Floyd or Supertramp — a musically intense group. It was no surprise that the relationship between Allen and the band's lead vocalist, Tom Cochrane, ended acrimoniously.

Much has always been made of a record going gold (fifty thousand copies), platinum (one hundred thousand copies), or even diamond (one million units). A lot of pomp and ceremony takes place when the artist or group in question receive the award. In the seventies and eighties this had become such a big deal that if a particular record was falling a couple of hundred or thousand units short of their target, the missing numbers would be shipped internationally as a way of topping up the sales. For the uninitiated, it was (and still is) illegal to export records to foreign countries.

"When the thunder from above decrees that you move X amount of units, you had to be creative," said former Capitol salesman Paul Church, who acknowledged illegally exporting units and storing product in warehouses was part and parcel of meeting those quotas. "There was a big hype about achieving a gold or platinum sales target for your releases so we did what we had to do to achieve those quotas. Everyone knew it was a bit unethical but it was an accepted practice so we all used whatever means was available to shift numbers."

A strange thing began to happen after we positioned *Music Express* with record wholesaler and retailer Records on Wheels. We started receiving subscription requests from strange countries like Argentina, Ecuador, Brazil, and even European nations. But how were these countries receiving our magazine? The answer came when an individual (who shall remain nameless — but you know who you are!) explained Records on Wheels was one of the companies that illegally shipped product to foreign countries, and had packed these boxes with copies of *Music Express*.

Advertising may have been a hit-or-miss affair with major record labels, but their press departments were happy to oblige us with story opportunities. Warner Music even arranged for my first junket in Toronto when I was invited to accompany Dave Tollington, Ontario sales rep Mike Gaitt, and Q-107 DJ Samantha Taylor to Buffalo to catch the first U.S. concert appearance by The Pretenders.

Being invited on a junket (a promotional trip) was an indication that *Music Express* had come of age and that our influence was being recognized by the industry. It was of course expected that you would report favourable on any artist that you were exposed to on these trips, but as *Music Express* was very promotionally minded, this was never a problem for us.

7

SETTING

UP SHOP

Summer in Toronto meant major concerts. Having connected with CPI's press chief Susan Rosenberg, *Music Express* was granted press passes to most of the company's big shows in 1980. Queen and The Who were on the Canadian Nation Exhibition schedule that summer, but the most memorable concert of the year (for all the wrong reasons) was to be Alice Cooper's August 19 gig.

The show's opening act, Toronto's Zon, did nothing for the audience, and following their performance there was an inordinate delay before Cooper's band started playing. From the press box positioned high above the crowd, I could sense something was wrong. I never knew Alice Cooper's band to be instrumental players, but they seemed to be dragging out the opening number without any appearance from Mr. Cooper. Then the band stopped playing. Still no Alice Cooper! Eventually an announcement was made that Alice was too sick to perform and that the rest of the show had been cancelled.

What followed was the infamous Alice Cooper riot, where a large number of the fold-out chairs laid out in front of the stage were hurled at police and their horses by a small but frenzied bunch of youths. A total of thirty-one people were arrested, and twelve people were injured by flying debris and taken to local hospitals. Now it is my contention that it wasn't Cooper's absence that sparked the riot. The real trouble started when Zon's lead vocalist, Denton Young, went to the microphone after Cooper's illness had been announced and offered to keep on playing! It was only then that the chairs started flying.

Four days later (August 23) the Heatwave Festival was staged at Mosport Raceway. The event was organized by John Brower, who had co-promoted the infamous Toronto Peace Festival in 1969 at Varsity Stadium (which marked the debut of John Lennon's Plastic Ono Band). Another Brower-promoted festival, The Strawberry Fields Festival, had been staged August 7–10, 1970, at Mosport with Ten Years After, Grand Funk Railroad, Jethro Tull, and Sly and the Family Stone on the bill. Brower also claimed responsibility for attracting Californians Sandy Feldman's and Lenny Stogel's interest in staging Canada Jam on August 26, 1978, pulling over one hundred thousand fans to see Triumph, Kansas, Prism, and The Doobie Brothers.

The logic behind Heatwave was that if over a hundred thousand fans showed up to a rock festival, how many more would support the cream of the world's new wave movement? Promoted as The Punk/New Wave Woodstock, Heatwave was supposed to present the best of the current crop of new wave bands. Yet The Clash, billed to appear, were no-shows, and all efforts to attract Blondie failed. Another major stumbling block was Elvis Costello's record label chief, Jake Riviera. Riviera insisted that, for Costello to perform, he had to be paid top dollar, and that Dave Edmunds and Nick Lowe's band Rockpile should also receive a hefty fee. Once word got out what Costello and Rockpile were being paid, suddenly Talking Heads and B-52's also demanded a major increase. Brower and his backers couldn't afford to pay everybody.

The day of the concert was pleasant and sunny and the promoters gave Canadian talent a shot with Vladymir Rogov, BB Gabor, and Teenage Head opening the festival, and The Kings closing it. In between, the Talking Heads were exceptional, Costello was okay, and The Pretenders were serviceable. Yet none of these bands projected enough live energy to set the festival alight.

As an epitaph, Heatwave was a financial disaster for the promoters (who reportedly dropped over a million dollars). Lots of suppliers didn't get paid and no music festivals were staged at Mosport again until the World Electronic Music Festival in 2005 (and that was struck by a freak tornado).

November 24 featured The Police performing to a sell-out crowd at Toronto's Massey Hall (2,600 fans) and marked a personal triumph for Gary Topp and Gary Cormier, who were the first Canadian promoters to take a chance on this then-unknown British trio and stuck with them through a series of sparse club appearances before their Massey Hall sell-out.

"I remember sitting on the toilet when I got a call from Gary (Cormier)," reflected Topp, maybe supplying too much information! "Gary says, 'We've been offered this new band called The Police. Interested?' I said, 'So who's in the band?' Cormier responds, 'Well the drummer Stewart Copeland used to be in Curved Air.' 'Okay. I've heard of him.' 'The singer/bassist is called Sting,' Cormier continued. 'Never heard of him.' 'And the guitarist is called Andy Summers.' 'Not the Andy Summers from Kevin Coyne?' said I. 'Yes I think that's him,' confirmed Cormier. 'Got to book them,' said I. 'I just love Kevin Coyne.' So we booked The Police based on Andy Summers and put them in The Horseshoe Tavern. First thing I said to Andy Summers when I met him at the gig was, 'So how do I book Kevin Coyne?'"

The Police had first played in Toronto with shows on November 2 and 3, 1978. Their debut album, *Outlandos D'Amour*, hadn't even been released yet in the U.S., and no one had heard of their debut single, "Roxanne," yet, so it was hardly surprising a total of sixty people (half of them industry by Topp's calculation) showed up at The Horseshoe for both nights. "Even though there was no one there, Gary (Cormier) and I sensed they would be a killer live band so we started plotting future dates with them," reflected Topp.

The Garys brought The Police back in early 1979, just as "Roxanne" started to get airplay. The concert pulled in four hundred fans over two nights at The Edge. Then, on November 12, 1979, The Police sold out The Music Hall (1,200) before pulling off their Massey Hall coup just over a year later. The band's management, FBI, fronted by Copeland's brother Miles, formed a solid relationship with the Garys that led to a trio of Police Picnic outdoor festivals. The first was held at The Grove in Oakville on August 23, 1981, followed by two more at the CNE in August 1982 and 1983.

The Garys's Edge venue at Gerrard and Church proved to be a Mecca for the new wave movement. Aside from The Police, the Garys booked The Smiths, The Cure, U2, The Specials, John Otway, Killing Joke, The Pretenders, virtually every happening underground band from the United Kingdom or the U.S., new Canadian talent like The Spoons, Martha and the Muffins, Nash the Slash, and the Payola$, and finally, Kevin Coyne, who closed the club June 5, 1981. The Garys had Joy Division booked for May 25, 1980, but the band's lead vocalist, Ian Curtis, committed suicide two weeks before the date.

Topp and Cormier were aware that *Music Express* was not actively involved in promoting the new wave scene. To be honest, aside from quasi-mainstream artists like Elvis Costello, the Talking Heads, and Blondie, the major labels did not actively pitch these releases to *Music Express* as we were viewed as a mainstream rock magazine at the time. That wasn't quite true, as we had featured Teenage Head on our cover, and had provided editorial coverage to local new wave bands like The Spoons, Blue Peter, and The Diodes.

Our first year in Toronto ended with a rock tragedy. On Monday, December 8, 1980, the day after my twenty-eighth birthday, I was watching the *Monday Night Football* game between the Miami Dolphins and the New England Patriots. I wasn't paying much attention when Howard Cosell interrupted the broadcast to announce John Lennon had just been shot outside his Dakota Apartment on New York's Upper West Side. And then Cosell carried on calling the football game!

I stood staring at the set in sheer disbelief. I couldn't fathom what Cosell had said. It wasn't possible. John Lennon, former Beatle ... dead! I started clicking the remote, trying to confirm Cosell's announcement, but this was before twenty-four hour news coverage and it was about twenty minutes before one of the news channels filled in those horrible details. Lennon and his wife, Yoko Ono, were returning from The Record Plant at 11:00 p.m. when he was shot four times in the back by a stalker, Mark Chapman. I called Greg Quill, our senior writer at that time, and he was equally shocked. We agreed to meet the following day to discuss what we should do in the next issue. Of course, in the days that followed there was blanket coverage of the incident, the fallout grief and memorial tributes that broke out around the world, including the Wednesday gathering at Toronto's Nathan Philips Square, which Greg attended.

Greg wrote a moving piece about Lennon in the next issue, while I wrote in my "Rockpiles" column that it was strange that after Lennon's death everyone was saying what a great record *Double Fantasy* was, when in reality, the album had been globally trashed before he got shot.

8

THE NETWORK
TARGETS LOVERBOY

In shopping for Loverboy's debut record deal, Bruce Allen and Lou Blair were determined not to sign a domestic deal as they rightly knew such a contract would severely limit their potential for U.S. exposure. But after a failed audition in Vancouver in front of Epic Records' New York A&R rep Larry Schnurre, Columbia's Toronto-based A&R chief Jeff Burns decided to go ahead with a domestic release.

The recording of Loverboy's debut album commenced March 18, 1980, at Vancouver's Little Mountain Sound, with former Prism musician Bruce Fairbairn recruited as producer, and the then-unknown Bob Rock (later the guitarist with the Payola$) working as assistant engineer. "The Kid Is Hot Tonite" launched their self-titled debut, but it was the band's second single, "Turn Me Loose," that stoked unit sales which approached five hundred thousand by late summer.

Having knocked their live show into shape, first by opening for KISS in Vancouver and then by opening for Prism on tour, Loverboy decided to take another shot at a U.S. deal by performing a second showcase concert for U.S. A&R reps, this time at Toronto's Danforth Theatre.

Allen and Blair invited Arma Andon and Mason Munuz from Columbia's A&R department to the July 1980 show, but when their impression of the performance was less than ecstatic, Blair and Allen knew they had to do something drastic.

"Bruce and I decide to take Arma and Mason for dinner," reflected Blair. "Bruce is driving and as he heads north on Church Street looking for

Bigliardi's Steak House, he drives past the restaurant and executes a U-turn before parking the car. 'Wow,' says our two American friends. 'You'd never see that in New York.'

"That one action broke the ice with the Americans. We spent the next three hours talking about the Sugar Ray Leonard–Roberto Duran fight, hardly talked about music. Bruce and I developed a great chemistry with them and Arma finally said, 'I'll tell you what, we won't tell New York about tonight's gig. You whip the band into shape, give them a couple of months and we'll take another look at them.'"

Dates opening for Cheap Trick further stimulated sales, and Columbia U.S. finally released their debut in November, with "Turn Me Loose" as the lead-off single. A glowing review in U.S. record tip-sheet *The Friday Morning Quarterback* announced that, "The lone survivor from Christmas is 'Turn Me Loose.'" This proved to be a half-million dollar review as the U.S. label president, Dick Asher, pressed the necessary buttons and Columbia's U.S. marketing machine swung into action, buying trade ads and providing the band with the necessary promotion and tour support to break into the States.

As 1981 rang in, Loverboy's self-titled debut album was erupting in the United States. Asher, seeing how well "Turn Me Loose" had performed during the Christmas holidays, made the release the number one priority at the label. What neither Blair nor Allen knew was that the American music industry was being riddled by a new payola scandal that drastically affected any singles trying to penetrate U.S. Contemporary Hit Radio (CHR) charts. By the time "Turn Me Loose" was released, a group of indie record promoters were controlling which singles charted and which didn't on key U.S. radio stations. Major labels were spending hundreds of thousands of dollars each year to ensure preferred placement on top-forty radio charts.

Known collectively as "The Network," an informal alliance of top independent promotion men headed by two key individuals, Joe Isgro and Freddie DiSipio, who operated a system in which they ensured maximum radio exposure by paying payola to key radio programmers. If you wanted to get your band or artist's new single on KFI Los Angeles or KAMZ in El Paso or WCIN Cincinnati, you had to deal with The Network, or that precious single would not be added to the charts. It was a problem CBS president Dick Asher tried to resolve by joining forces with other major labels, mainly the Warner Music Group, to reject indie payola. In response, The Network succeeded in removing certain singles from the charts. Loverboy's "Turn Me Loose" was one of the first targets of The Network's revenge tactics.

As superbly documented in Frederic Dannen's insightful *Hit Men* (Vintage Publishers), which illuminates the sordid inner workings of the U.S. music business, we learn that The Network's treatment of "Turn Me Loose" was designed to show that they had the power to manipulate the fate of singles if key stations didn't receive appropriate financial compensation. "Turn Me Loose" broke into *Billboard*'s Hot-100 chart at number eighty-seven during the week ending January 31, 1981, earning the star awarded to records showing the greatest airplay and sales strength.

Over the next seven weeks, the single made a rapid ascent to number thirty-seven, but then lost its star and fell into a rapid free-fall before disappearing off the chart altogether by May 30. "The indie promoters chose to wipe our noses in it," said Asher in Dannen's book. "We still had independent promotion on that record so their boycott shouldn't have affected that record. But it affected Loverboy that way because they wanted to send me a message."

"We didn't have a clue what was happening," admitted Blair. "We just thought the single had run out of gas because it was a rock track anyway. It was only afterwards that we learned the song had been targeted. Fortunately for Loverboy, we were more of an AOR band and we racked up the album sales by intense touring. So a CHR boycott didn't really affect us. But you can imagine how other Canadian bands made out."

Blair and Allen also countered The Network by racking up major album sales by touring incessantly. A tour with April Wine took the band to Las Vegas in April 1981. Allen's connections with top U.S. promoter Don Fox hooked the band up with Kansas, and Fox then used his influence with ZZ Top's manager, Billy Ham, to keep the momentum going. *Loverboy* eventually sold two million copies in the U.S. and four million worldwide.

"Besides me and Bruce, Don Fox was the most influential person in Loverboy's career," noted Blair. "With Don providing such high-profile tours with Kansas and ZZ Top, Columbia just couldn't say no! You cannot imagine how big Loverboy was in the States through 1981. They would eventually play more than two hundred shows that year."

A meeting I had with Bruce Allen around this time resulted from the flames of a controversy that was raging with CARAS (Canadian Academy of Recording Arts and Sciences) over the results of the 1981 Juno Awards. Staged at the O'Keefe Theatre on February 5, with SCTV's Andrea Martin hosting, it was assumed Loverboy's seven hundred thousand domestic sales counted for something in the award balloting. That assumption would be wrong!

Loverboy hadn't even been nominated for Group of the Year. That award went to Allen's other band, Prism. Yet Loverboy also lost the Most Promising Group of the Year award to Vancouver's Powder Blues Band, and weren't even nominated for Album or Single of the Year awards even though, clearly, they had both the top-selling album and most-played singles. And to add salt to the wound, in Allen's opinion, Bryan Adams lost the Most Promising Male Vocalist award for a second time, this time to True North artist Graham Shaw.

The 1981 Junos were a travesty for a number of other reasons. Anne Murray continued her boycott of the live show, but still won Female Vocalist of the Year, Country Female Vocalist of the Year, Album of the Year (for her *Greatest Hits* album!), and tied for Single of the Year with her "Could I Have This Dance" track, sharing honours with Martha And The Muffins' "Echo Beach." Her refusal to appear on-stage, despite receiving this plethora of awards, continued to undermine the show's credibility.

The dissatisfaction shown by Bruce Allen focused on the obvious oversights in the voting procedure. These lapses are easily explained by going over the history of the Junos. Launched in February 1969 as The Gold Leaf Awards by *RPM* magazine's Walt Grealis and Stan Klees, the awards originally simply marked the fact that a Canadian independent music industry actually existed, and so there was not a great deal of importance put on how the winners were decided. Yet, as the awards grew in stature (renamed the Junos in 1971 in honour of Pierre Juneau, head of the CRTC, which established Canadian content regulations for all domestic radio stations), and began to fall under media and public scrutiny, questions began to get asked about the voting procedure.

To participate in the voting process, you needed to be a member of CARAS. Now, anyone in the industry can pay an annual fee and secure a CARAS membership. Yet as most CARAS memberships were purchased by the major record companies, accusations were aired that certain labels were voting as a block and trading favours amongst each other. Say Record

Company One wanted to win the Album of the Year award and Record Company Two wanted to win the Female Vocalist of the Year award, they would agree to swap votes to win their desired award.

"The machinations were Machiavellian," pronounced Bryan Tucker, former Western Canadian VP of Marketing for Columbia-Epic Records. "People out West knew what was going on so we ignored the whole process. Guess who won? What a surprise! Initially the whole balloting process was considered an advertising ploy between *RPM* publisher Walt Grealis and the industry to sell magazine subscriptions. As far as I was concerned, I never had a Juno ballot and if I did, nobody told me about it."

Considering the dissatisfaction with the Juno balloting process from our readership standpoint, and the obvious injustice that had been directed at Loverboy, it was a no-brainer for *Music Express* to decide that we should look into starting our own awards show.

9

THE PULSE OF CANADIAN ROCK

As 1981 rolled along we mixed magazine covers to feature Canadian bands like Klaatu (a band briefly thought to be the secretly reunited Beatles), Toronto, Goddo, and Carole Pope, with major international artists like The Clash, Styx, Tom Petty, and The Rolling Stones. *Music Express* was attracting writers from England, New York, and Los Angeles, and we had also started mailing out copies to U.S. record companies and music public relation companies like Rogers and Cowan and Paul Levine to get the word out on our existence. Gordon and Gotch magazine distributors also started racking our magazine in newsstands and traffic terminals, not only in Canada, but also in Australia and the United Kingdom.

Domestically, Canadian bands and artists were releasing a slew of top-selling albums in 1981. Rush was hitting their progressive peak with *Moving Pictures*. Featuring "Tom Sawyer" and "Limelight," the album made it to No. 3 on the *Billboard* album charts. Later that year, they would follow with their second live album, *Exit Stage Left*, which featured a composite of their *Permanent Waves* and *Moving Pictures* live shows.

Loverboy continued their U.S. domination with their second record, *Get Lucky*, which was fuelled by "Working for the Weekend," their most successful single to date. The album was released on November 3, after being recorded at Little Mountain Sound and co-produced by Bruce Fairbairn and guitarist Paul Dean. *Get Lucky* eventually reached No. 7 on the *Billboard* album charts and sold over four million copies in North America. After touring as Journey's opening act, Loverboy began 1982 with a fourteen-date headlining tour of the Pacific Northwest.

Bryan Adams was still an unknown entity. His second album, *You Want It, You Got It*, was co-produced by Bob Clearmountain in New York City and enjoyed one hit single, "Lonely Nights." Adams wanted to call the release *Bryan Adams Hasn't Heard of You Either*, in reference to his debut being largely ignored, but cooler heads prevailed. Those sessions marked the performance debut of drummer Mickey Curry and keyboardist Tommy Mandel, who featured prominently in future incarnations of his band. Adams was still playing high schools and small venues, getting his live show together, but he did appear in the U.S. opening for Foreigner and The Kings.

One Saturday evening in mid-May, I was watching an episode of Citytv's *The NewMusic* show, produced by an affable Mancunian called John Martin and hosted by Jeanne Becker and a mullet-haired young guy called J.D. Roberts. *The NewMusic* aired a segment on the exploding metal scene in England that featured such new acts as Def Leppard, Saxon, and, the focus of that show, Iron Maiden. Shot at some London pub, Maiden performed a great live gig, with double lead guitars, and for their encore this guy (I assumed a member of the road crew) appeared on stage wearing the skeletal mask of Iron Maiden's mascot, Eddie.

David Munz, Capitol's new VP of marketing, was fresh over from England and he was cluing me in to all these hot new bands springing up over there. The movement was nicknamed NWBHM (New Wave of British Heavy Metal), and I was particularly impressed with Iron Maiden, who of course were on Munz's EMI label. Maiden's self-titled 1980 release was already attracting attention throughout Europe, where the band had opened for KISS and Judas Priest. Sure enough, I got the word Maiden were launching their second album, *Killers*, with a concert appearance Friday, June 19, at Toronto's Concert Hall. I was asked if I was interested in chatting with them.

I agreed, and in advance of a phone chat with bassist Steve Harris, I noticed in the band's bio Harris previously had tryouts with the West Ham United Football (soccer) Club. Great! Something I could focus on to break the ice. Harris was on the phone just before heading out to the airport, and we naturally got around to talking football. He told me Maiden actually had team made up of band members, and when I mentioned *Music Express* also had a team, it was agreed that the day before their Concert Hall debut Maiden would drop by our office and play *ME* in a kick-about match. Trouble was *ME* didn't actually have a team!

It wasn't quite a lie. We had a bunch of writers who could play football, but we hadn't actually formed a team. There was me, of course, and New Zealander Kerry Doole, who was decent enough if he could remember to stop picking the ball up and running with it like they do in rugby. Roman Mitz's Germanic background qualified him as a player. Lenny Stoute had joined our writing staff and claimed he had played in Mexico. For the rest, we called upon Triumph's Rik Emmett and his brother Russell, industry types like Warner Music salesmen Mike Gaitt and John Deighan, and musicians like Teenage Head's Steve Mahon, Malcolm Tomlinson, The Bopcats' Sonny Baker, BB Gabor, David Bendeth, and we even got bluesman Matt Minglewood to slip on some cleats.

A call to John Martin ensured *The NewMusic* cameras were at the soccer field behind our office, and J.D. Roberts himself donned our red and black kit to join in the activities. A fleet of vans arrived and we said hello to Iron Maiden and their crew. The geezer wearing the Eddie mask in the film clip turned out to be the band's manager, Rod Smallwood. We quickly befriended band members Harris, Adrian Smith, Dave Murray, lead vocalist Paul Di'Anno, and drummer Clive Burr, and with the TV cameras rolling, we executed a kick-around that basically amounted to Harris scoring six goals on yours truly. It was a fun encounter and Maiden proved to be terrific blokes. It was a great way to launch their North American tour, and we agreed that with every future visit to Toronto Maiden would play *Music Express* at soccer. The game was also a catalyst for musicians and industry types who wanted to play future games for *Music Express*, which proved to be a valuable public relations outlet for our magazine.

The following day (Friday, June 19, 1981), Mike Gaitt and I were at the Concert Hall for Maiden's first gig in Canada. They had Anvil opening and the place was about three-quarters full. Anvil played so loud Gaitt and I retreated to W.C. Fields patio bar on Cumberland Avenue where we could still hear them clearly while knocking down a pint. Anvil was one of Canada's most promising heavy metal bands, but fell foul to poor American management and never reached their potential. An award-winning documentary of their exploits was produced in 2008.

At the end of their gig, we dropped by Maiden's dressing room. I gave Harris a soccer ball and a Toronto Blizzard soccer shirt (worn by top English player Peter Lorimer), and we promised to do it again in 1982. A firm friendship had been established between *Music Express* and Iron Maiden.

While hard rock/heavy metal was looming large on the global landscape, new wave music wasn't receiving the same amount of support from the major labels. The Garys had been forced to close The Edge after the building owners sold the property. After Gary Topp–favourite Kevin Coyne closed the curtains of the bar on June 21, their next project was the August 23 Police Picnic. As previously documented, the Garys had joined forces with band-manager Miles Copeland to plan a special outdoors concert, a selected site being an expanse of property called The Grove which was located in Oakville at the junction of Trafalgar Road and Fifth Line.

The Garys had not been impressed with John Brower's 1980 efforts to stage a New Wave Woodstock at Mosport, and felt that with their connections they could execute a more significant production. "I hated Heatwave," snorted Topp. "The whole event was too corporate. Artists like Elvis Costello, the Talking Heads, and The Pretenders weren't what real new wave music was about. The Police were the hottest band of 1981. Their mix of punk and reggae was what music was about then. And also, we could present a show with bands that we were excited about. To see John Otway, Willie P Bennett, and Killing Joke live on stage on the same bill was a major thrill for us."

The Police Picnic was impressive to say the least. Aside from The Police (who were riding high on the charts with their second album, *Zenyatta Mondata*), the lineup also featured The Specials' final concert appearance, Iggy Pop, Oingo Boing, The Go Go's, Killing Joke, and John Otway, as well as Canadian talent such as The David Bendeth Band, the Payola$, Willie P. Bennett, and Nash The Slash. "We could have had a young Prince too but Miles Copeland turned him down flat," revealed Topp. "Copeland thought Prince was too R&B and they were more into reggae."

A warm late-August day attracted a crowd estimated at 29,000, which remained relatively well behaved except for a bunch of kids who were throwing slices of watermelon at John Otway. "My wife was selling the watermelon from a kid's plastic wading pool. Kids would buy the watermelon and then turn around and throw the slices at Otway," admitted Topp. "When he complained to me afterwards I didn't have the heart to tell him that it was my wife who was selling the projectiles!" The Garys, by their own admission, didn't make any money on the gig, but had presented The Police in the best possible light, which earned them the right to stage the concert two more times.

It was during the Picnic that I first met Payola$ Paul Hyde and Bob Rock. After the initial buzz created by their first single "China Boys," A&M Records agreed to test the waters with a four-track EP, titled *Introducing Payola$*, in 1980. Rock was moonlighting as a record engineer at Vancouver's Little Mountain Sound (having worked on Loverboy's debut release). It was a practice A&M indulged in when they weren't sure of a band's potential. They released EPs by both The Payola$ and Barney Bentall's first band, Brandon Wolf, to sample public reaction before making a contract commitment. A&M was sufficiently impressed to sign the Payola$, but passed on Brandon Wolf.

Miles Copeland had also heard "China Boys" and originally arranged to have their debut released on his I.R.S. Records. However, there was a parting of the ways over material for the band's *In a Place like This* 1981 debut. "We had a song called 'Kill the White Man,' which Copeland demanded we pull from the album," reflected Hyde (now a contract plasterer). "Also, I don't think Copeland was too impressed about Bob [Rock] coming onto his wife in a New York nightclub."

Paul and I got along famously. He's from Harrogate, Yorkshire, across the Pennine Hills from Manchester, and we were both huge fans of Mott the Hoople's Ian Hunter. Bob told me the Payola$' new manager was Cliff Jones, who I had met via his connection with The Hometown Band, and I promised to provide whatever editorial support I could generate.

That promise was fulfilled when, on a visit to Vancouver, I dropped by A&M Records' office where band manager Cliff Jones previewed the Payola$' latest album, *No Stranger To Danger*. "Listen to this," he requested, with the boastful look of a proud new father. Out of the stereo speakers came that haunting percussive, reggae refrain that marked the intro to the Payola$' new single, "Eyes of a Stranger." "This is going to be huge," boasted Jones. "And Bruce Allen isn't going to get this band."

Jones filled me in on how they were able to get legendary Spiders from Mars guitarist Mick Ronson as the producer and handed me a cassette of the yet-to-be released *No Stranger to Danger* album. The following day I met Hyde and Rock at an outdoor cafe on Granville Street to discuss their new project. Both sensed they had a huge single with "Eyes of a Stranger," and both reiterated Jones's comment on how they were determined to make their mark without the involvement of Allen's management regime. "No bloody way do we want to look like Loverboy," quipped Hyde over his pint of beer. "Their whole image is so plastic. There's nothing authentic about them."

The Payola$ reached top four in Canada with "Eyes of a Stranger," and also registered a hit with "Be a Soldier," which wasn't included on the album, and toured nationally opening for New Zealand's Split Enz, with Ronson guesting on keyboards. Yet the band's failure to penetrate the U.S. meant that by the time the Payola$ released *Hammer on a Drum* in 1983, they would indeed be managed by Bruce Allen.

Bob and Doug McKenzie (alias comedians Dave Thomas and Rick Moranis) were the TV cult heroes of 1981. Their three-minute vignettes, where they played supposedly typical Canadians with their "Take off, eh!" and "You hoser" catch-phrases, propelled their SCTV show (about characters in the make-believe town of Melonville) to huge ratings in the U.S., at one point threatening the existence of *Saturday Night Live*. Responding to the Great White North mania, I suggested we run a cover story on the McKenzie Brothers, providing I could interview Thomas and Moranis in character. Fortunately, SCTV producer Andrew Alexander was familiar with *Music Express* through our contacts with Anthem Records, and he agreed to set up an interview for our January 1982 cover.

Early December I arrived at Alexander's office (which I believe was on Bloor Street West) and met with Thomas and Moranis. I explained I wanted them to stay in character throughout the Q&A, and the resulting dialogue was hysterical. There was one bit where I asked them to compare Canadian beer with European beer (me being English), and Moranis (as Bob) says, "Yeah well I like German beer, Heineken!" When I pointed out Heineken was a Dutch beer, Thomas (as Doug) went off an a rant about Bob being a real hoser because he doesn't know the difference between Dutch and German beer that finished with both of them yelling at each other to "Take off, eh!"

The dialogue was so funny that I was in tears transcribing the conversation. Our January issue, with Bob and Doug positioned in front of their Great White North map, came out just as they executed their Bob and Doug parade down Yonge Street. That issue literally flew out of the stores. The McKenzies went on to star in their own movie, *Strange Brew*, but their popularity became a source of jealousy with the rest of the SCTV crew, and by mid-1982 Moranis and Thomas had left the show.

As 1981 rolled to a close a Canadian superstar band was on its deathbed. Prism's 1980 *Young and Restless* release had failed badly and the band had needed to restrict most of their touring to Canadian dates. They had finished the year by headlining at Toronto's Danforth Theatre, and had gone down well with a capacity crowd. However, that same night in his suite at the Delta Chelsea Hotel, manager Bruce Allen shocked me by confiding that he (and the band) had decided to fire lead vocalist Ron Tabak. No clear reason was given, although Tabak's lack of writing proficiency, his poor interview skills, and the rumour that he was prone to gambling debts all made him a liability.

Replacing him was Henry Small, former lead vocalist of Scrubbaloe Caine. From the get-go there was internal trouble between Small and the remaining group members. Their first LP together, *Small Change*, featured only one song co-written with another member, Mitchell, and the album's only hit single, "Don't Let Him Know," was a Bryan Adams–Jim Vallance composition. Bassist Al Harlow felt Prism's direction took a turn for the worst during the band's L.A. recording sessions for *Small Change*. He agreed it was a unanimous decision to purge Tabak and that they were initially receptive to Small being their new front man. "However, right from the start, Henry made it clear he was going to be the focal point and we were just a rock 'n' roll band he was committed to work with," noted Harlow. "It was also obvious he had the full support of manager Bruce Allen and the executives at Capitol Records. Right from the beginning, we felt we were being used. Keyboardist John Hall quit right away but guitarist Lindsay Mitchell convinced the remaining members to go along with the new project and give Allen the benefit of the doubt."

A national tour concluded back at the Danforth Theatre in late December. It was there Prism discovered just how badly they had slipped. Klaatu were booked as openers and delivered a sensational performance. Prism followed, but with a new singer delivering the band's past hits and a batch of unfamiliar tracks, another capacity crowd, which had wildly cheered last year's band, sat in stunned silence. When Prism returned to the stage for their perfunctory encore, there was no one left in the building! That proved to be the last straw for Mitchell, Harlow, and Norton. With U.S. dates still pending, Small recruited an entirely new band, and even released a new album in 1983, titled *Beat Street*, that was Prism in name only.

"They quit because they couldn't face the challenge," snarled a defensive Allen. "They complain to me Ron Tabak is holding them back so I get them the best possible replacement in Henry Small. You'd think they'd want to rise to the challenge and try to improve themselves. But all they did was bitch and complain. I'm mortified at what has happened but I'm even more disappointed in their attitude. They didn't even try to make a go of it."

There was a buzz of excitement at our 209 Kingslake Road office as we launched into our third year in Toronto. We hired our first in-house employee, Greg Quill, who agreed to be our full-time editor and effectively took about half the writing burden off me. We had a Toronto freelance writing staff that comprised of Kerry Doole, Chris Churchill, Lenny Stoute, Roman Mitz, Angela Calderone, Norman (Otis) Richmond, who covered the black music scene, plus Lola, who was our celebrity columnist, and Davida Watson, who wrote a four-part series on jobs in the music industry.

In publishing our debut issue of 1982, Greg was assigned to execute an in-depth feature on April Wine, covering the band's roots in Waverley, Nova Scotia, through to their rise to prominence as one of Canada's premiere rock acts. The feature was set to appear in two parts, the first featuring the band's lead vocalist Myles Goodwyn on the cover, with the second part to run in our March/April issue. Myles was happy to oblige and engaged in a lengthy interview with Greg, agreeing to continue the conversation for the second part at a later date.

April Wine had been one of the first bands to benefit from the CRTC's Canadian-content regulations, with their debut single "Fast Train" justifying Aquarius Records' decision to make them the label's first release. The band suffered a major breakup when brothers David and Ritchie Henman and their cousin Jim Henmen left the band after the release of their second album, but lead vocalist Myles Goodwyn stayed and recruited new musicians to keep the band intact.

Goodwyn wasn't happy with the first part of our historical piece because Greg had spent a large portion of the feature interviewing Ritchie Henman, so Goodwyn refused to complete the second part of the feature. Much panic ensued, frantic calls to Aquarius were made, and Goodwyn finally agreed to be interviewed for part two. The focus of the second part was on

April Wine's August 1977 gig opening for The Stones at the El Mocambo in Toronto, their battle to maintain credibility against the rising disco and punk scenes, the introduction of a third guitarist in Brian Greenway (who debuted at the El Mo), and subsequent *First Glance* and *Harder Faster* albums which tried, unsuccessfully, to crack the U.S., despite the radio impact of "Say Hello" and "I Like To Rock."

With Capitol-EMI's money supporting April Wine, they toured Britain and Europe with *Harder Faster*, and even performed at the first Monsters of Rock festival on August 16, 1980, at England's Castle Donington raceway. That bill featured Ritchie Blackmore's Rainbow, Judas Priest, The Scorpions, and Saxon.

"Bad mistake," reflected April Wine lead guitarist Brian Greenway. "Everyone was dressed in black and there's us with our red-and-white outfits and red stage gear. We stood out like the Village People at a Blues convention. We were heckled unmercifully, everyone at the front of the stage telling us to piss off. It was a very uncomfortable gig."

With EMI's encouragement, April Wine pushed their presence in England, recorded a live concert at London's Hammersmith Odeon, and even recorded their next album, 1981's *Nature of the Beast*, at The Manor Studios in England. Unfortunately, the album jacket, depicting the band's three guitarists in a live shot, gave the impression April Wine was adopting an Iron Maiden or Def Leppard hard-rock direction. Fans who attended their gig at Birmingham's Odeon theatre voiced displeasure at the band's reliance on pop ballads, and their subsequent Hammersmith gig in London was cancelled. "EMI definitely misrepresented the band," noted Brown. "There was no way April Wine could be compared to Iron Maiden or Judas Priest. They even had us touring Europe with Motorhead and Uriah Heap."

In Toronto, Streetheart were facing a race against the clock to complete their fourth album — simply titled *Streetheart* — at George Semkiw's Amber Studios. Facing a mid-day deadline from EMI to complete the sessions, Semkiw, lead singer Kenny Shields, keyboardist Daryl Guthiel, and bassist Spide Sinnaeve, were agonizing over the final mix of the last track "Look in your Eyes."

"Maybe it would sound better if Kenny added a tambourine line," suggested Semkiw.

"We don't have time," protested Sinnaeve. "Besides, I don't think it'll make much difference."

"Oh, what the hell," quipped Shields as he grabbed a tambourine and re-entered the recording booth. Thirty minutes later, said tambourine had been added to the final track, and everyone was in agreement — Semkiw's perception had indeed increased the impact of that song.

Following the initial success of their first two albums, *Meanwhile Back in Paris* and *Under Heaven Over Hell*, which had gone gold and platinum respectively (earning Streetheart Most Promising Group of the Year Juno honours in 1980), the band's fortunes suffered a nosedive. Having survived the drama of losing Paul Dean and Matt Frenette to Loverboy, Streetheart were scheduled to execute a national tour in support of their *Under Heaven Over Hell* album. Some bright spark at Warner felt an ideal opening act for Streetheart would be AC/DC, who had just replaced the late Bon Scott with new vocalist Brian Johnson and released the album *Back in Black*.

Having AC/DC open for Streetheart was a classic mismatch. By the time the tour reached Toronto the order had been reversed, and although Streetheart held their own on the tour, the damage to their psyche had been done. Their 1980 *Quicksand Shoes* failed to generate a hit single, and a switch to EMI later that year for their next *Drugstore Dancer* LP was hampered by their guitarist John Hannah suffering a nervous breakdown.

That release did feature their cover of The Small Faces' "Tin Soldier" that helped them to score another platinum album. This created a wave of optimism for their 1982 project. With the addition of former Shama guitarist Jeff Neill, and fuelled by tracks like "What Kind of Love is This" and "Look In Your Eyes," the self-titled *Streetheart* proved to be their most successful release, selling over two hundred thousand units in Canada. However, their 1983 follow-up, *Dancing with Danger*, flopped badly and Streetheart entered a prolonged retirement later that year.

Suffice to say, the Canadian record industry was really humming in 1982. All the big bands — Loverboy (*Get Lucky*), Triumph (*Allied Forces*), Red Rider (*As Far As Siam*), April Wine (*Nature of the Beast*)— had mega-selling albums in retail and constant play on the radio. Rush was about to release their synth-driven *Signals*, and Solid Gold Records boasted three major bands in Chilliwack (*Opus X*), Toronto (*Head On*), and the newly launched Headpins (*Turn It Loud*).

It wasn't just commercial rock bands either. Being such a multicultural melting pot, Toronto boasted a plethora of varied styles and trends. The Bamboo Club was the host to a vibrant reggae scene, with The Satellites, Hopping Penguins, Messenjah, Leroy Sibbles, and, later that year, The Parachute Club, all adding a presence of ethnicity to the scene. The Copa and The Diamond Club were also reggae hotspots.

Country still flourished at The Horseshoe and Matador clubs with The Good Brothers, The Mercey Brothers, and Family Brown dominating the scene, while the success of Downchild Blues Band, Vancouver's Powder Blues Band, and David Wilcox in outlets like The El Mocambo, The Brunswick, Grossman's Tavern, and Club Bluenote provided Toronto with a strong Blues vibe. The Gasworks was still *the* venue for hard rock acts, but Gareth Brown's Heaven was about to transform from a Studio 54 disco venue to the city's hottest rock bar.

Heaven, located in the concourse level of the Hudson's Bay Centre at Bloor and Yonge, had been operating as a high-class disco in the same vein as New York's Studio 54, but was only open on Fridays and Saturdays. This changed one fateful day when Gary Slaight, vice president of rock station Q-107, wandered into the club. Q-107 was located in the adjacent office tower and Slaight was looking for an ideal venue for the station's fifth anniversary party, to be staged May 22, 1982.

Slaight was impressed with the club's layout and booked it for the party. The surprise headliner was Bryan Adams, and the club was packed full of local rock celebrities. Brown, who had been brought over from the CN Tower disco, Sparkles, to run Heaven, noted that club owner Victor Morton was impressed by the amount of alcohol consumed by the rock crowd, and soon warmed to the prospect of more rock music activity in his venue.

"The club's sight lines weren't the greatest," admitted Brown. "Yet the layout was designed so you could wander around, hang out at the horseshoe-shaped bar at the front and watch the stage on the monitors or go to the back and watch the stage. There was a great ambiance about the place. As the disco phase died, rock bands took control and the venue was eventually renamed Rock N Roll Heaven on June 13, 1986."

Near the end of the summer in 1982, I found myself heading down Russell Hill Road in Toronto's tony Forest Hills area to interview Rush drummer Neil Peart about the band's new *Signals* album for our September cover. As I have stated previously, I wasn't a great fan of their earlier work. Yet, having relocated to Toronto and spent a fair amount of time at Anthem Records Oak Ridges office being force-fed a steady diet of Rush, I had grown to appreciate the complexities of their compositions. Having agreed to meet with Peart on his home turf, I was forewarned by Anthem's Tom Berry to do my homework on the album as Peart did not appreciate journalists who had not done their research.

No worries. Peart greeted me warmly, we headed upstairs to his attic office and spent a good hour talking about how Rush was incorporating synthesizers into their sound and how Peart had assumed virtually all the lyrical duties. He seemed to be impressed by my awareness of his Ernest Hemingway references in "Losing It," and he even mentioned the band's conflict with producer Terry Brown over their reggae direction on "Digital Man" and how Brown didn't want that track on the album. The result of the argument was that *Signals* was Brown's last production involvement with Rush. *Signals* produced the bands only top-forty U.S. hit with "New World Man," and spawned a major Canadian hit with "Subdivisions." Both tracks continue to be featured prominently on current concert set lists.

As 1982 rolled to a close, I got back in touch with Bruce Allen about utilizing *Music Express* and a network of national rock radio stations to launch a national public music awards program. Understanding Bryan Adams and Loverboy would likely win something, it was imperative Allen agreed to have his acts present at the awards, this he promised to do.

Next question: where to stage the awards? Since the Junos were always held in Toronto at that time, we wanted to do it somewhere else. We elected to go with Montreal. The city was close enough that we could organize it from our Toronto offices, and we could stage a bilingual event, something the Junos had never done. There were so many details to take care of: the event's date, venue, possible television coverage, sponsorship, talent etc. But for some reason, none of these details fazed us. We had no comprehension of how much time, money, and energy such an undertaking cost. It was just a matter of thinking, let's do it!

10

MUSIC EXPRESS
HAS A BETTER IDEA!

In deciding to stage our first annual Music Express Awards, I wanted to correct the faults continually made by the Junos. First off, I wanted a live show. I also wanted to schedule our show ahead of the 1983 Junos, which were set for April 5 in Toronto. The tight squeeze between conceiving the idea and the projected date didn't give us much time.

Opting to put on the show in Montreal, the first call I made was to Martin Melhuish to solicit his support. I had met Marty and his partner Doug Pringle during their staging of the Rock Cirkus in Edmonton, and understood he and Doug knew the Montreal music scene inside out. These two Englishmen had worked together on a syndicated radio show out of Montreal and had joined forces to execute two major concerts in Edmonton in both 1979 and 1980. Pringle, from London, developed a lucrative career as a radio programmer, while Melhuish authored several rock books, including *Heart of Gold* and a Bachman-Turner Overdrive biography.

My first visit to meet Marty was during the second week of January. That trip introduced me to the legend of 7 Burton Street in the Westmount section of Montreal. Marty invited me to stay over at his place, which proved to be a commune for displaced musicians and industry types. During my first stay, I was introduced to RCA Records publicity coordinator Kathy Hahn, and to a precocious seventeen-year-old girl called Sass Jordan. She had just left her first band, The Pinups, and was also crashing at Marty's. I still remember her bouncing on a bed, playing air guitar to Def Leppard's "Rock! Rock! Till You Drop" off their newly released *Pyromania* album. Sass eventually developed into a major recording artist with Capitol-EMI and also served as a judge on *Canadian Idol*.

It was Marty who suggested The Spectrum as a logical venue. Located downtown on Sainte-Catherines Street and with a seating capacity of 1,325, The Spectrum was the city's prime live club venue and received strong sponsorship support from CHOM-FM, our targeted radio liaison. Using Marty's connections, we met CHOM's music director Ian McLean, who instantly warmed to our anti-Juno project and agreed the station would co-promote the live performance. With CHOM-FM on board, the venue agreed to stage the show on Sunday, February 27 in exchange for the drink concessions.

With a projected date set, our next quandary was how to execute a television broadcast. Again, never thinking of all the obstacles that prevented us televising the show, I responded to a suggestion from Marty that we might want to touch base with Andre Perry, the owner of Le Studio recording studio in Morin Heights, located north of Montreal in the picturesque Laurentian Mountains. Marty knew Perry very well and was aware Perry had just installed television production equipment at Le Studio and might want a debut project to play with his new toys.

Now, Morin Heights was *the* recording studio in North America at that time. Key albums by Rush, April Wine, and David Bowie had been recorded there. Arriving at Le Studio, we were told The Police were currently using the facilities to record their *Synchronicity* album. Perry, a big bear of a guy, met us at the studio and instantly enthused about shooting the show. He showed us his new television consoles, and bubbled with enthusiasm over shooting both an English and French version of the event. I was so overwhelmed by Perry's enthusiasm that I didn't confirm at the time how much he was going to charge us.

Perry was fine with Marty and I producing the show with him producing the television program, a concept that made both Marty and me giddy with enthusiasm. After slagging off the Junos, the onus was on us to deliver something fresh and new. Using the NME Awards as a template, we wanted live bands, winners determined by a public vote, a live audience, and most important to us, at least one host who could relate to the event.

We contacted nine major Canadian FM stations and asked them to promote the fan-pick ballots on air, and as an additional twist we invited them to designate a band/artist from their area to receive a Most Promising

Group/Artist award. This solidified our radio support and we were able to generate over twenty-two thousand votes. Also, we wanted our awards to be special, not just a chunk of acrylic. To that end we had gold-plated working microphones made, courtesy of Shure, who were happy to link their mics to the cream of Canada's music industry.

As for the host, the name that immediately sprung to my mind was Long John Baldry. Having watched Baldry host British TV specials and met him several times, I loved his dry British wit and the fact he knew the history of contemporary music inside and out. Recognized as a central figure in the development of London Blues movement of the early sixties, Baldry had personally discovered Rod Stewart playing harmonica at a London railway station, and his first name "John" was usurped by certain Reginald Dwight, who renamed himself Elton John. I wanted someone who didn't need cue cards to introduce people and who could fill in the gaps with his own anecdotes. Long John Baldry was the perfect choice. So I tracked Baldry down at his Village by the Grange apartment in Toronto. He loved the idea and agreed he could ad lib the show.

More trips to 7 Burton Street ensued. Marty and I plotted out the show; we needed a French element, so Marty suggested Nanette Workman as Baldry's co-host. Nanette was fluent in French and English, was popular in the Quebecois music scene, and a meeting with her and her manager Francine Herschorn at a bar in Old Montreal convinced us she would be the ideal co-host who could carry the French segment of the show.

Having secured Baldry and Workman, we booked Martha and the Muffins, the Payola$, and then decided on Corbeau as the third live act. Formed by former Offenbach members, Pierre Harel, Roger Belval, Michel Lamonthe, and Donald Hince, and fronted by the magnetic Marjolaine Morin, Corbeau (which translates to "raven") dominated the Quebecois rock scene through the late seventies and early eighties before breaking up in 1984.

Deciding that we needed a stand-up comedian to fill some of the gaps, Marty and I dropped by Yuk Yuks on Bay Street in Toronto where we scouted Steve Brinder. As part of his stand-up, Brinder executed this tribute to Motown that was absolutely hysterical. We tackled him backstage, briefly explained the concept, and told him we needed him for at least one spot in the show. Hearing it was going to be televised, Brinder accepted our offer of two hundred dollars, a return train ticket, and two night's accommodation in Montreal.

Now that we had all the talent, we needed to plan out the show. I had been in contact with most record companies, talent managers, and booking agencies, and together we cobbled together a list of award nominees (CHOM handled the French categories), and Marty and I agreed we would tell the winners in advance to attract as many artists as possible.

The plan was for Martha and the Muffins to play three songs, after which they would execute an equipment switch with Corbeau while the awards were handed out. Corbeau would perform three songs, Brinder do his routine, and then we would finish off with three Payola$ songs. Fine on paper but we still had some major gaps to fill. The Spectrum was one of the first concert venues to feature a video screen, and it quickly occurred to us that we could fill in the gaps by airing artist videos.

Music videos had become a new art form in 1983. There was still no MuchMusic or Music Plus, but with MTV established in the U.S., many Canadian acts had already started to invest in creating their own videos. The Juno Awards had yet to embrace this technology, so the Music Express Awards became the first Canadian music awards show to utilize this new art form when we used them as brief clips aired while presenting the winners. We played lengthier clips when we needed time to switch equipment.

One priority was to make sure the winners were going to be in attendance. Headpins' Darby Mills had won Top Canadian Female Vocalist, and she was thrilled to attend and to pick up her award and also accept the Most Promising Group award for her band. The Payola$ had won Top Single ("Eyes of a Stranger"), and they were booked to perform so they weren't a problem. Ditto Montrealer Aldo Nova, who had won as Most Promising Male Vocalist.

But surprisingly, or maybe not surprisingly, a stumbling block came in the form of Bruce Allen, someone who had strongly pushed for the original concept. Loverboy had won Top Canadian Album (*Get Lucky*) and Bryan Adams had won Top Canadian Male Vocalist. Yet when I tried to nail Allen down to commit to both acts being present in Montreal, he started to waffle.

In a heated phone conversation, I totally lost it with him. I yelled at Allen, calling him two-faced and sundry other barbs and insults, when suddenly he started to laugh. "Just winding you up, of course we'll be there," he cracked. "Just testing you." Allen brought in Reno and Dean, and Adams was playing at McGill opening for Aerosmith in support of his newly released *Cuts Like a Knife* album, so he was in the neighbourhood.

The problems started with Andre Perry. He had taken hands-on control over the production, sound systems, and even acquired some impressive looking stage props from the CBC. Everything looked great until he dropped the cost bomb on us. He wanted forty thousand dollars to execute the production. I think he saw me turn white, so he explained that we could generate those funds securing corporate sponsors, and he knocked off any monies he generated from selling the French show.

It was a huge financial risk; Conny went ballistic when she found out. But we rationalized that we could raise about fifteen thousand dollars from admissions (I believe the tickets were fifteen dollars each), and I did expect to solicit corporate sponsors once they had viewed the taped show, and Perry was confident he could generate about fifteen thousand dollars from the French broadcast rights. So I did have a shot at breaking even, and we would have the prestige of televising the broadcast. Problem was, I didn't have any corporate sponsors going in, and didn't even have a TV broadcast network lined up. But true to form, we went for it anyway!

On the day of the show, Marty and I met at the venue late morning with Steve Brinder, Baldry, and Nanette Workman to go over the production. We ran through the order of winners so John could familiarize himself with anyone he didn't know, and we established when we were going to run the video inserts, the band performances, and Steve's stand-up spot. We did realize we had one spot in the show still to fill, so Steve offered to do an additional routine ... but what to do? Then I had one of those flashbulb moments. "The Junos are always honouring Anne Murray, even though she is sick of winning those awards. So why don't we execute a tribute to Anne ... as performed by Ozzy Osbourne!" said I, laughing at the sick idea I had just thought up.

The idea was to get Steve in a mullet wig. We would start to play Anne Murray's "Snowbird," and he would come out, prancing about, holding a white snowbird (a Christmas ornament), and then the song would change to Black Sabbath's "Ironman" and Steve would bite the head off the bird! For realism, we went down the street to a Harvey's restaurant and got a handful of ketchup packets, then we drilled a hole in the fake-bird's neck and filled it up with ketchup.

With the venue totally sold out, the show couldn't have gone better. As a host, Baldry was brilliant, funny, entertaining, and able to respond to any occasion with his dry humour and commanding presence. The Junos really missed out in not selecting John to host one of their shows. At one point in his opening monologue, John told a story about his mate, Rod Stewart, performing in Germany. "A fan jumps out of the audience and strikes Rod in the face. Which is the first recorded case of a fan hitting the shit!" cracked Baldry. Whoa, I thought they were mates!

Martha and the Muffins were well received by the mainly Francophone audience and the Payola$ concluded the show with their trio of songs, including "Eyes of a Stranger." But the night's biggest hit was Corbeau. I had never seen them before, and Marjolaine Morin was absolutely amazing — energetic and extremely sexy. At one point she ripped off her dress to reveal a scanty mini skirt. The shock effect almost knocked Bruce Allen off his chair.

Steve Brinder's Anne Murray tribute brought the house down. When he bit into the dove's neck and ketchup squirted all over his face, you could hear a gasp of shock followed by uncontrolled laughter. The videos were also a great success as a lot of people had yet to see Men Without Hats' "Safety Dance," Martha and the Muffins' "Echo Beach," or the Payola$' "Eyes Of A Stranger" videos before.

Nanette was also brilliant, and the fact we had a Francophone element to the show, which featured Aldo Nova, Corbeau, Diane Tell, and Claude Dubois all receiving awards, made our show unique. The event was so relaxed we solicited some great comments from the recipients. Aldo Nova, examining the phallic shape of his award, cracked, "I wish I'd had this award on tour. I could have tucked it in my pants and pulled a few babes."

Bryan Adams acknowledged his Music Express Award as the first award he'd ever won, and by knowing in advance who had won we were able to receive a funny acceptance video from Australia's Men at Work, who had won both Top International Album (*Business As Usual*) and Top International Single ("Who Can It Be Now"). Lead vocalist Colin Hay cracked, "We'd like to thank *Music Express* and youse blokes and sheilas out there in readershipland for voting our record the grousest!"

The following day we paid off the bands and settled their hotel bills. Revenues from ticket sales covered our immediate expenses, yet we still had to deal with Andre Perry's bill. Conny headed back to Toronto and Marty and I drove up to Le Studio to see how Perry was making out with the footage.

Perry was like the proverbial kid in a candy store. He had the concert footage on his monitors and was editing through it to fashion a tight ninety-minute package in both French and English. He delighted in re-running the footage of Allen almost falling off his chair when Morin whipped her dress off. The fact Perry could edit the raw footage, splice in tons of special effects, tweak the sound quality, and edit down John's monologues in post-production provided a first-class end result. Something the Junos had never accomplished.

Perry was still adamant he wanted forty thousand dollars, but he did release a final version of the telecast for me to shop to corporate sponsors. Fortunately, there was a major beer war brewing between Molson and Labatt for musical properties, and my first call to Brent Imlach (former Maple Leafs coach Punch Imlach's son) at Molson produced a positive response. He viewed the cassette at his downtown office and was very impressed with the package. He offered me fifteen thousand dollars for full rights to the show — not quite the amount I was looking for, but time was of the essence so we accepted.

The next step was to secure a television broadcast network. I knew Citytv was always on the lookout for new properties, and based on Molson's sponsorship it wasn't going to cost them anything. One viewing of the tape and Citytv's Jay Levine enthusiastically cobbled together a national network of independent stations to air the show on a staggered basis, starting around May 22, with the Quebec version going out on TVA May 14. Perry released the tape to us on receiving the Molson monies, but he insisted he couldn't obtain funds from his TVA broadcast and held us accountable for the balance of twenty-five thousand dollars. We ended up making a settlement, but I don't believe we paid him the full amount. Still, our credibility in the industry soared and CARAS made it clear to me they were pissed off we had successfully executed an indie awards show, but we didn't care. This, at the time, was our crowning achievement.

11

SPREADING

OUR WINGS

Buoyed by the success of our awards show, we stormed into 1983 on a tidal wave of activity. First duty was for yours truly to serve as one of the judges for Q-107's Homegrown Talent Contest held that April. Promoted as an initiative to stimulate local talent, Q-107 invited regional artists and groups to submit songs to the contest. About twenty-six songs were selected by the station and judged by a group of local industry A&R types and music writers who listened to the tracks in one marathon three-hour session. An overall winner was announced later by the station based on points awarded by the judges, and the top eight or ten tracks were included on the station's annual *Homegrown* album, released by Attic Records.

A big problem with the voting process was that by the time you, as a judge, had heard the fourteenth song, you started to get a bit punchy. But all this changed as we gathered at Heaven nightclub in late April to listen to that year's entries. About the fourth or fifth track in, a catchy drum/guitar intro led into Honeymoon Suite's "New Girl Now." The entire club fell deadly silent, absorbed by the song. Talk about instant hit.

One person seen frantically scribbling away was new Warner Canada A&R chief Bob Roper. "It was like, Wow! Who are these guys?" said Roper, now an instructor at the Harris Institute in Toronto. "That song had everything, great lyrics, great instrumental hook, and it was also well produced." Suffice to say, Q-107 shuffled through the remaining tracks without much of a ripple. As everyone munched through their post-voting pizzas and beer, the talk was still centred on that one track.

Roper soon became familiar with Honeymoon Suite as band manager Steve Prendergast had targeted Warner as the right label for his project. I had met Prendergast the previous December at Heaven, where he had mentioned his then-current band, Lennox, had broken up but that the band's lead singer, Johnnie Dee, had joined forces with guitarist Derry Grehan and keyboardist Ray Coburn to form a new group. He also mentioned top local producer Tom Treumuth had already recorded some material and he was going to the MIDEM music conference (a major gathering of the world's record industry staged annually in France) in January to shop the tracks to potential foreign labels.

While at MIDEM, Prendergast found receptive ears in Warner U.K. A&R rep Robin Godfrey, but Godfrey wondered why he hadn't first pitched the band to Warner Canada, which was the correct protocol. To create some local buzz, Prendergast entered "New Girl Now" in Q-017's Homegrown Contest, and by the time he pitched the band to Roper, he was preaching to the converted.

"We really wanted Warner," acknowledged Jeff Rogers, part of Prendergast's management team who enjoyed later success managing Crash Test Dummies. "I remember going to Pennington's and buying a mannequin so I could rip it apart and send Bob a package containing an arm and a leg saying 'We would give an arm and a leg for you to sign Honeymoon Suite.'"

"Stan [Kulin, Warner Canada president] wanted to generate U.S. interest so we staged a showcase gig at the Roxy in Brampton and brought in personnel from Warner and Elektra," continued Roper. "We didn't tell the band anything to make sure they wouldn't get too nervous, but Derry goes to the front door to make sure his girlfriend was on the guest list and sees [top U.S. producer] Roy Thomas-Baker walking through the door."

Honeymoon Suite passed the audition, signed a U.S. deal with Warner, and after Treumuth was able to re-record existing tracks and complete the rest of the material, the band's debut album was released in early June 1984 (missing the intended Valentine's Day target).

Bryan Adams had released his third album, *Cuts Like a Knife*, in January and was preparing for a slot opening for Loverboy's tour by staging some warm-up gigs around Toronto. I had Paul Suter, our London correspondent, visit us in Toronto while he was checking out some stories for his *Kerrang!* magazine, and I was anxious for him to catch Bryan playing at the Roncesvalles Tavern. So I got us great seats right in front of the stage and Bryan started to play. Ten minutes into the set, Paul looked at me and said, "This guy is nothing but a Bruce Springsteen wannabe, anything else in mind?"

My mind was spinning. What else was going on in town that night? "Well, we could go and see Lee Aaron playing at the Queensbury Arms," said I.

"Sounds good to me," responded Suter.

So off we go up Weston Road to catch Ms. Aaron. By this point, her debut indie-released *Lee Aaron Project* LP had been picked up by Attic, she had appeared on the front cover of *Oui,* and her stage act was quite salacious in that she did this number where she seemed to strip behind a silhouetted screen with her female form quite clearly outlined. Paul Suter was gob smacked! "Got to meet her," he bubbled. "She would be sensational in *Kerrang!*"

Within weeks of retuning to England, Suter had arranged a centre-fold shot of Lee, real name Karen Greening, to appear in *Kerrang!*, which triggered a chain reaction of interest from other European magazines. By May he had arranged for her to fly over to England to perform at the famous Marquee Club, supported by a Manchester band called Sam Thunder. All this activity led to a slot on day two of the Reading Festival playing on a bill with Black Sabbath, Marillion, Suzi Quatro, and Stevie Ray Vaughan. Lee's debut album grew in demand as a result and ended up being imported all over Europe.

"The British media said that I was 'flat and flaccid' compared to my promo shots," laughed Belleville, Ontario, native Aaron. "But they were astonished by my powerhouse vocals. I took great heart in that and was invited back to play at the Reading Festival."

I was soon heading over to England myself to visit the major record companies, interview a few new British acts, and promote *Music Express* overseas. We had used this trip to run a contest for a winner and a friend to catch Rush in concert at Wembley Arena, and writer Kerry Doole agreed to go over a couple of days before me to escort the winners to the concert.

I arrived at London's Victoria Station, dragged my luggage out into the bustling city, and went in search of the bed and breakfast that was hosting

Kerry and our winners. I finally tracked down the place, and I was greeted by Kerry and the two winners, who were still buzzed about the Rush concert. But there was one problem! "Hey Keith, remember that promise you made to them if there was any other shows they wanted to see in London whilst they were here, you would try to arrange it?" said Kerry.

"Er, yes," yawned I, craving to hit the sack to shake off my jet lag.

"Well they have read Iron Maiden are playing in Birmingham tonight and want to know if you'll take them." Oh, no, me and my big mouth. I had said to them I would try to arrange something for their last night in *London*! But a trip two hundred miles north to Birmingham wasn't part of the plan.

Still, a promise is a promise, so I reluctantly agreed to the trip provided they gave me at least a couple of hours sleep. Mid-afternoon, I dragged my butt out of the B&B and with our two winners in tow headed off for Euston Station to catch the train north to Birmingham. The two winners, both nineteen-year-old guys who were heavy metal fans, were even more ecstatic about seeing Maiden than they were about Rush. The gig was at the Odeon Theatre in Birmingham. I had no idea where that was, but as the train pulled into Birmingham New Street station the theatre's Odeon marquee was clearly visible.

I was on the verge of collapse, yet struggled to the venue, arriving about 4:00 p.m. as Maiden were completing the sound check. A few quick enquires and I was told to take the winners down the road to the Hilton Hotel where manager Rod Smallwood was thrilled by our unexpected visit. The rest of the band were also happy to see me and were great with our winners, signing autographs, posing for photos, handing them backstage passes, and even giving them those signature Maiden T-shirts.

The gig was part of the English portion of their World Piece Tour, and the winners received the additional thrill of standing by the soundboard to watch the show. I stood with them next to Rod, trying to fight an overwhelming drowsiness, when I suddenly keeled forward and collapsed headfirst into the soundboard. Fortunately, no damage occurred to their equipment, and I was carried backstage and revived. Told I was planning to take the winners back to London that night, Rod said, "No way," and arranged for me and the two winners to stay that night at the Hilton at the band's expense before heading south the following morning. Just another example of what a class act Smallwood and Maiden were then and would be again in the future.

With our winners winging their way home to Toronto, Kerry and I started making contact with British labels in the hopes of getting a few high-profile interviews. Some of the labels wouldn't give us the time of day, but Columbia was particularly enthusiastic and arranged for us to interview two of their latest acts, Wham! and Fastway. As the interviews were scheduled at the same time, Kerry volunteered to chat with George Michael and Andrew Ridgely of Wham! while I was entertained by Fast Eddie Clarke and Pete Way of heavy metal band Fastway.

Clarke had been a member of Motorhead, but had left under less than amicable circumstances and had nothing positive to say about band leader Lemmy Kilmister. Way had joined Fastway after previously playing bass for UFO. Nobody in Canada had heard about either of the bands we interviewed yet, but Kerry was particularly enthused about his chat with the Wham guys and their album soon conquered North America.

Another artist Columbia raved about was Paul Young. They sent us copies of his *No Parlez* debut release. During the rest of our visit, we dropped by RCA where they tipped us off about the Eurythmics and Haysi Fantayzee, with Kerry getting to interview Eurythmic's Annie Lennox and Dave Stewart at their home studio.

Whilst Kerry and I were tripping around Old Blighty, my editor Greg Quill was out in San Bernardino, California, covering the second US Festival. Apple Computer co-founder (and future *Dancing with the Stars* contestant) Steve Wozniak had decided the best way to promote Apple was to fund a major music festival, rather than spend his company's marketing dollars on traditional advertising outlets. The first US Festival was staged Labour Day weekend, September 3–5, 1982, with a lineup of new wave talent, including The Police, Talking Heads, and The Ramones, and more corporate acts like Tom Petty and Fleetwood Mac. San Francisco promoter Bill Graham provided the talent, and the festival at Glen Helen Regional Park was surprisingly well executed, even though Wozniak dropped about twelve million dollars on the event.

Such was the positive response to US Festival that Wozniak decided to repeat the format, this time during the Memorial weekend of May 28–30, 1983, with a special country music day set for June 4. Again using

Graham to line up the talent, Wozniak assigned a special theme to each day. New music took over the first day's lineup (The Clash, English Beat, Stray Cats, INXS), the next day featured hard rock (Quiet Riot, Motley Crue, Ozzy Osbourne, Judas Priest, Triumph, The Scorpions, Van Halen), and a corporate rock night closed the show on May 30 (David Bowie, U2, Simple Minds, The Pretenders). The country night featured Alabama, Willie Nelson, and Waylon Jennings.

Van Halen was originally contracted to be paid one million dollars with a clause that they would be the highest paid act. So when Bowie was brought on, also for a million dollars, Van Halen's fee was hiked to 1.5 million dollars. When quizzed about this exorbitant fee at a press conference prior to their performance, Van Halen lead vocalist David Lee Roth responded, "Yes, well sure it's a lot of money, but we do have costs! By the time we've paid for our crew, our accommodation, and our out-of-pocket expenses, we only have enough money left to buy a small ocean-going liner."

The hard rock day was a major event for Toronto's Triumph. With Citytv's *The NewMusic* VJ, J.D. Roberts (now Fox News and former CNN morning host John Roberts) along for the ride, Triumph flew into the site by helicopter with *The NewMusic* cameras capturing the view of some 450,000 spectators and the band's resulting spectacular late-afternoon performance.

"Steve Wozniak loved us so he insisted that we be on with Van Halen, Ozzy, and Judas Priest," reflected Triumph guitarist Rik Emmett, whose band was at the time enjoying huge success with their *Allied Forces* album and Emmett's "Magic Power" single. "The crowd stretched as far as your eyes could see. We played great but the longer the day went the drunker the bands got. By the time Van Halen went on they were totally pissed." Wozniak had seven cameras shooting the concert, "But the footage was so bad, the tape just sat there," noted Emmett. "We asked for our footage and Steve was happy to give it to us. So we re-edited our clip and the final tape looked like it was our concert."

Sending Greg out to cover the US Festival was an expensive hit for *Music Express,* but we were determined to promote ourselves at as many major events as possible. Imagine Conny's shock when she picked up the Sunday May 29 *Toronto Star* to find a full-page feature on the festival courtesy of one Greg Quill! Now, Greg claimed he mentioned telling Conny about writing something for the *Star,* but she couldn't have imagined he would be scooping his own magazine. The following day, the same thing; another major feature on the hard rock day in the *Star.* Worst of all, the *Star* gave Greg a by-line but didn't credit him as *Music Express* editor. Conny called the *Toronto Star*'s entertainment department and went ballistic on them. She wanted to know what right they had using our writer and demanded they reimburse us for his expenses. They politely told her to get stuffed!

Greg returned to face the music about the same time I arrived back from England. He claimed he didn't know the *Star* planned to play up his stories the way they did. Worse was to follow. The *Star,* obviously impressed by his writing talents, assigned Greg to write a series of columns investigating claims Michael Cohl's CPI operation was scalping their own concert tickets and had been cheating acts playing at the CNE by surcharging them a non-existing tax on their performances. The *Star* made him an offer to join their staff full time, and by September he was gone.

Our *Music Express* soccer team came out of mothballs when I received a phone call from Q-107. The station was sponsoring a concert by Teenage Head at the CNE right after a Toronto Blizzard–Tampa Bay Rowdies Major League Soccer match. The problem was they needed to retain the crowd after the Blizzard match while they moved the portable stage into position in front of the grandstand. So they asked if we could organize a charity match against Q-107, to be played while they were setting up the stage?

Ask anyone in the music industry at that time and they will say Teenage Head were unlucky not to break in the States. Launched out of Hamilton in 1978 at the peak of England's punk invasion, lead singer Frankie Venom, guitarist Gord Lewis, bassist Steve Mahon, and drummer Nick Stipanitz arrived with a self-titled debut on local indie label Ready Records. They played a prominent role in the infamous Last Pogo Riot, which occurred on December 1, 1978, at The Horseshoe Tavern.

The two Garys had promoted a lineup of Toronto's top punk — The Scenics, Cardboard Brains, The Secrets, Mods, The Ugly, Viletones, and Teenage Head — that night. The show dissolved into a riot when over-zealous police and firefighters ended the show one song into Teenage Head's performance. This event triggered national attention and spawned a documentary shot by Colin Brunton, now on DVD, called *The Last Pogo*, that detailed all the mayhem resulting in all future punk bands being banned from the building.

Such was Teenage Head's notoriety that they were picked up by Attic Records for their 1980 release, *Frantic City,* which resulted in two major hits, "Let's Shake" and "Something On My Mind," an opening appearance at Heatwave, plus a gig at Ontario Place (which triggered another riot). Showcase dates in New York City were set up to break the band stateside, but a near fatal car accident involving Lewis forced cancellation of these dates. And although David Bendeth filled in for Lewis during his recovery, the subsequent 1982 release, *Some Kinda Fun,* failed to recapture that buzz and their shot at U.S. exposure was lost.

For the pre-concert soccer match, we gathered our usual writers and record industry types, but we held a couple of key players back just in case Q-107 brought in a few new players. One young chap playing for Q-107 that we did meet before the game introduced himself as Mark Holmes, lead singer for a new band called Platinum Blonde. The fact he was English had me thinking Q had brought in a few ringers but we had nothing to fear as we trashed them 6–0.

After the match, Mark and guitarist Sergio Galli told me they were playing at the Queen Elizabeth Theatre as part of a Canadian Musician Magazine Expo on the CNE grounds and I was invited to check them out. Kerry and I went along and caught the show and were quite impressed. Promoted as a Police clone band, Mark, Sergio, and drummer Chris Steffler mixed a few original tunes into their set plus a couple of Beatles covers, including a passable reggae-tinged version of "Twist and Shout." Next time I heard of them, Platinum Blonde had released an EP on Columbia called *Six Track Attack* and were storming the national airwaves with "Doesn't Really Matter."

By May 1983, a new concert venue called Kingswood Theatre had opened up north of Toronto at Canada's Wonderland, a Disney-inspired theme park that had opened its gates in the summer of 1981. Kingswood Theatre was in direct competition with Michael Cohl's CPI Productions, which had assumed ownership of CNE concert events. This led to a "Beer War," with Labatt sponsoring Kingswood and competing against Molson's exclusive sponsorship of the CNE. Kingswood trying to lure big names like Eric Clapton and Don Henley caused a major bidding war broke out between the rival promoters. This bidding war also included domestic acts like Bryan Adams, Kim Mitchell, Honeymoon Suite, and Platinum Blonde, who all earned headline status at Kingswood. New York promoters, The Nederlander Group, were recruited to supply many of the venue's big names.

A few major problems faced Kingswood, the biggest one being how to differentiate park visitors from those who had just bought concert tickets. Obviously, patrons who shelled out twenty-five dollars to catch a concert didn't also want to pay a regular park admission. This problem was resolved by allowing concert ticket holders access to the park two hours before the show — which meant they could hit the rides before attending the concert. Yet when Iron Maiden was booked for Monday September 5, Kingswood management rescinded this policy. Maiden fans did not get that two-hour window and were asked to go straight from the box office to the venue. I guess they didn't want fifteen thousand Maiden fans wandering around the park prior to the concert.

Kingswood's excuse was that an Italian wine-tasting festival was being staged at the same time as the concert. However, the same festival was also staged on the Saturday while a Culture Club concert went on, yet no fan restrictions were in place. I pointed this discrepancy out to Rod Smallwood, who went ballistic at this obvious discrimination. A few heated phone calls from EMI to Canada's Wonderland eventually smoothed out the problem.

Our soccer team was at it again for its annual soccer match against Maiden. It was set for the Sunday before their Kingswood concert, but needed a better venue than our Kingslake location to play the game. On my travels I had passed Upper Canada College on Avenue Road quite a few times. The college was vacant for the summer, and I had noticed their soccer field was still marked for regular soccer matches. On a whim, I pulled into the parking lot and noticed no one on site acting as security. Taking a wild risk, I designated Upper Canada College as the venue for the match.

Pre-promoted by Q-107, we had quite a crowd gather at the college for the afternoon kick-off. The *Music Express* team featured Rik Emmett; Frankie Venom and Steve Mahon from Teenage Head; Roots' Ray Perkins,

Kerry Doole; Roman Mitz, Lenny Stoute, and photographer Dimo Safari from the mag; and industry types like Mike Gaitt and John Deighan from Warner Music. Maiden were obviously set on reversing the previous year's loss as they had a full contingent of group members and road crew.

Knowing Maiden had a concert the following day, I told our players to go easy on them, no rough stuff. Five minutes into the game, Roman ran back to my goal and said, "Keith, they're kicking the crap out of us." So I told them to go for it and we had a highly spirited game which ended in a 3–3 tie. We pulled a couple of hundred spectators, including Platinum Blonde's Mark Holmes and Sergio Galli, and we all agreed to reconvene at the Rose and Crown Pub at Yonge and Eglinton for a post-game reception.

Good job it was a Sunday afternoon, as the pub didn't know what hit it. Both teams and the spectators invaded the place. Maiden commandeered about four tables and ordered every plate of British pub grub on the menu, setting up this huge smorgasbord of food. Then Maiden took over the two dartboards, with Steve Harris and sundry other Maidens playing anyone that offered to take them on. The sight of Iron Maiden mingling with the regular punters was typical of how they connect with their fans in England. There was no rock musician ego present, just a bunch of guys with long hair happy to play arrows with the locals.

In reflecting why Maiden were becoming so successful, Smallwood noted, "Maiden never compromised their principles or tried to win fans by following the latest musical trends — and people respected that they feel Maiden is something they can trust and believe in and it's an attitude which translates globally."

During our Sunday get-together, Rod asked me how our soccer team was making out and I let it slip that we had been invited by Montreal's CHOM-FM station to send a rock star team to play a station X1 at Montreal's Olympic Stadium on the next Sunday. The intent was for our game to serve as the opening act for a Montreal Manic (NASL) playoff final against the legendary New York Cosmos. I told Rod I doubted we could scramble a team together in time. "Why not, we'd love to play," responded Rod, with Steve Harris, Bruce Dickinson, and Dave Murray all nodding in agreement.

"Yes, but aren't you performing next week?" stuttered I.

"Well we have Lansing, Michigan, on Saturday and Madison, Wisconsin, on Monday — but we have Sunday free," noted Smallwood, totally unfazed by a potential scheduling conflict.

"Let me get this straight," said I. "You are prepared to travel from Lansing to Montreal at your own expense and then continue on to Madison, Wisconsin — just to play in a soccer match?"

"But it's the Olympic Stadium, and we are opening for the New York Cosmos," responded Smallwood, somewhat perplexed at my concern.

"Well, if you are up for it, no worries," said I before frantically running around the pub to round up the rest of our squad for next Sunday's match.

Backstage the following night, several Maidens were sporting obvious limps from the previous day's game, yet Harris, in particular, was enthusiastic about the match and about next Sunday's game in Montreal. Again, Maiden presented an amazing concert, with their star mascot Eddie becoming the centre point of their finale. I have never seen so many Maiden T-shirts in my life. It appeared that all fifteen thousand fans were decked out in Maiden attire.

Opening for Maiden in Montreal were Anthem's Coney Hatch, who had just released their second album, *Outta Hand*, produced by Canadian producer Jack Richardson. Their self-titled debut had produced three major singles: "Hey Operator," "Monkey Bars," and "Devil's Deck," which earned an opening spot on thirty-five Maiden dates for band members Carl Dixon (lead vocals/guitar), Andy Curran (lead vocals/bass), Steve Shelski (lead guitar), and Dave Ketchum (drums). *Outta Hand*'s failure to spark a hit single resulted in the band removing Ketchum in favour of new drummer Barry Connors, and when their 1985 *Friction* album also failed, Dixon quit the band and they eventually folded, only to be revived twenty-nine years later with the original lineup intact!

On Monday morning I was making frantic phone calls to Ian McLean at CHOM to confirm the game and to announce Maiden would be in our starting lineup. He, of course, was thrilled and arranged free accommodation for us at the Queen Elizabeth Hotel, and promised CHOM would go heavy on game promotion. I quickly recruited Paul Hyde from the Payola$, Mark Holmes from Platinum Blonde, Malcolm Tomlinson (a Londoner who had a decent solo album on A&M), David Bendeth, and Teenage Head's Frankie Venom and Steve Mahon. We were to travel to Montreal by train and meet Maiden Sunday at the hotel.

I mentioned to Ian that Maiden were going out of their way to play the match, so it would be appreciated if they wouldn't stack their lineup with ringers — and also to go easy on the guys physically, as they did have a concert the following night. "No problem," said McLean. "[I'll] just use station jocks and a couple of outsiders to make up the numbers." We all assembled at the hotel, sorted out our rooms and I was thrilled and relieved Maiden showed up promptly to join us as we took a chartered bus out to the Olympic Stadium. A crowd of about thirty thousand were on hand and many of them were obvious Maiden fans. Our kick-off was late afternoon with The Manic and New York Cosmos set to play early that evening.

CHOM's team took the field and, as promised, was full of radio jocks, male and female. "No problems," said I to Paul Hyde. "This is going to be a walk in the park." Then their jocks walked off the field and were instantly replaced by another group of players who definitely weren't on-air talent. Their goalie played for Quebec's youth team and the forward line was full of Italians. Now I knew CHOM was partially francophone, but I didn't know they were that multi-cultural! The only familiar faces on the opposition were my mates Martin Melhuish and Nanette Workman.

What ensued was a real battle between two evenly matched teams. CHOM took a 1–0 lead, Steve Harris tied the score in the second half, but some Italian geezer blasted the winner for CHOM just before the final whistle. As Ian McLean came to thank me for the game, all I could mutter was, "You swine!" which left him laughing. We took a shower and walked out into the dressing room only to hear this female laughter coming from a corner of the room. Workman and her manager, Francine Herschorn, had snuck into the men's dressing room and were getting an eyeful of the players coming out of the showers.

Emerging from the changing room and heading towards the elevator that would take us to the VIP suites where the post-game reception was to take place, I was suddenly exposed to what it was really like being in a famous rock band. Walking along with Steve and Bruce we were suddenly confronted by a mob of kids surging towards us. Maiden are usually gracious to their fans, but some of this group were decidedly unruly. Security had to help us force our way through the crowd, and I got to feel what it was like to be swarmed by fans.

Several Canadian albums had blossomed during 1983. As previously noted, Bryan Adams racked up major U.S. video exposure on MTV for *Cuts Like a Knife* and had toured successfully with Loverboy and Supertramp. Loverboy themselves achieved equally strong MTV coverage with their third album, *Keep It Up*, with Lenny Stoute executing the interview honours for *Music Express*.

The Payola$ released their follow up to *No Stranger to Danger, Hammer on a Drum,* and it proved to be their biggest-selling album. To achieve this fame, though, they made the move they had vowed they never would — they agreed to be managed by Bruce Allen.

"Our problem was that our current manager Cliff Jones had no idea how to break us in the States. So he did a deal with the devil and entered into a co-management deal with Allen," muttered lead vocalist Paul Hyde at the time. "Bruce got us some dates with Supertramp and ZZ Top but he wanted to change us. Change our appearance, change our songs, and change our show. Next thing you know I am singing a duet with Carole Pope!" "Where Is This Love" proved to be a powerful anti-domestic violence anthem but Hyde's cheesy duet with Pope on "Never Said I Love You" killed off any remaining street credibility the band had.

At Solid Gold, Brian MacLeod and Ab Bryant finished off their work with Chilliwack's *Opus X* album and went on to launch the Headpins' second release, *Line Of Fire*. Yet the label's third key band, Toronto, were having problems and their fourth album, *Girls Night Out,* marked the last time Brian Allen and his wife Sheron Alton recorded with the group. Toronto's problems went back to the band's 1982 *Get It on Credit* record. Allen and Alton had written a song, "What About Love," that was submitted for the album but Holly Woods was dead set against recording the track. The band Heart picked up the song and scored a global hit with it. It is significant that only Woods and Alton appear on the cover of Toronto's 1983 release *Girls Night Out,* and by the time their 1984 release, *Assault and Flattery,* hit the stores, the band had been renamed Holly Woods and Toronto, with Allen and Alton having moved on (Allen assumed A&R duties at Attic Records).

Montreal's Luba Kowalchyk burst on to the scene in 1983 with a four-song EP on Capitol-EMI that included what shaped up to be a mega hit in her ode to her dead father, "Every Time I See Your Picture I

Cry." Her manager, Paul Levesque, had taken Luba on the rebound after initially discovering an eleven-year old prodigy named Celine Dion. He had received a one-song demo Dion had written with her mother, met the youngster and her mother, but thought she was a bit young at the time so he signed a provisional contract with her mother confirming he would work with Celine in a couple of years' time. Big mistake!

Rene Angelil, who had just finished working with Ginette Reno, was also looking for a new project and received a copy of the same one-song demo. He also met with Celine and her mother but promised to immediately work with Celine. Owing to the family's cash-strapped situation, Celine's mother was more than happy to have her youngster start generating income. The problem, of course, was that she had already signed an agreement with Levesque. Naturally there was a legal conflict, but Levesque accepted a cash settlement and good-naturedly bowed out of his agreement. I'll bet he kicked himself afterwards. Yet Luba reigned as Juno Female Vocalist of the Year winner for three years straight, from 1985 to 1987, though she never crossed over to the U.S.

Toronto's Ready Records, run by Andy Crosby and Angus McKay, ruled Eastern Canada in the early eighties by investing in a number of popular indie acts including The Santers Band, Blue Peter, The Extras, Colin Linden, and Stevie Blimpkie. But their biggest discovery was The Spoons. Created in 1979 in Burlington, Ontario, by manager Peter Abrahams, original members Gord Deppe (vocals/guitars) and Sandy Horne (bass) were soon joined by drummer Derrick Ross and fifteen-year-old keyboardist Rob Preuss.

Riding the tide of the new Romantic Movement, which was headed by the likes of Duran Duran and Spandau Ballet, The Spoons launched with *Stick Finger Neighbourhood* in 1981, with Hamilton's Daniel Lanois producing. They then released *Arias and Symphonies* the following year, charting with the singles "Nova Heart" and "Smiling in Winter."

This success earned them tour dates with The Police and Culture Club. Although The Spoons failed to make any waves in the States, they did come to the attention of Chic-member and producer Nile Rodgers, who agreed to produce their 1983 album, *Talkback*, which featured a more sophisticated sound as reflected in the album's two hits "Romantic Traffic" and "Tell No Lies."

Probably the year's hottest new release was The Parachute Club's self-titled release in July. The single "Rise Up" climbed high into the Canadian charts. Produced by Lanois, their soca-infused dance track, supported by one of the year's top videos, ideally mixed sexual politics with an irresistible dance arrangement. Featuring Lorraine Segato, Lauri Conger, Julie Masi, Margo Davidson, and band quarterback (and drummer) Billy Bryans, bassist Steve Webster, and guitarist David Gray, The Parachute Club took Canada by storm. Released on Gerry Young's Current Records, The Parachute Club was the poster band for Toronto's burgeoning gay music scene.

My soccer-mate Mark Holmes's Platinum Blonde got on the charts in October with the release of the EP titled *Six Track Attack,* which Jeff Burns scooped for Columbia/Epic. Before that EP came out, Holmes and new band members, guitarist Sergio Galli and drummer Chris Steffler, had sent a seven-track demo to English producer David Tickle (who had just recorded Red Rider's *Neruda*). Tickle was so enthused he met the band at Triumph's Metalwork Studios in the Toronto suburb of Mississauga, and within three weeks had recorded the six-track EP, which featured "Doesn't Really Matter." Columbia were pleasantly surprised to see that EP soar to No. 37 on the Canadian album charts and the band and Tickle were quickly back in the studios to complete an additional four tracks.

Ironically, Holmes had been fired by other band members in the original Platinum Blonde lineup. "When we started, cover bands were all the rage and were making great money. So I thought, I can do a decent Sting impression and we could work in some of our own songs." Yet Holmes was stunned when his original guitarist and drummer fired him and brought in a replacement bassist. "That lasted about three dates," reflected Holmes. "The club owners wanted to know what happened to that crazy Englishman who ran across the tables. So Bruce Barrow, who had been booking the original band, stepped in and told me that if I could form a new band, he could get us dates. So I brought in Chris and Sergio and their enthusiasm was infectious. We played our first gig at some nightclub out by the airport and Sergio is going 'Yeah, and next year we'll be playing at Maple Leaf Gardens' — and he was right."

Holmes continued, recounting the early shows, "We get to this bar and the girls start screaming and going berserk. It became a word of mouth thing that the girls would see us play and start screaming."

Columbia moved to capitalize on this hysteria by rush-releasing their debut EP, which hit Canada by storm. Airplay for "It Doesn't Really Matter" and "Standing in the Dark" was so strong it was almost inevitable a complete album would be rush released in the New Year. In anticipation of this, I met with Mark (and his dad) at the Rose and Crown pub in November and conducted the first of many interviews. What struck me as odd was Mark brought questions to the interview that he wanted me to ask him. A true Brit rock star in the making! The band's debut LP, *Standing in the Dark,* was indeed rushed out early in 1984 and would go on to achieve triple platinum sales.

↗ (top) The Stampeders — the band that sparked my desire to launch *Alberta Music Express*.
Photo courtesy of The Stampeders.

↗ (bottom) The Who, live in Edmonton. Shots from this concert would grace the cover of the first issue of *Alberta Music Express*.
Photo courtesy of Ian Mark.

Alberta Music Express

CANADA'S ONLY MONTHLY MUSIC TABLOID

Vol. 1, No. 1, 1976   October, 1976   25¢

The Who sell out

The Who is probably the biggest rock act ever to appear in Alberta. No wonder Brimstone Production's Dave Horodezky is wearing a permanent smile.

"It's the biggest act I've ever handled," reports Horodezky whose Oct. 16 concert at the Edmonton Coliseum is already sold out.

"This concert gives us credibility. It'll make it easier for us to book other major acts now that the Who has played here."

The 10-year career of Peter Townshend, Roger Daltrey, John Entwistle and Keith Moon has been well chronicled.

Products of London England's Mod scene, the Who sprung to prominence with songs like My Generation, Magic Bus and I Can See For Miles.

It was the rock opera Tommy which established the Who as one of the world's top attractions. A level that has been maintained with recent albums, Who's Next, Quadrophenia and The Who By Numbers.

Rumours persist that The Who are on the verge of breaking up. But these rumours are continually disspelled as the band tours the continent showing their vast legions of fans that the magic is still there.

Another album is expected to be released shortly proplonging The Who's recording career even more. Who's to say when the band will finally call it a day. Their longevity has been phenominal. Hopefully, they'll be around for at least a few more years.

Nazareth are loud n' proud

BY JOE SORNBERGER

Onstage, his voice comes rolling out of his throat like un-wound barb-wire: all scratch and thorny and a little bit rusted. It's almost a painful voice.

But in conversation, when he doesn't have to compete with Manny Charlton's decibal-busting slide guitar work it's a soft voice. Quiet. Polite, even.

"Canada is where it really happened for us," the polite-soft voice of Nazareth's Dan McCafferty explains. "Our first two albums did really well in Europe. Then about three years ago, we

DAN McCAFFERTY

did a Canadian tour. We talked to A & M Records to see if they could set it up for us to come here and play. They said: 'Oh, yeah.' We figured that Canada was a big country. There had to be more places to play in it besides Montreal, Toronto and Vancouver.

McCafferty and Nazareth were right. The group has become one of Canada's and Alberta's favorites.

A & M boasts that Nazareth's Love Hurts is their best-selling single yet, bigger than even The Captain and Ternilles' Love Will Keep Us Together. The group that still calls Scotland home know their albums sell incredibly well, particularly in Alberta where just about every 16year-old worth his or her stacked heels owns at least one Nazareth LP.

"It's a case of touring here, playing quite a lot. We came and played..." And conquered.

McCafferty, who says he

likes to listen to "everything from light classics to old blues records — the only thing I can't stand is disco" is, at 29, married and a father still happy to play good, loud, raucous rock and roll.

"What we did originally was just play the songs we liked as best we could. It just sort of built up. As it built up, we've just tried harder.

"With rock and roll you never look behind. You're ahead of yourself all the time. After this tour, we've got something else. You just keep thinking ahead.

"We enjoy playing rock and roll. To say that we should do something different just to prove to people that we can do it is ridiculous."

McCafferty explained that Nazareth (who got their name from The Band's song The Weight; "I pulled into Nazareth, I was a' feeling 'bout half-past dead") works about 10 months of the year, with eight months of touring and two months of recording. It's a tough schedule to keep.

"On the road, you live in a sort of a bubble. If you didn't, it wouldn't be efficient, things would not get done. All we have to do is concentrate on the stage, so everything is done for us.

"When you're a rock star, people want you to be weird. But you're not really. If Alice Cooper went into a bar, dressed normally in his street clothes, he'd probably never be recognized. People recognize the weirdness, and the real person.

"But us, we've not got an image. We're just a rock and roll band."

McCafferty doesn't feel Nazareth needs any image because of their loud and proud outlook on music.

"They've been predicting the death of heavy rock since the Stones. Well, the biggest band in the States right now is Aerosmith and they're pretty heavy. Kids want it. Kids still want to boogie. We've been doing this for five or six years and we've been building our following steadily.

"If you play a concert and you give the kid what he wants to hear, he'll come back the next time to hear you. We've always played like that."

PINBALL WIZARD — Besides commanding the front-stage spotlight as The Who's lead vocalist, Roger Daltrey is a star in his own right. He made a tremendous impact as Tommy in Ken Russell's movie adaption of the Who's rock opera and is set to appear in several more films. Daltrey also has two solo albums to his credit.

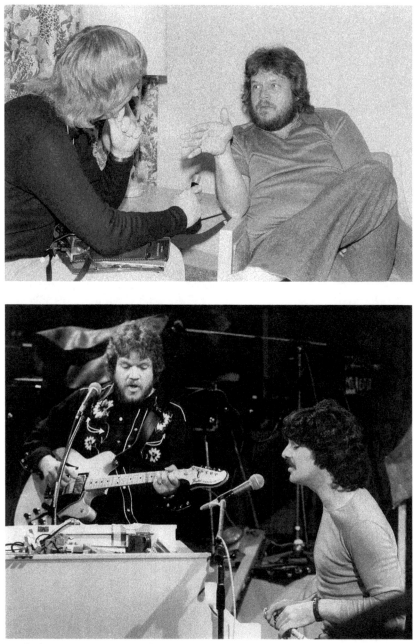

↗ (top) Interviewing Randy Bachman, of The Guess Who and Bachman-Turner Overdrive, for the first time.
Photo courtesy of Ian Mark.

↗ (bottom) Two Canadian rock legends, Randy Bachman and Burton Cummings.
Photo courtesy of The Guess Who.

↖ (opposite) Our debut issue, *Alberta Music Express*, October 1976.

↖ Bruce Allen, godfather of the Canadian music industry.
Photo courtesy of Dee Lippingwell.

↗ Gene Simmons, KISS guitarist and one of the most amenable interviewees I've ever met.
Photo courtesy of Charles Hope.

↗ (top) Frampton comes alive at the Edmonton Rock Cirkus, 1979.
Photo courtesy of Charles Hope.

↗ (bottom) Loverboy's Paul Dean and Mike Reno make their Vancouver concert debut.
Photo courtesy of Charles Hope.

↖ (opposite) Lisa DalBello at the Blindman Valley Festival. Scott Smith, who was being scouted by the members of what would become Loverboy, is in the background.
Photo courtesy of Charles Hope.

↖ Brian "Too Loud" MacLeod was a great performer who came to a tragic end.
Photo courtesy of Charles Hope.

↙ Queen's Freddie Mercury (with drummer Roger Taylor) was one of the most majestic performers I ever saw.
Photo courtesy of Ian Mark.

↘ Triumph's Rik Emmett. We nicknamed the band Ontario Hydro in reference to their extensive light show.
Photo courtesy of Charles Hope.

↘ Max Webster's Kim Mitchell, an eclectic performer who raised his level of fame after going solo.
Photo courtesy of Charles Hope.

↗ Conny Kunz and I, just before we moved the magazine from Calgary to Toronto.
Photo courtesy of *Calgary Albertan*.

↗ (top) The *Music Express* soccer team joins forces with Iron Maiden in Montreal.
Photo courtesy of Dee Lippingwell.

↗ (bottom) Rick Moranis (Bob Mackenzie) and Dave Thomas (Doug Mackenzie) with
Rush's Geddy Lee.
Photo courtesy of SRO-Anthem Entertainment.

↘ Iron Maiden front man Bruce Dickinson is a multi-talented individual — he even pilots the band's plane!
Photo courtesy of Sanctuary Music.

12

HOW NOT TO INVADE EUROPE!

The Canadian band that enjoyed the biggest breakthrough in 1983 was Helix, from Kitchener, Ontario. A hard-working rock band that *Music Express* had covered as they released two indie LPs, *Breaking Loose* in 1979 and *Black Leather White Lace* in 1981, the band were great at self-promotion (they had their own print mag).

David Munz, who had taken over as VP of marketing at Capitol, had been looking to break a Canadian metal band in the image of Iron Maiden, and even though Helix had been turned down several times, Munz heard something that clicked with his British sensibility. He and A&R chief Deane Cameron took a gamble on Helix and released their *No Rest for the Wicked* album, which created a buzz with their "Heavy Metal Love" track and the controversial video for it (which featured a girl killing guy with a flaming guitar). Munz went one step further in sanctioning funds for Helix to tour Europe in October as the opening act for KISS.

Having unmasked themselves in advance of their *Lick It Up* album, KISS hit the road in Europe with Helix tagging along in support. Munz, knowing the value of magazine exposure in promoting Helix, had invited me to document their experience. So Thursday November 1, 1983, found yours truly arriving at Frankfurt Airport at 6:00 a.m. to link up with the band for the German leg of the tour.

I flew in to Frankfurt in possession of a scrap of paper that stated Helix had checked into some obscure hotel in the city of Offenbach, which is located on the south side of the Main River. The original plan was for the band to pick me up at the airport, but two hours after arrival I am on to Plan B, which was for me to find them in Offenbach.

After checking with the information desk (and finally finding someone who spoke English), I was directed to the airport's bus terminal where a bus was about to depart for Offenbach. I showed the scrap of paper to the bus driver who helpfully let me off right in front of the band's hotel.

Arriving at reception, I somehow managed to communicate I was there to meet Helix, and the hotel manager explained they were all fast asleep as they had just arrived from Paris. I planted myself in a giant armchair in reception and fell asleep as well. About three hours later the Helix entourage began to stir. First to greet me was Kenny Heague, the band's roadie. Kenny had been with the band since day one in 1979. Originally from Liverpool, England, Heague boasted a thick Scouse (Liverpool) accent. He was a dead ringer for then-current Liverpool soccer hero Kevin Keegan, so I instantly nicknamed him "Keegan."

One by one, the members of Helix staggered down to reception, and we climbed into the somewhat dilapidated Fiat Iveca van that was to serve as the band's transportation for their entire tour. Five band members, manager Bill Seip, the sound tech, Keegan, and yours truly crammed in this van — with the band's gear. With no back seats, or seat belts, and just a piece of plywood covering the floor, you can image how dangerous it was. Any accident and everyone would have been tossed across the autobahn like rag dolls.

We arrived at the Offenbach Stadthalle and I was shocked at how small the venue was; it looked like some high-school gymnasium. The only thing that convinced me it was a legitimate venue were posters on the wall promoting a future gig by Def Leppard! There couldn't have been more than three thousand kids at the gig, yet Helix went down well and was obviously winning over new fans.

I thought we were going to watch the KISS set, but Bill Seip, concerned I would have a difficult time adopting to the band's van transportation, suggested I and drummer Greg (Fritz) Hinz might want to travel on to Munich in the record company rep's Mercedes Benz. So we met the local EMI rep, a nice enough geezer, and were soon tooling onto the autobahn heading south to Munich. Talk about a white knuckle trip. We zipped along at about 160 miles per hour, but cars were going by us like we were standing still!

We rolled into Munich and headed for the Sugar Shacke nightclub, which was going to be the venue for the after-party. As I ascended the stairs,

I noticed a vast collection of backstage passes plastered on the walls. I offered my Offenbach KISS pass, which was gratefully received. We stayed only long enough for the EMI rep to ascertain that everything was in order for the festivities, before Greg and I headed for our hotel room.

Greg and I awoke the next day to discover the band's van had broken down on the autobahn and the rest of the entourage had only arrived at the hotel earlier that morning and had crashed out in their rooms. Still, there was a day of promotion which involved the band visiting a major German heavy metal magazine for an interview and photo shoot, and despite being almost comatose, Helix staggered through the interview and we headed to that night's venue, Munich's Olympiahalle, located in the shadows of Lowenbrau Brewery.

Again, I was amazed at how small the venue was considering the global status of KISS. Their stage props had obviously been scaled down, and word was that their makeup-free persona wasn't going down too well in Europe. Still, Gene Simmons recognized me from previous interviews and he introduced me to Paul Stanley, new guitarist Vinnie Vincent, and drummer Eric Carr, and I was given the full backstage treatment. Watching KISS on stage from the sidelines was a rare treat. Simmons executed the fire-breathing act where he gargles a mouthful of gasoline and spits it into a torch, igniting a massive flame. After the fireball died away, he retreated backstage to gargle a mouthful of cleansing water, which was quite revealing for me to see.

Following the concert, we headed off to the Sugar Shacke for a private party co-sponsored by PolyGram Records and Helix's EMI label. Admission was restricted to just the two bands, their road crews, record executives, and select guests, including Queen's Brian May (who was recording at the band's Munich studios at the time). Also in attendance were about sixty of Munich's hottest female party goers!

Now the rule was that these girls had to buy their own drinks unless band members bought their drinks for them, which meant the drinks went on the party tab. It didn't take long for the girls to latch on to any guy in the room — which meant before long everyone, including yours truly, had attracted an entourage of about three stunning beauties each.

Of course, just as things were getting interesting, manager Bill Seip announced all Helix members had to head out to the van for an all-night drive to the next venue, Basle, Switzerland. The Helix crew were yelling in anger as they were dragged out of the club, kicking and screaming as their new female friends doubled up with the KISS guys and waved us a cruel farewell.

Saturday, November 3 found us arriving at Basle, Switzerland. As had been the case on many of the band's tour stops, we rented one hotel room. Whoever had been driving the van last got to crash out on the bed while the rest made do with whatever else was available. First thing they did was use the room's showers before heading over to the venue where lunch and dinner catering was laid out by the promoters. This was about as budget a concert tour as you could possibly execute. No luxury buses or concert guides here. We were all sardined into this Fiat Iveca van, and all we had was a written tour itinerary and a road map to find the next gig. And, of course, our lack of command of the German language proved to be a hindrance.

Bill Seip had obviously seen one too many episodes of Hogan's Heroes because he believed if you spoke English with a faux-German accent the locals would be able to understand you. This led to a series of hysterically funny episodes of Bill trying to obtain directions using his Colonel Klinke impersonations.

Driving East from Basle, the location for the next gig was Stuttgart Sindelfingen Glaspalast. Bill surmised that if we hit the middle of downtown Stuttgart we would have no problem asking directions to this Sindelfingen place. The problem was Sindelfingen is an actual U.S. army forces base located about twenty kilometres outside of Stuttgart. And there we were in the middle of Stuttgart, trying to find this place with Bill's fractured German offering no help.

The following day we traveled to Nuremburg where we stayed for two days, giving me one full day to interview Vollmer, Hinz, lead guitarist Brent Doerner, guitarist Paul Hackman, and temporary bassist Mark Rector. This was obviously another world for Helix, and even though the hardships of this tour were staggering, the band endured all challenges with a great team spirit.

Again, it was shocking to find the venue, the Hammerleinhalle, was actually attached to a hotel. We heard rumours that KISS had severely downscaled their operations yet again and had let a number of their crew go mid tour. But in talking to Simmons and Stanley after the Nuremburg concert, they were quite stoic about the response to their Unmasked tour, and were upbeat about the audience's reaction to their uncovered facade

In his book *Gimme an R*, Helix lead vocalist Brian Vollmer confirmed that the coverage his band received in *Music Express* allowed them to generate a tremendous amount of credibility —not just in Canada but also in the States and in Europe, where they returned to tour as headliners.

13

HANGING OUT
AT THE MADISON

By early 1984 we had moved our offices to 37 Madison Avenue in the heart of the Annex, directly across the street from a number of University of Toronto frat houses. The Madison Avenue Pub was conveniently located just down the street. Occupying a historic building created by the same architect who built Casa Loma, we had replaced the ad agency Ambrose DeCarr Forest as prime tenants, and had assumed control of the first floor and basement. An accounting firm occupied the second floor, and the third floor remained mysteriously empty, for a good reason — the building was reputed to be haunted.

A series of strange events occurred that supported this theory. Returning for the second day at the office, we found a bottle of hand cream had been smashed against the boardroom wall and a stack of albums had been strewn across the floor. Lights on the unoccupied third floor flickered off and on, and I personally heard doors opening and closing above me when I knew I was the only inhabitant in the building ... scary stuff!

Our first visitor to our new HQ was Corey Hart. His *First Offence* album had been recorded with studio session help from both Eric Clapton and Pete Townshend. Certainly, the first single, "Sunglasses at Night," was racking up airplay, yet when Corey dropped by our office he appeared to be in a surly mood, especially when he met Kerry Doole. "So you're the guy who trashed me in Montreal?" snapped Hart as Doole melted into his chair (this was a reference to Doole's less than flattering review of Hart's opening stint for Culture Club).

"The scary thing was he could recite every word in my review," noted Doole. "He definitely came across as someone you wouldn't want to tangle with."

One thing you had to say about Hart was he backed up his brashness. His debut was picked up by EMI in the U.S., where heavy airplay for "Sunglasses at Night" and constant video exposure on MTV pushed his album to No. 7 on the *Billboard* charts with sales of over five hundred thousand copies (gold status). In Canada he went to No. 8 on the domestic charts, with sales of over three hundred thousand units (triple platinum). That night at the El Mo, Corey delivered a classy performance that oozed star power. (He must have had an off-night opening for Culture Club!)

Having settled into our new digs, our focus was now on executing the second annual Music Express Awards. We had targeted Sunday, April 15 for the show, and planned to stage it in Vancouver. Everyone associated with our Montreal show was enthusiastic about the readers' poll concept, and Bruce Allen in particular wanted his home city to showcase the second event. Having learned valuable lessons from our first effort, we zeroed in on securing our advertising sponsors before moving forward.

Through our association with covering bands at the Kingswood venue we had formulated a great liaison with Labatt, and with their Beer Wars with Molson still raging, company marketing VP Barry Snetzinger and his promotions director Jo-Anne Wilson were happy to meet and discuss sponsorship of the Vancouver show. Conny and I took them to lunch at posh downtown Toronto eatery Winston's Steak House, provided them with a copy of the Montreal show, and walked out of our meeting with Labatt firmly on-board to foot expenses in return for prime sponsorship.

Jay Levine at Citytv, on confirmation of support from Labatt, promised to assemble a similar indie TV network to the one that aired the first show. With television and corporate sponsorship in the bag, the 1984 Music Express Awards was taking shape nicely. It also didn't hurt that CARAS had decided to reschedule the 1984 Juno Awards for December 5 at the CNE grounds. Their explanation was they wanted the Junos to tie in with Christmas sales? But by shifting their show to December it meant many of the artists and records that were released in late 1983 would be ignored — this particularly hurt Platinum Blonde and Honeymoon Suite. Hardly surprising CARAS was now vying for a live concert venue at the CNE, and had even gone into partnership with CPI to produce the show. I guess our Montreal awards concert had triggered a reflex reaction.

Long John Baldry was definitely on board to co-host the show again, but we needed a female foil based out of Vancouver. I think it was Tom Harrison, then working as music scribe for the Vancouver *Province*, who suggested Shari Ulrich might be interested. I had known Shari from her stint as lead vocalist for The Hometown Band, and apparently she had been doing some local TV hosting as well as launching a successful solo career. I used my press conference trip to track down Shari at her West End condo, and she loved the idea of co-hosting with John.

Knowing it was a lot to ask for John and Shari to carry the whole show, I had an idea for secondary hosts to fill in during the show's mid-point. I zeroed in on Ian Thomas, who I knew was not only a talented singer but also hysterically funny. And like Baldry, he knew the Canadian music scene and wouldn't need a teleprompter to announce winners. Thomas, who enjoyed early success with his "Painted Ladies" single, was not only a gifted singer/songwriter, but had a sense of humour that rivalled his brother Dave (one of the McKenzie Brothers off SCTV). A quick call to his manager, Val Azolli, secured Ian's involvement. Now I needed someone else from Vancouver to partner with Ian.

The name Doug Bennett instantly came to mind. As lead singer of Doug & the Slugs, Bennett combined great songs with a droll comedic performance in recording two popular albums, 1980's *Cognac and Bologna* (which featured the hit single "Too Bad") and 1981's *Wrap It*. I just had this feeling he would be an ideal fit to work with Ian. On another trip to Vancouver, I got Doug to a lunch meeting at the Sandman Hotel on West Georgia. In what proved to be a lengthy liquid lunch, I got Doug on-board with the concept.

Talent-wise, Bruce was adamant that his acts were not going to perform on their home turf, so I thought it would be great if we could introduce a selection of new talent emerging from Toronto. Platinum Blonde were up for making their national television debut, Lee Aaron was about to introduce her "Metal Queen" persona, Carole Pope and Rough Trade were willing to join the show, and for our fourth act we picked our national indie band winners, who proved to be Q-107's Honeymoon Suite.

To spice up the show, and to honour Michael Jackson, whose *Thriller* album was dominating world airwaves in 1984, we tracked down this hip-hop troupe from Saskatoon called Street Scape to perform a dance tribute. Also aware we didn't have any Vancouver acts on the show, I invited Chilliwack's Bill Henderson to execute an all-star performance of "Dance to the Music" for the show's finale.

Hiring Andre Perry to fly from Montreal to Vancouver to oversee the show's television production was out of the question, so we negotiated with a Vancouver outfit named Polaris Entertainment, which had a pretty decent track record for independent TV production. The Hyatt Regency Ballroom stage was big enough for two separate sets of gear, which allowed for a clean transfer between the four bands. Overall, the production seemed to be a lot smoother than the Montreal show, in which we virtually flew by the seat of our pants.

The Second Annual Music Express Awards show was set to tape at 2:00 p.m. We walked the hosts through the program, and although the production crew insisted on some form of loose script, we left enough gaps for our talent to ad lib their intros. The first problem occurred during Honeymoon Suite's sound check. Someone (we believe it was the rep from Ray Coburn's keyboard manufacturer) apparently adjusted Coburn's keyboards after the band's sound check. The change left a humming sound emitting from his instrument. Baldry and Ulrich launched the show with an opening monologue only to be told to stop by the producer, who had detected the humming sound. It would take about four or five false starts before the offending noise was located and corrected.

Suddenly, I realized why it may not have been a good idea to go with a totally live broadcast. Honeymoon Suite debuted their "New Girl Now" single and received their Top Indie Group award, which was now a gold microphone sponsored by Sennheiser. Lee Aaron's new Metal Queen image also went down well, but as Platinum Blonde started to perform "Standing in the Dark," one of Mark's bass strings snapped and we had to halt the show while he restrung his bass.

Further delays dragged the show's running time to over four hours, and I felt the whole thing was turning into a disaster. Yet Ian Thomas assured me it wasn't that bad and we would be able to fix most of the problems in post-production — which we of course did. Despite the ordeal, the audience hung in there and were well entertained by all four groups, plus the

Saskatoon hip-hop troupe, who were sensational. Allen, despite rumours to the contrary, showed up with Adams and Loverboy, who received Top Male Canadian Vocalist and Top Canadian Group award, respectively, and we were able to utilize other celebrities to receive awards for those artists who couldn't make it.

Stealing a trick from Montreal, we had arranged to shoot a video clip of The Police accepting Top International Album award for *Synchronicity*, which photographer Dimo Safari and I had recorded while they were performing their final concert date (at that time!) in Buffalo.

One incident at the awards sparked a prolonged feud between Corey Hart and Bryan Adams. Knowing Corey was in Vancouver doing press for his debut album, I had suggested to Keith Brown it would be great if we could get Corey on the show accepting the award for the Most Promising Group winners (and fellow Montrealers) Men Without Hats. Corey was compliant and seemed happy to accept the gold microphone on the band's behalf.

"Corey wanted to leave right after making the presentation but I told him it would be disrespectful to go," noted Brown. "So I am wondering how I could keep him occupied when I notice Bryan and Bruce out by the bar in the foyer. I said to Corey, 'Now there are two people you should meet.' So we walk across the foyer and I introduced Corey to Bryan. Bryan said something polite like, 'Nice to meet you and congratulate Ivan (Men Without Hats) when you see him in Montreal.' Corey extended his hand to shake Bryan's but then abruptly pulled it back and walked away. I chased after Corey and said to him, 'What was all that about?' 'Well Bryan didn't ask me about my album. He just asked me about Men Without Hats — and I've never even met them.'

"Of course Bruce saw everything," noted Brown. "So he wrote this scathing column in *The Province* calling Corey a spoiled brat, a column that was reprinted in *RPM*. Of course Corey was pissed off and that triggered bad feelings between him and Bryan."

By far, the hit act of the night was the twinning together of Ian Thomas and Doug Bennett as co-hosts. Think of Abbott and Costello or Laurel and Hardy; the chemistry between the two of them was magic. Thomas had the quick quips while Bennett served up the droll responses. They had the audience rolling in the aisles. In presenting Adams with his Top Canadian Male Vocalist gold mic, Thomas, straight-faced, read out Bryan's current record company bio, but changed the emphasis on the material into a funny monologue. And it was all ad libbed. Adams himself congratulated the pair upon receiving his award. It was a shame CARAS never followed through and hired them for a future Juno telecast. They would have been sensational.

The show ended with a Vancouver all-star band jamming to "Dance to the Music." Onstage performers included Chilliwack's Bill Henderson, Streetheart's Jeff Neill and Ken (Spider) Sinnaeve, Shari Ulrich, Kathi McDonald, Lee Aaron, and Stonebolt keyboardist Steve Webster, plus the Powder Blues horn section which combined to provide the telecast with an upbeat finale.

Next problem: what to do after the show? We had just assumed the hotel lounge would be open after the gig, but due to some archaic liquor laws in Western Canada, no alcohol was being served on Sundays! To the rescue came Gary Taylor, who invited everyone over to his club, Gary Taylor's Rock Room, for a private soiree. Taylor's Rock Room was a famous (or infamous) Vancouver club that booked all the top Canadian touring bands upstairs, while downstairs some of the city's raunchiest strip acts were staged. Every time a band took a break upstairs, everyone raced downstairs to catch the strippers.

We all reassembled over at Gary's on Hornby Street. The disc jockey pumped out the tunes, Street Scape reprised their hip-hop choreography, and then out came Taylor's special feature — a male and female sex show! I was mortified wondering what Jo-Anne Wilson from Labatt's would think, but she seemed to enjoy the spectacle, so I ran around the building with photographer Dimo Safari, snapping candid snaps of everyone, including some great shots of Lee Aaron and Krokus front man Marc Storace posed in the men's washroom!

Returning to Toronto, *Music Express* was about to be inundated by a slew of top-notch Canadian albums. First out of the blocks was Platinum Blonde's *Standing in the Dark*, which was launched in front of an estimated crowd of some thirty thousand fans at Nathan Phillips Square on May 24. Initially conceived as a CHUM-FM radio broadcast and expected to pull about three thousand kids, this event triggered Platinum Blonde mania.

"We couldn't believe the response," reflected Holmes. "We wondered how many people knew about us. We thought there must have been some other band on the bill. I had only finished six songs at the time and a few songs that I had bits and pieces of lyrics. So when it came to the new songs,

I faked the lyrics, made up stuff as I went along. I just sang something in faux Swahili. The crowd was screaming so much it didn't matter what I sang."

Platinum Blonde was tailor made for the video generation. Billed as Canada's Duran Duran, the Blondes were Canada's first sex-symbol rock band in that they appealed to their audience in so many different levels. Their music was danceable pop, their fashion sense and hair styles set new trends, and their videos, which would soon be staples on MuchMusic, attracted a young teen demographic.

"We thought of ourselves as a British band," explained Holmes. "All the bands in Britain at that time were fashion conscious, wore makeup, eyeliner, and cared about their hair and their appearance. People from MuchMusic have told me we virtually kept them in business at the start."

The Blonde's debut chalked up over three hundred thousand units in domestic sales. They soon opened for Bryan Adams and Billy Idol, before headlining three straight nights at Kingswood in front of a combined total crowd of over seventy-five thousand fans. So why didn't the Blondes catch on in the States?

"In a way, we were lazy," admitted Holmes. "We didn't want to go down to the States and start from scratch. We already thought we were stars. And our management didn't have it together to break us down there. In retrospect, we should have gone down there, started from scratch, and toured our arses off. But when you've got twenty-five thousand fans screaming for you in Canada, it's hard to play some obscure American club date. And it was bad in the U.S. at that time with all that payola scandal. I don't think Columbia knew how to break a new band without all the payoffs and bribery."

The following month, Honeymoon Suite launched their self-titled album. The singles "New Girl Now," "Burning in Love," "Stay in the Light," and "Wave Babies," propelled the album to two hundred thousand units sold in Canada.

The record's producer, Tom Treumuth, was not surprised Honeymoon Suite's debut was successful. "For one thing, they had a great front man in Johnnie Dee. He's got that great sandpaper vocal quality and those Italian good looks. Having a great vocalist is so important. And then they had his sidekick, Derry Grehan on guitar. Think of Steve Tyler and Joe Perry in Aerosmith, the dynamic was identical," noted Treumuth, still managing the band through his Hypnotic Agency in Hamilton. "And then they had great songs. All I had to do was capture them on tape and present them correctly. On that first album it was all there."

Another album launched early in 1984 was Lee Aaron's *Metal Queen*, produced by Paul Gross and recorded at Toronto's Phase One Studios. The album had attracted attention from Al Mair's Attic Records, who signed her to a multi-album contract.

The video for "Metal Queen" featured Lee in a Conan-the-Barbarian setting, tied to posts and being attacked by sinister characters as well as python snake and a tarantula. The video was so over the top it received an R rating in the States and no Canadian program touched it. This meant "Metal Queen," as a single, ran into trouble and Attic had to substitute "Steal Your Love" with Aaron's manager patching together some live concert footage for the video.

"I loved the idea of empowering women by creating this mythological goddess-like character for the ['Metal Queen'] video," noted Aaron. "I had no idea it would have such an impact. I've had albums which have sold much better — yet I am still known as the Metal Queen. It's funny what people won't let go of. I have written far better songs and made far better wardrobe choices since then, thank you!"

Following his 1983 Juno win as Most Promising Male Artist, Kim Mitchell finally released a full album, *Akimbo Alogo*, which featured a stack of great songs in "All We Are" (one of my all-time favs), "Lager and Ale," and "Diary for Rock 'N' Roll Men," but would be dominated by "Go for Soda," his one legitimate U.S. hit and a track that was adopted as an anthem for the MADD organization (Mothers Against Drunk Driving).

In releasing the album, Mitchell left Anthem to join Tom Berry, who had just launched his own Alert label. "I just got sick of being in Rush's kid brother band," reflected Mitchell. "Max Webster never made any money with Anthem. It was so refreshing to tour solo and return with a couple of thousand bucks in my pocket."

Rush released their first post–Terry Brown album, *Grace Under Pressure*, which they self-produced. A heavy nuclear holocaust lyrical theme was noticeable on hit singles "Distant Early Warning" and "Red Sector A," which displayed the band's progressive development. The album went platinum in both Canada and the U.S.

Helix released *Walking the Razor's Edge* in July, becoming one of the many hair bands to cash in during the mid-eighties. The original song, "Rock You," plus two covers; Crazy Elephant's "Gimme Gimme Good

Lovin'," and A Foot in Cold Water's "Make Me Do Anything You Want," pushed the album to platinum sales in Canada and netted them over four hundred thousand copies internationally.

The album spawned two videos, for "Rock You" and "Gimme Gimme Good Lovin'," which were unique in that Helix decided to try to cash in on the developing adult video channel market by cutting two versions of each video, the second versions featuring topless porno models (including a sixteen-year-old Traci Lords). The X-rated versions served as time fillers on the Playboy Channel and other adult sites.

Other established bands were not so fortunate. Triumph left RCA for MCA to release *Thunder Seven*, but despite two decent singles, Gil Moore's "Spellbound" and "Follow Your Heart," the album failed to replicate the success of *Allied Forces*. "We were selling platinum but Journey was selling seven times platinum," noted Emmett. "So our success failed by comparison. My working relationship with Gil started to break down. By the time we had recorded *Thunder Seven*, Gil didn't want to be in the same studio as me."

Yet the biggest flame-out would be April Wine. Their 1982 release, *Power Play*, had not sold well. Rumours of discord were ripe, with Myles Goodwyn seeming to distance himself from the rest of the band by moving with his family to the Bahamas. It took the best part of two years for the band to record *Animal Grace*, and when I was summoned to Montreal to interview Myles to discuss the new opus, I had no idea what I was in for.

The session started amicably enough. But then I started talking to him about their 1981 *Nature of the Beast* album, in which the band was presented to England as a hard rock unit. I casually asked him about why April Wine had three guitar players considering most of their songs were of the soft rock variety. I was not prepared for his bitter response.

"We don't *need* three guitar players," spewed Goodwyn. "Matter of fact, if I could play all the guitar parts I would do. If I could play the drums, I'd do without a drummer," Myles continued working himself into a slow burn. "I seem to be doing everything myself anyway. After *Power Play*, everyone else was bitching about why they weren't getting any writing credits so I said, right. I'll leave you alone, you write the songs. So I purposely left them alone, returned a few months later and *nothing* had been done. It was a joke. So I said, right, I'll write the songs, as usual, yet everyone else was bitching about the sessions. The whole process of recording *Animal Grace* was a total joke."

I repeated to Myles several times, "Are you sure you want to say that?" He insisted that was exactly what he wanted to say. So I published the story in our April issue.

Within days of that issue being published, Aquarius president Terry Flood was on the phone. "You realize your story has destroyed the band," fumed Flood. "No one is talking to each other."

My response was, "I have the tapes if you'd care to listen."

Terry sighed and said, "No I don't think that's necessary."

April Wine launched a tour with the foreboding title One More for the Road. Corey Hart was the opening act, but the crowds were so bad that he bailed by the time they reached Ottawa (feigning some mysterious sickness). Their date at Kingswood was embarrassing. Most of the prime seats remained unsold and only a few thousand fans were scattered across the grass. The first thing Myles did was tell everyone to move forward and fill up the seats, much to the consternation of Kingswood's security. By the time April Wine concluded their final date at Kelowna, that lineup was finished as a touring band.

Aquarius still milked the tour for one more live album, *One for the Road,* and contractual obligations meant Goodwyn and Greenway joined forces with studio musicians for *Walking through Fire* in 1986, but their fans weren't fooled and April Wine remained dormant until their 1993 *Attitude* comeback CD.

To say we were flooded with pop star interviews at Madison Avenue would be an understatement. Within a short time of us relocating, we interviewed Corey Hart, the Payola$, Lisa Dal Bello, Sinead O'Connor, Paul Young, Squeeze, A-ha, and Pink Floyd drummer Nick Mason, who was racing sport cars at Mosport. Sean, a busboy at the Madison got a special kick out of meeting the celebs, but even he was overcome when confronted by Mason. When asked why he froze on the spot, all Sean could say was "What do you say to a God?"

August 31, 1984, marked the launch of MuchMusic, Canada's first national music video channel. Based on the success of MTV in the U.S. and Europe, it was inevitable Canada would succeed in securing its own channel. Several bids were organized, but Citytv president Moses Znaimer had already compiled an impressive music programming library with his *The NewMusic* show and, in John Martin, he had an ideal person to helm this new venture. I had worked with Martin on many previous occasions, he being a fellow native of Manchester, and once it was confirmed that Citytv had the new channel, I proposed a synergistic relationship between *Music Express* and MuchMusic, which he seemed agreeable to.

As MuchMusic's launch date approached, I followed up with John on the working relationship, and we designated our September issue as a MuchMusic special. I attend the channel's launch at their cramped 99 Queen Street East location — Rush's "The Enemy Within" being their first broadcasted video.

The following day I turned on the channel to check out their content and I was horrified to see their VJs waving copies of a new magazine called *Graffiti*. I grabbed a phone, finally got through to Martin, and asked him what the hell this *Graffiti* connection was all about? He sputtered an apology about not knowing that some friends of Moses's were launching a magazine and had used their connection with him to establish a link with MuchMusic.

Considering everything *Music Express* had done to establish ourselves as *the* national music magazine, it was a bit of a kick in the teeth to have Canada's first music channel publicizing a brand new magazine. Although *Graffiti* tried to succeed purely on newsstand sales, they did give us a bit of a run for our money for about three years before their publishers ran out of gas trying to make it work financially. Suffice to say, we never did succeed in establishing a viable working relationship with MuchMusic.

14

GETTING

RECKLESS IN THE U.S.

Early in the summer of 1984, Conny, her son Raymond, and I moved from Kingslake Road to a house on Brunswick Avenue in the Annex. It was a handy location to commute to our office and to also check out the Brunswick Tavern, located at the end of the street. When Richard Flohil called to hype us on his new client, Consort Alberta's k.d. Lang, and her band, The Reclines, set to debut in Toronto at Albert's Hall, the upstairs club at the Brunswick House, we couldn't really refuse.

And it's a good job we didn't, as k.d. totally rewrote the rules for country music. Her spiky hair, granny glasses, punk boots, and her amazing voice marked her as a totally unique performer. She sold out the rest of the week at the Brunswick, generated tons of positive media attention, and her *Truly Western Experience* CD proved to be a revelation. It was hardly surprising she won the Most Promising Female Vocalist Juno award in 1985.

Platinum Blonde chose a mid-week date in late September to launch their official fan club. They did this by inviting about four hundred of their most ardent fans to a lunchtime function at Gareth Brown's Heaven night-club. The plan was to launch the fan club, cut a ceremonial cake, receive their platinum album for *Standing in the Dark*, and informally press the flesh with their fans. The resulting chaos almost triggered tragic consequences.

Heaven was packed to the rafters with tweens and teens shoehorned into the venue. They were initially entertained by Blonde videos and concert footage beamed onto the club's video screens. Then Mark Holmes, Sergio Galli, and Chris Steffler emerged from the back of the stage to accept their platinum album from Columbia VP of Sales Don Oates. Cue a massive surge forward by the crowd, which forced the Blondes to retreat backstage. Managers Bruce Barrow and Tony Tsavdaris tried to quiet a crowd that was ramping up the hysteria level. Once more, the Blondes appeared and tried to execute an organized Q&A with their audience. But the kids weren't having it. They surged forward against what limited security Barrow and Tsavdaris had hired, and it was clear the Blondes were facing a losing battle.

Now, if the band had stayed backstage and security had cleared the club, no further problems would have occurred. But inexplicably, Barrow and Tsavdaris led the Blondes towards a glass enclosed lounge where they cut the ceremonial cake — in full view of the departing kids. Suddenly, there was a mass surge against the glass door, with hundreds of kids trying to push the door open to get at their idols. I was in the lounge with the band and I could see the door starting to buckle. The glass door threatened to give way, and numerous kids could have been decapitated.

"I couldn't believe what was happening," reflected Brown. "No one could have anticipated such a reaction. I had never witnessed anything like it. There was hardly any security present but the adults that were there started grabbing kids and hauling them away from the door before anyone got hurt. It was a close escape but it did show how powerful the Blondes had become."

One Friday evening in early October, Conny and I were enjoying our usual after-work ritual, imbibing on the Madison Pub patio, when A&M's director of promotion, J.P. Guilbert, tracked me down to tell me he had something special to play for me on his car's cassette deck. I followed him out to his car parked outside the pub, and he started playing "Run to You," Bryan Adams's debut single from his new CD, *Reckless*. "Going to be huge, this album," remarked Guilbert, "At least five singles. Probably go multi-platinum."

"Nah, easily a million," said I. Guilbert laughed at the sales figure, which had never yet been reached by a Canadian artist.

Recorded at Vancouver's Little Mountain Sound and self-produced by Adams and Bob Clearmountain, *Reckless* was released October 29, 1984, and produced six singles that reached the top fifteen in the U.S. charts, sold five million copies in the U.S., topped the *Billboard* charts by August 1985, and yes, my prediction was correct. Adams hit the diamond mark of over one million copies sold domestically.

A week before Christmas, I received a phone call from Bruce Allen. Adams was executing a brief headline tour of Chicago, Detroit, Cleveland, Philadelphia, and New Jersey (with Honeymoon Suite opening) between December 26 and 31, and Bruce wanted to know if I was interested in tagging along. "What the hell," I said. "It's only Christmas." I agreed to hook up with them in Detroit on the twenty-seventh.

The day before heading out to Detroit, I received news that former Prism lead singer, Ron Tabak, had died in Vancouver under controversial circumstances. With plans to reform the band, guitarist Al Harlow invited Tabak to spend Christmas with him, so Tabak jumped on his bike Christmas Eve to head over to Harlow's house. Problem was the headlight on Tabak's bike wasn't working and he wasn't wearing a helmet. At some point during his brief ride, he was clipped by a passing vehicle and hit his head on the pavement.

Tabak was rushed to hospital where an initial examination did not detect any problems. However, he became abusive when released from the hospital, and two police officers arrested him on suspicion of being intoxicated. A few hours later, he was discovered unconscious on the floor of his jail cell and was rushed back to hospital where a further examination found a blood clot had developed on the right side of his brain. Tabak died before a neurosurgical operation could be performed.

Saddened by the news, I found myself heading out to Windsor, Ontario, by train. I hired a cab at the station to take me across the St. Clair River to hook up with the Adams/Honeymoon Suite touring party at the plush Marriot Hotel in downtown Detroit. Adams's *Reckless* album had been making positive strides in the U.S. at this point, his debut single "Run to You" had positioned itself at No. 6 on *Billboard*'s Hot 100 chart, and this tour was meant to give Bryan his first baby steps toward establishing himself stateside.

I arrived in Detroit early afternoon and just had chance to settle into my room before I was on the band bus to the famous Fox Theatre, scene of many great Motown showcases. Honeymoon Suite opened to a sea of empty seats, save yours truly. I cut a conspicuous figure sitting alone in the tenth row; Johnnie Dee and Derry Grehan waved at me and I waved back at them. The Suite had received decent initial support from Warner Music, but were finding it a tough slog working their debut album. But as their brief set progressed, seats started to fill, and there seemed to be a healthy contingent of Canadians in the audience.

Adams was obviously blooming as a live performer. His band, led by guitarist Keith Scott, had jelled into a solid unit and his new songs, particularly "Summer of '69," showed great potential. The Fox holds over five thousand spectators and seemed to be at least three-quarters full, with Bryan playing an energetic set.

Retiring back to the Marriot Hotel bar after the concert, Bruce introduced me to top U.S. concert promoter Don Fox, who had been responsible for breaking both Bachman-Turner Overdrive and Loverboy in the States and would play a major role in establishing Bryan's international career. Originally from Atlanta (he now runs Beaver Productions out of New Orleans), Fox controlled an impressive talent roster, which included ZZ Top, Heart, and Kansas; all major touring acts in the eighties.

Fox's history with Allen goes back to when Bachman-Turner Overdrive released their third album, *Not Fragile*, in 1974. The album boasted their biggest single, "You Ain't Seen Nothing Yet," as well as "Roll on Down the Highway," and topped both U.S. and Canadian charts.

In the early seventies touring was very territorial in the States. If you wanted your act to play in the New York area, you had to go through Ron Delsener. Conversely, if you wanted to play San Francisco, you had to negotiate with Bill Graham. Which of course meant you had to play by their rules and agree to their terms.

As BTO became a hot concert commodity, Allen changed these rules. Frustrated by touring politics which he had encountered with the band's previous *BTO II* album, Bruce decided to hand the band's entire U.S. itinerary over to Fox. If any of these regional promoters wanted BTO, they had to negotiate with Fox. This, of course, created a great deal of uproar, but the band was so popular that the promoters eventually caved in and booked BTO through Fox.

It was understood Fox owed Allen big time, and Bruce used this leverage with Loverboy, employing Fox to feature his new band on a series of key U.S. tours with ZZ Top and Kansas. It was these dates that launched Loverboy as a major international force in the early eighties. Similar tactics would be employed with Adams, although in fairness, as 1985 rolled out, Adams didn't need much help to crack the charts. Still, listening to Fox and Allen spinning tour anecdotes was a great experience and Bruce showed his class by sending a bottle of white wine to my room with a note thanking me for giving up my Christmas vacation.

The following morning we had climbed aboard the bus set for Cleveland when I noticed Bruce in conversation with a group of men who turned out to be A&M Record executives from L.A. "Hey Sharp, we need your input," yelled Allen. "We need your opinion. What would your choice be for the next single off the album?"

"Run to You" had pretty well run its course and they had settled on "Somebody" as the second single. They were planning to shoot a video for the third single, but were in conflict what that choice should be. "If you are asking me, I'd go with 'Heaven.' I still think it's the best song on the album," said I.

"Can't go with that," interjected Adams. "The song has already been used on a movie soundtrack (*A Night in Heaven*) and it stiffed."

"Yes, the movie stiffed, but the song didn't receive any exposure," responded I. "I'd still go with 'Heaven,' but that's just my opinion." Nothing more was said, but I could see Bruce was deep in thought.

I have had the pleasure of knowing Bryan since those early Sweeney Todd days and have interviewed him on several occasions. One thing you quickly learn from Bryan is he rarely surrenders much personal information. He is just as likely to quiz you on why you asked such a question rather than surrender an answer. He is also very sensitive about his work and does not respond well to criticism.

As we sat on the bus travelling to Cleveland, Bryan told me he had been particularly hurt by what he perceived as a negative review of *Reckless* by Tom Harrison in the Vancouver *Province*. "I thought he was a friend of mine, how could he write this," fumed Adams waving the offending review in the air.

Relaxing during that trip to Cleveland, Adams offered an in-depth insight into his career. In preparation for this tour, he said, "I just threw two pairs of jeans, two T-shirts, ten pairs of socks, and four pairs of underwear into a bag, phoned up the boys and said 'let's go.' We didn't have to rehearse much because we'd played the songs together while recording the album."

Adams was aware of a strong critical support of *Reckless* and was particularly buzzed about his duet with Tina Turner on "It's Only Love." "That was a real 'Beauty and the Beast' situation," offered Adams. "She was in Vancouver performing and seemed genuinely excited about doing the song."

That night's gig in Cleveland was at the Music Hall, which was part of a three-venue complex that held multiple events at the same time. Bryan's concert had been assigned one of the side venues while a World Wrestling Federation (WWF) event was taking centre stage. In the communal hospitality area prior to the concert, Allen obviously knew who these wrestlers were as he glad-handed a group of the athletes while they dined together before going out to pound the crap out of each other. The Cleveland crowd seemed knowledgeable of both bands, and Adams again showed confidence in working with his audience while Honeymoon Suite met with recognition for "New Girl Now," which had been featured on a recent *Miami Vice* episode.

Philadelphia's Tower Ballroom was the venue for the next gig, and the Suite were buzzed this was the same venue which had hosted David Bowie's 1978 *Live* album. I spent the afternoon chatting with the band about the Canadian success of their debut and their battle to gain acceptance in the States. This tour would do them no harm, and there were a few Honeymoon Suite signs in the Philly audience. All the seats occupied even before the Suite appeared.

Adams executed his best performance to date and was beaming when he came off stage. The following day, the two bands travelled on to New Jersey for a New Year's Eve show, but I flew back to Toronto as I had promised Platinum Blonde I would catch their Maple Leaf Gardens debut as headliners for their own New Year's Eve event.

Adams continued his *Reckless* tour with a three-night stand at Massey Hall, commencing January 3. Luba took over the opening slot and was absolutely sensational. January 2, I got a call from Bruce Allen's office inviting me down to Massey Hall. I walked in on a video shoot. The whole hall was filled with television sets. Bryan was shooting the video for his next single — "Heaven." Suffice to say, this would be his first No. 1 single on *Billboard*. I don't know how much weight my comments in Detroit carried, but I like to think I had some influence in Bryan's decision to go with that track. Bryan also shot a live version of "Somebody" for his second video during that same three-night stint.

Adams had finally broken through the U.S. barrier with *Reckless*. We had featured Adams with Tina Turner on our November front cover and that partnership paid dividends for Adams in the New Year when he opened for Turner during a major European tour.

15

LIVE AID –

CAN-AID – FIRST AID

The year 1985 could be summed up as one in which the eight previous years of hard work and progress were almost destroyed by one bold attempt to promote a major music event in Canada. Can-Aid was a projected concert that turned previous industry supporters against us, pitched us against bands and artists who we had previously considered friends, and forced Conny and I to discover the consequences of Bruce Allen turning nasty on you.

However, events couldn't have gotten off to a more positive start. I had cemented my friendship with Allan Gregg by producing a pair of U2 concert tickets for him and his son to catch the band's March 28 concert at Maple Leaf Gardens. I had gotten to know Allan in 1983, when he booked an ad to promote an EP recorded by an Edmonton colleague of his, Peter Panter. Gregg, chief pollster for Prime Minister Brian Mulroney, was also interested in music. He identified with what Conny and I were trying to achieve with *Music Express,* and even invested fifty thousand dollars for a share of our ownership.

As well, Allan displayed his government contacts by producing a cheque for one hundred thousand dollars that *Music Express* was to use to stage a concert event (sponsored by the Canadian Government) to celebrate the United Nation's "International Youth Year." Allan's political cohorts felt it would be a great gesture if *Music Express* executed some high-profile initiative and gave us the funds to create such an event — no strings attached!

But events were bubbling elsewhere that scuppered that opportunity. Boomtown Rats' frontman Bob Geldof (in conjunction with Ultravox pal Midge Ure) had successfully launched a fundraiser for Ethiopian famine relief with his "Do They Know it's Christmas" celebrity-loaded Band Aid single in November of 1983. The U.S. had followed suit with their "We are the World" song, which was created by many of America's top names after the Grammy Awards in Los Angeles (Monday, January 28). Shortly after the single was recorded, producer Quincy Jones phoned top Canadian producer David Foster to see if Canada was interested in recording its own contribution for a *We are the World* album, to be released by CBS in April.

"It all happened while the Payola$ were doing our album with David [Foster] at Little Mountain Sound," recalled lead vocalist Paul Hyde. "After David got the call from Jones he came back into the studio and started plonking away on the piano. Bob and I told him we had a song about starvation called 'Tears are not Enough.' We told him the words but he thought they were a bit too graphic for public consumption. We wrote it about three years before but it never made it on to an album."

Sample lyrics: "Help save the children cried the hungry, pleading eyes. The bony ribs that stick out, the faces full of flies. Switch off the TV; I can't stand to watch that stuff. Tears are not enough."

"David did like the title, so that's mine and Bob's minor claim to fame," laughed Hyde. Foster, Bryan Adams, and Jim Vallance created new lyrics and arrangements, and two weeks later the cream of the Canadian music industry descended on Toronto's Manta Sound, and under Foster's direction recorded and filmed "Tears are not Enough."

Disappointingly, *Music Express* was not invited to attend the recording sessions, but we did hook up with Platinum Blonde's Mark Holmes, who agreed to be our spy inside for the proceedings. His report waxed enthusiastically about the recording experience, meeting SCTV comedy stars John Candy and Eugene Levy, and sharing a post-recording dinner with Joni Mitchell and Bryan Adams. Not one to reject a global opportunity, Bruce Allen grabbed the rights to Canada's involvement in Bob Geldof's Famine Relief Project, calling the Canadian division "Northern Lights." All revenues for that song and video would be channelled through this charity.

But what were we to do with hundred grand? That was the dilemma we faced in discussing how to go about executing that International Youth Year gig. One idea was to stage our awards concert with a lineup featuring Corey Hart, Platinum Blonde, and Luba, by the end of May. We certainly had the funds to pay them. Yet this whole Band Aid, USA for Africa, and Northern

Lights blitz meant the bands were more focused on Ethiopian famine relief.

Our next option was to look at international talent. Tears for Fears were suggested based on the success of their new *Songs from the Big Chair* LP, which featured a huge hit in "Shout." Bob Ansell, VP of marketing for A&M Records, who had never been a big supporter of our magazine, even warmed to the idea and dropped by our office to discuss this opportunity. Simple Minds were another option, and we were told Jim Kerr and the boys might be open to the gig, even sharing a bill with Tears for Fears.

This concept was torpedoed by an announcement from Bob Geldof claiming he was planning two Live Aid concerts for Saturday, July 13 — one at Wembley Stadium in London and a second in New York City — to raise funds and awareness for his famine relief efforts. With an all star cast projected for both concerts, neither Tears for Fears nor Simple Minds were available to us.

As July approached, the upcoming Live Aid concerts were top priority. We still hadn't decided what to do with that hundred grand, but we decided to defer a decision until after the event. It was a given I would cover the London show, while Lenny Stoute was assigned the U.S. concert, which was now set for Philadelphia's JFK Stadium after organizers couldn't find a suitable locale in New York. Rogers and Cowan handled concert publicity, so I called my contact Bernard Doherty in New York, who assured me we could easily obtain press credentials for both gigs.

I flew out to London, arriving Thursday, July 11, and set up base at my usual bed and breakfast lodging behind Victoria Station. I had to drop by Rogers and Cowan's London office on Friday to pick up my press pass, which cost the princely sum of twenty-five pounds (approximately sixty dollars). Then I took the tube to deepest, darkest Brixton to meet with my latest English correspondent, Johnny Waller, as I was going to use his office on the Sunday to file my story back to Canada.

That night, back at my hotel, I watched Geldof being interviewed about Live Aid at his Phonogram Records office. He mentioned he was disappointed in Canada's participation and had expected more of a fundraising effort on this country's part. Geldof had previously worked as a reporter for Vancouver's *Georgia Straight* magazine, but I wasn't sure what his current beef with Canada was about. Turns out, although Northern Lights was Canada's official Live Aid outlet, nobody at the charity had considered organizing a telethon component for the broadcast which was being aired by MuchMusic.

A phone call from Geldof to John Martin at MuchMusic pointed out the discrepancy of staging a telecast without a telethon, the onus being left with Martin and his staff, who executed a heroic two-day scramble to organize the telethon. The Royal York hotel donated their Grand Ballroom, and Bell Canada worked around the clock installing telephone lines.

"It's amazing it happened at all," noted MuchMusic publicity director Bill Bobek at the time. "This telethon was put together in two days. Events like this usually two months to get organized. Marty Simon was a huge help but even he doubted we could pull it off on time. We got all the donation forms printed Friday. We asked for people to show up to take the pledges and received almost eight hundred volunteers. All the help we asked for, we got. The response from both businesses and the general public was amazing." Of course, Northern Lights laid claim to all funds raised by the telethon.

London was bathed in sunshine as I packed my backpack full of pop, potato chips, and sandwiches before heading out on the tube and taking the Jubilee line up to Wembley Stadium. The temperature was approaching eighty degrees Fahrenheit as I arrived at the stadium around 10:30 a.m., very unusual for London. It was if the gods were conspiring together to forge a memorable day. The stadium was almost full to its 72,000 capacity when I located my press seat at the centre of the stadium, just to the right of the Royal Box, which would soon be occupied by Prince Charles and Princess Diana.

Spot on at 12:00 a.m., the familiar beeping of the Greenwich Mean Time Clock was followed by a booming stadium announcement from the BBC's Richard Skinner. "It's twelve o'clock in London, 7:00 a.m. in Philadelphia, and around the world it's time for Live Aid. Please welcome the Prince and Princess of Wales." A fanfare from the Coldstream Guards accompanied Charles and Lady Di, who assumed their positions in the Royal Box. "God Save the Queen" followed before Status Quo hit the stage to launch sixteen hours of music with John Fogerty's "Rockin' All Over the World." Couldn't have picked a better opener, the song lyrics magically captured the spirit of the day and 72,000 people, en masse, sang the chorus.

Geldof had joined Prince Charles and Princess Diana in the royal box with David Bowie and assorted members of Queen, but after being prompting by Lady Di, was convinced to put his Boomtown Rats on early as she wasn't sure she could stay for the whole concert and wanted to see Geldof perform.

Geldof was nursing a painful back injury, but this did not prevent him from executing his Global Jukebox event. He admitted the night before that none of the bands were under contract and he had nightmares no one would show up. "Thirteen hours of the Boomtown Rats could get a little monotonous," he cracked.

Sir Bob had nothing to fear. A virtual who's who of the world's rock fraternity assembled in both London and Philadelphia. Connected by a network of satellites, this complex communications system reached over 1.5 billion television viewers in some 169 countries — more than double the audience that witnessed Neil Armstrong's Moon landing in 1969.

The day's first highlight, occurred when Johnny Finger's distinctive piano intro to "I Don't Like Mondays" summoned Sir Bob and his Boomtown Rats to the stage. Geldof was definitely a performer to seize the moment and there was a point in the song where he sang, "And the lesson today is how to die." He then created this dramatic pause of about ten seconds, in which you could hear a pin drop, before wrapping up the song. Geldof concluded with "Rat Trap" and "Drag Me Down," leaving the stage to an impromptu crowd cheer of "For He's a Jolly Good Fellow" — very British!

Then the heavyweights started to appear. First was Sting, dressed all in white, who launched into an acoustic version of "Roxanne" accompanied by Branford Marsalis on saxophone. A cheery "Hello London" came from Phil Collins, who sat down at the piano for a run-through of "Against All Odds," before joining Sting for duets on "Message in a Bottle," "In the Air Tonight," "Long Way to Go," and "Every Breath You Take." Collins was then spirited away to Heathrow Airport where a British Airways Concorde flew him to Philadelphia to continue his day's exploits.

Philadelphia beamed into Wembley with Jack Nicholson introducing Bryan Adams singing "Summer of '69." But the crowd is already restless in anticipation of the day's first super group, U2. The Irish band was just breaking through as major artists, and they certainly boosted their credibility on this day. Their "Sunday Bloody Sunday" struck a religious fervour with the crowd, and Bono then performed an elongated version of "Bad," which incorporated the Rolling Stones' "Ruby Tuesday," "Sympathy for the Devil," and Lou Reed's "Walk on the Wild Side," which he concluded by pulling one lucky young lady from the audience to slow dance on stage.

That fifteen-year-old girl, Londoner Kal Khalique, later claimed Bono's actions probably saved her life. "I was being crushed at the front. Bono noticed my plight, signalled for security guards to pull me on stage, and even jumped down himself to help rescue me," she later told British press.

I had always been a huge Queen fan, and even if some people were put off by Freddie Mercury's somewhat effeminate persona, even the most cynical person had to be won over by Mercury's sheer magnetism that day. Starting off at the piano with the recognizable refrain of "Bohemian Rhapsody," Mercury then bounded off his stool and launched into "Radio Ga Ga." Suddenly 72,000 fans were singing the chorus, performing the video's signature hand claps, and swaying in tune with the song.

Wembley had become a Queen love-in. "Hammer to Fall" and "Crazy Little Thing Called Love" continued the excitement before they wrapped with "We Will Rock You" and "We Are the Champions." A fabulous set, one rated by a majority of critics as *the* performance of the day.

Bowie and Mick Jagger's "Dancing in the Streets" video was then aired on the screens. The original intent was for Bowie (in London) and Jagger (in Philadelphia) to perform "Dancing in the Streets" together via satellite, but engineer Dave Richards nixed the idea because satellite delays would have thrown their performances out of sync. A video of the pair dancing in some London backstreet was quickly shot and aired at both stadiums. Bowie appeared in person after the video, running his new band through a danceable set with "TVC 15," "Modern Love," "Rebel Rebel," and "Heroes," pushed along by some snazzy keyboard work from Thomas Dolby.

Then Bowie pulled the purpose of Live Aid into its true perspective by introducing a video, shot by the CBC and edited by Colin Dean, which graphically showed the horror of people dying of starvation in Ethiopia. With the Cars' haunting "Drive" as a musical soundtrack, the effect of that vignette on the assembled crowd was devastating. There wasn't a dry eye in the stadium. Surprisingly, Geldof almost cut this clip from the show due to time constraints and only reinstated it when Bowie agreed to cut the song "Five Years" from his set. Such was the effect of that video, telethon donations skyrocketed.

We were into the final stretch. Everyone was glued to their seats as Elton John continued the parade of superstars. "I'm Still Standing" segued into "Benny and the Jets" and "Rocket Man." Kiki Dee romped onstage for "Don't

Go Breaking My Heart" and a decidedly scruffy George Michael sang a duet with her on "Don't Let the Sun Go Down on Me."

Queen's Freddie Mercury and Brian May delivered their Live Aid message, "Is This the World We Created," which proved to be a smokescreen to set up the finale — Paul McCartney alone at the piano singing "Let it Be." But something was wrong!

McCartney started to sing, but no sound emitted through the speakers. First the crowd started to jeer, but then sang along to cover the awkward silence. Promoter Harvey Goldsmith realized he had accidentally unplugged McCartney's microphone during the final scramble, and quickly plugged it back in, causing McCartney's vocals to finally kick in for the balance of the song. Wembley went berserk and the thought crossed my mind, surely the Beatles would have reformed this day if John Lennon had not been assassinated five years earlier.

McCartney was joined on stage by Bowie, Geldof, Allison Moyet, and Pete Townshend to finish his song before Geldof stepped forward into the spotlight. "I think you know what's coming next," he said to a deafening cheer. "We may cock this up. But if you are going to cock it up, you might as well cock it up it in front of the entire world."

With that, David Bowie started off "Do They Know it's Christmas," and the entire cast and crowd joined in, 72,000 voices singing in harmony. To be a part of that crowd was a spiritual moment, something I will never forget. Geldof thanked us and sent his regards to Philadelphia, the performers shuffled off stage, the stadium lights went out, yet the crowd kept singing and continued to sing all the way back to the tube station.

I still had a chance to catch a pint at the local pub before closing and was able to watch some of the Philadelphia Live Aid show. Organizers had pulled a crowd in excess of ninety thousand people, yet it was obvious from the clips we had seen from Wembley that the vibe in the States wasn't the same. Something Lenny Stoute concurred with following his return from Philadelphia.

Geldof had executed the London Live Aid show to deliver a message, and his lineup of talent respected that message. Yet U.S. promoter Bill Graham seemed content just to load up the Philadelphia show with as much talent as he could squeeze in, with little respect to the actual charity. Artists like Michael Jackson, Stevie Wonder, Bruce Springsteen, Ray Charles, Huey Lewis, Cyndi Lauper, Kenny Rogers, Jeffrey Osbourne, and James Ingram, who played significant roles in performing "We are the World," were conspicuous by their absence. Whether they had passed on the show or had not been invited was a mystery.

Looking to reward myself with a drink following my journalistic exertions, I agreed to meet this Japanese lady who was a photo-journalist for a number of top Japanese magazines the following evening. The excuse was to check out her Live Aid photos (which weren't very good) and to possibly hook up with her magazines in the hope that they would promote Canadian talent.

As we chatted, I became aware of a young chap sitting close by who seemed to be listening in on our conversation. As my Japanese cohort got up to leave, he slid over and said, "Sorry, I couldn't help but overhear, are you Keith Sharp from *Music Express*?" I confirmed the correctness of his observation, and he introduced himself as Hugh Dillon, said he was an avid reader of my magazine, and informed he had moved to London to pursue a music career. I bought him a drink and he started telling me about problems in his native Kingston, Ontario; how he was trying to get something going in London, but was fast running out of time, patience, confidence, and money.

I tried to cheer him up and when he asked if I was interested in going to this club in Brixton that night, I felt obliged to accept his offer. Now, Brixton is a dodgy area at the best of times, but Dillon seemed familiar with this particular club, and I settled in for a couple of drinks. Adam Ant enlivened the place by sticking his head through the door and immediately suffering verbal abuse from local punters for his lacklustre performance at Live Aid.

Years later, Kerry Doole interviewed Dillon, now lead singer for the Headstones, and he mentioned our meeting and how influential my words had been in encouraging him to return to Canada and form a successful group. Dillon is now a highly successful actor starring in TV shows like *Flashpoint* and *Durham County*, as well as movies like *Hardcore Logo*, and still pursues a recording career with the Headstones. I have met him on quite a few occasions since, and we always chat about that initial meeting.

Still buzzed by Live Aid, I reflected how many countries — Australia, Germany, Holland, and even Russia — had staged their own concerts. Yet Canada's sole contribution had been the efforts of Adams and Neil Young. Understanding *Music Express* was committed to spending that hundred thousand, I started to think maybe we could do a belated Live Aid–type show in Canada. On the Monday before flying back to Toronto, I called Vinny Cinquemani, president of The Agency, Canada's premiere talent booking agency, and casually asked if there might be some interest in a Canadian show, keeping in mind we did have the seed money to spend.

Vinny confirmed quite a few of his acts regretted they couldn't have participated more and had wondered why Canada hadn't taken such an initiative. He advised me Platinum Blonde were staging a press conference on that Wednesday to launch a national tour for their *Alien Shores* release and we should touch base.

I appeared at the press conference, admired how MacLean had actually executed a change in his hair colour (from strawberry red to a reddish platinum), and chatted with Cineqemani about the feasibility of cobbling together some kind of lineup. What really got things rolling was the unexpected support of MuchMusic's John Martin. He had wondered himself why Canada had not taken the initiative of a Live Aid concert and said he would love to televise such an event. With both Cinquemani and Martin on board, it seemed such a show wasn't a pipe dream after all.

Let me state emphatically: *Music Express* never professed to know how to execute a major concert. Yes, we had enjoyed great success with our two awards shows, but this would be show on a much grander scale. If anyone from the industry had called to say there was no way we could pull this gig off, we would have happily stepped back and instead organized some kind of low-brow event to facilitate our International Youth Year commitment. Yet no one from the industry made that call! At the beginning, everyone I talked to couldn't have been more supportive.

With MuchMusic supposedly locked, and Cinquemani in charge of the talent, Martin and I both agreed we should look at CNE Stadium for the venue. As this facility was the concert domain of CPI, I called Arthur Fogel for a meeting. I invited CPI to actually run the concert and to join The Agency in securing the talent, and confirmed we had MuchMusic on board. "Have you talked to Bruce (Allen)?" asked Fogel.

The answer to that question was no. My feeling was Bruce had done enough with his involvement in Northern Lights. I knew Bryan Adams was setting up for a major national tour in the fall, and besides, I wanted to get all my ducks in a row before calling him. It wasn't until after Fogel implied that CPI would be involved that I decided it was the time to call Bruce.

I informed him of what was being planned, told him MuchMusic, The Agency, and CPI were on-board. I had also called Labatt to confirm their potential corporate sponsorship (assuming we could pull the concert off). I said to Bruce that I totally understood if Bryan passed on the gig, but felt he should be aware of what we were planning, and I invited Allen to participate in any way possible — with funds going to his Northern Lights charity.

Bruce acknowledged the call, put the phone down ... and set about destroying the event. At that point, everything went pear shaped. Again, and I repeat this, if Bruce was against the concept, all he had to do was say so and I would have respected him enough to pull the plug.

In fact, over the next few weeks, he convinced The Agency not to participate. He made the same call to CPI, and probably tried the same with MuchMusic, though he didn't carry any clout with John Martin. What made things worse, Randy Bachman had somehow found out about our intentions and had called to ask what was happening. I told him nothing had been confirmed but he should call Vinny.

Next thing I know, Bachman mentioned the gig in a press interview and *Music Express* was being inundated with calls. Apparently, Bachman had his own axe to grind after Allen's office rejected his offer to participate in the "Tears are not Enough" recording session.

We soon learned it was not kosher to piss off Bruce Allen. He had anointed himself as the Godfather of the Canadian music industry and, as such, wanted to control everything that was going on. It had worked to our advantage when he backed us against CARAS with our music awards. But now he vented his full fury against us for the unforgivable sin of trying to execute an initiative without his blessing.

Next thing I know, Bruce and Anthem's Ray Danniels are on CHUM Radio at six in the morning totally trashing our gig and saying there was no way they were going to let it happen! Shortly after, Bryan Adams staged a press conference at the Bellair Cafe in Toronto to announce his forthcoming Canadian concert tour. When a journalist asked if he was planning to perform at Can-Aid, his curt answer was, "No, it's not going to happen." All of this should have been a sign for us to pull the plug. But stupidly, as it turned out, the more grief we suffered, the more determined we were to stage the show.

Aware CPI would be no help, we brought in Wolfgang Siebert, whose past experience had been staging The Police Picnic at Oakville and promoting Mosport concerts. He was convinced if we locked in a date at the CNE, people would believe the gig was a go and bands would commit. A call to Gord Walker at the CNE resulted in us finding out Sunday September 29, was available, and for a non-refundable fee of ten thousand dollars, the gig was ours. So we fired him over a cheque.

Apparently, CPI went ballistic when they discovered we had nailed down a date. Furthermore, through his connections, Siebert found out Bruce Springsteen was bringing his own stage setup to the CNE for his August 26 and 27 dates and, according to his tour manager, we might be able to use the same stage and Springsteen himself might agree to perform at Can-Aid.

The tour manager informed Siebert that Springsteen had kicked himself for not agreeing to perform in Philadelphia, and a cameo at Can-Aid might be his way to give something back. We were sworn to secrecy over any possible appearance, but Springsteen did add fuel to the fire when he closed off his August 27 date at the CNE by saying, "You might see me back here faster than you think." Nobody but us knew what he was talking about.

Phil Collins became another international target. Ritchie Yorke and I chased him down to the Pine Knob amphitheatre north of Detroit to pitch him on our show, which resulted in a call from his manager, Tony Smith. But still, all these barriers were being erected against us. Bands who were our friends, like Helix and Honeymoon Suite, were being warned not to play Can-Aid. We hired Stuart Raven-Hill to co-ordinate talent, but he reported back that no one wanted to play.

Things finally came to a head when Martin, trying to resolve Can-Aid once and for all, called me into a meeting at MuchMusic and placed a call to Bruce Allen. Allen took the call, said Can-Aid was "Ill-conceived, ill-timed and ill-planned," and said if we agreed to cancel the date, he would convene a meeting of key industry members during the forthcoming Juno Awards in November to discuss possible future opportunities.

We subsequently cancelled Can-Aid and lost our ten thousand dollar deposit to the CNE. This whole fiasco severely hurt *Music Express*'s relationship with certain industry types and was stressful enough to put Conny in hospital.

True to his word, Bruce Allen staged that meeting with us to discuss Can-Aid, and what a meeting it was! Held at a conference room at the Harbour Castle on Saturday November 3, this meeting was attended by a who's who of the Canadian music industry. Aside from Allen, there was Anthem's Ray Danniels, Donald Tarleton, and Terry Flood; from Aquarius, Sam Feldman; Anne Murray's manager Leonard Rambeau; Gordon Lightfoot's manager Barry Harvey; plus Arthur Fogel from CPI; Vinny Cinquemani from The Agency; and John Martin from MuchMusic. Facing this entourage on the other side of the table was Conny, Allan Gregg, and I.

I should have been flattered *Music Express* could draw such a prestigious turnout. The joke was that if the roof had collapsed, Canada's entire music industry would have been wiped out. The session itself was brief and quite blunt. Gregg made a brief speech about International Youth Year and what we were trying to achieve. I talked about how I picked up on the vibe Canadian artists wanted to do more for Live Aid and how I had originally rallied enough support to execute the gig. But then Allen jumped in, and speaking for the entire room, quickly derided our Can-Aid notion. He said he felt the Canadian industry had done enough and that future charity efforts were not welcome or viable. So goodbye Can-Aid.

This was supposed to be a closed meeting, yet Allen smuggled a Canadian Press reporter in, and I was clearly rattled when that reporter started firing questions at me at the meeting's conclusion. In retrospect, I should have dropped that cheque for a hundred thousand dollars on Cinquemani's desk and said, "Hey Vinny, book me some bands." But I got carried away with the potential of doing something profound, and in the process got my fingers burned. Note to self: In future don't take on the Canadian music industry. Nasty things happen when you do!

So what to do next? We had already depleted our hundred thousand with the loss of the CNE deposit and funds that had been paid to Siebert and Raven-Hill. With no possibility of moving forward with Can-Aid, we decided to sink some funds into our Music Express Awards, which we were now scrambling to schedule December 5 at the Copa in Toronto. We also made a ten thousand dollar donation to United Way to fund tickets for Platinum Blonde's United Way concert December 6.

Unlike our previous two award shows, which had been major productions, the December 6 event at the Copa was a virtual non-event. Because of all the drama surrounding our Can-Aid fiasco, we didn't have time to organize a proper ceremony, most of the winners didn't bother to show up to accept their awards, and to top it off, the show's headline artist, Vancouver's Paul Janz, got into a backstage confrontation with Conny and had her ejected from the building. Not a great way to end the year!

16

RACKING UP

THE AIR MILES

Despite all the problems with Can-Aid, 1985 wasn't all bad. I spent a memorable week jet-setting around Canada to judge all three semi-finals of the CBC-sponsored *Rock Wars* show, I checked out Bryan Adams performing with Tina Turner in London, and I also ended up in sunny Jamaica, where Kerry Doole, photographer Phil Regandanz, and I covered Jamfest 1985 in Kingston.

Early in February 1985, before the Can-Aid disaster began, I received a phone call from Ken Gibson, television production mogul and one half of the Griffiths-Gibson jingle empire. They had initiated a CBC show called *Rock Wars*. The contest pitted three regional bands against each other each week, with the finalists from each of these shows moving on to compete against each other. The ultimate winner was to receive their own thirty-minute CBC-TV special as well as studio recording time. This segment was to run Fridays, dropped into the middle of *Good Rockin' Tonite*, a rock show hosted by Terry David Mulligan and Stu Jefferies (now a Boomer 97.3 radio DJ).

Gibson asked if I was interested in participating as one of three semi-final judges. The caveat being I had to be available to judge all three semi-finals (in Regina, Halifax, and Toronto) in just five days! Realizing it would be good press exposure for *Music Express,* I accepted Ken's offer. The following Sunday I found myself meeting fellow judges, *Video Hits* host Samantha Taylor and CFNY radio mogul David Marsden, as we prepared to fly out from Toronto to our first semi-final in Regina.

I had watched a few of the regional contests on earlier telecasts and detected an error in the voting process. I remembered watching a Maritime regional in which two of the three judges voted for one band (I believe they were Price Edward Island's Haywire), but the third judge voted for another band. But the third judge's voting score was so drastically different than the other two, when the total points for all three bands were tabulated, the third judge's choice beat out the picks of the other two judges. It was my opinion if one band received top score from two out of three judges, they should be declared the winner. I mentioned this possible discrepancy to Taylor and Marsden and both agreed with my observation.

It was understood we weren't supposed to be familiar with any of the three bands in order to retain our neutrality. So when we arrived at the CBC studios for the 4:00 p.m. taping, the three contestants, Edmonton's Peter Mann & the Lonely, Regina's Mad Shadows, and Winnipeg's Instructions, meant nothing to me — or so I thought. *Rock Wars* was hosted by Brad Giffen (now CFCN news reporter), and he explained the show's format to us. First, we would be introduced to the live studio audience. Then we would judge each act out of one hundred points, based on material and presentation (the bands lip-synced), and after observing all three bands perform one song, we would step out in front of the audience, offer a critique, and deliver our scores. The band with the highest total points went through to the finals in Vancouver.

After our briefing, we headed into makeup and the first person I see is Peter Bodman, former lead singer of The Models. "Hey Keith, me ol' mate, what are you doing here?" he quizzed.

"I am one of the three judges," responded I. "And what are you doing here?"

"I am in the contest, lead singer of Peter Mann & the Lonely," said he. Can you say conflict of interest boys and girls? And, of course, this conversation is observed by members of the other two bands. So I quickly found Brad Giffen and explained my problem. But with thirty minutes to go before airtime, there was no time to find a replacement. So he told me to try to judge the talent purely on merit.

Bodman almost had another problem when his drummer decided to give Samantha the ol' groupie rap, with an explicit invitation to meet him after the show, not knowing that she was a judge. Just in time, Bodman spotted the danger and spirited the miscreant drummer down the hallway screaming, "You stupid swine, she's one of the judges."

First band up, Mad Shadows, showed plenty of promise in a Duran Duran, teenybopper fashion. Unfortunately, the guitarist decided to milk the fact they were miming to the track by going Jimi Hendrix on us and he launched into some behind-the-back guitar histrionics. His guitar strap snapped and his instrument fell limply to the floor while the track kept playing. Winnipeg's Instructions adopted a surly pose with both the audience and judges, smoking and tossing cigarette butts into the crowd and adopting an arrogant attitude. It didn't help that their performance was woeful.

Which left things for Peter Mann & the Lonely, and they didn't disappoint. Their Sheila E–type percussionist provided real eye candy, and the quality of their delivery was streets ahead of the other two bands. Samantha and I immediately targeted The Lonely as our first choice, with Mad Shadows and the Instructions numbers two and three respectfully. But as the show's producer was pushing for our final results, we found Marsden reluctant to show us his scores.

Sure enough, by the time we received Marsden's scores from the producer, we discovered he had done exactly what the girl in the Maritimes had done. He had scored Mad Shadows as his first choice and jigged the second- and third-place scores so those bands couldn't win. It looked like Mad Shadows would win, despite being the final choice of only one judge!

Quickly, with the producer yelling for a final tally, Samantha and I recalibrated our scores to ensure Peter Mann & the Lonely won — which meant lowering the scores of the other two bands. The live audience didn't seem to mind, Marsden was cheesed we had circumvented his plan, and of course, Mad Shadows registered a protest, claiming that I was friendly with Peter Bodman and had fixed the final outcome, but this was to no avail.

We flew out of Regina late Sunday, and by Tuesday afternoon were back at the airport for our flight to Halifax. Samantha and I conferred about Marsden's refusal to go along with our voting formula, and we vowed if we both liked the same band we would ensure they won.

Halifax proved to be much more intimidating. We were literally scooped off the plane and hustled into the downtown studios before we had even had time to deposit our bags in our hotel room. From the sanctity of the green room, we could hear the rumble of five hundred kids chanting, "Steps, Steps, Steps." "Don't be intimidated by the audience," said our friendly producer. "It's just that they are sort of partial to the home band, Steps Around the House."

The first band out was Newfoundland's 12 Gauge, a run-of-the-mill blues band that were okay, but no threat to win the contest. Next came Steps Around the House, and it was like U2 had hit the stage. They were a good looking band, kind of like Spandau Ballet in sound and appearance. The band's lead singer, Peter Baylis (who we would later find out is the son of the head of CBC Halifax), was extremely polished. As they walked off stage to a rapturous applause, we felt pretty sure Steps would win. But then came Montreal's Tchukon.

All three of us judges let out an oh-no gasp at the same instant. This black jazz/funk fusion band bounced onto the stage fronted an extremely attractive white girl singer. They were in full costume, had slick dance moves, and sang live to track (not lip-synching). The girl guitarist, Kat Dyson-Oliver, was so good she later performed with Prince, Cyndi Lauper, and more recently, P!nk. This was George Clinton/Parliament meeting Earth, Wind & Fire. Tchukon were totally awesome, and should not have been in this contest — they were too good!

Even Marsden turned pale. There was no question who had won, and for once he was in total agreement. Even the crowd seemed to acknowledge Tchukon's talent, yet started chanting "Steps, Steps, Steps," even more voraciously. So we agreed to mark Tchukon as the winners but make the points spread between them and Steps extremely tight ... like three points.

All three judges had to run the gauntlet of presenting our final submissions, and we acknowledged Steps were terrific but Tchukon just slightly better. I can remember standing on the stage looking at this young girl as the point scores were announced. She had a calculator in hand, had tallied up Steps scores, and when she tallied up Tchukon's scores and realized they had won by three points, a look of horror flashed across her face. She was crestfallen! Normally, the show's judges go back on stage for the final credits. Yet this time the show's producers thought it would be wise to avoid any potential conflict with the audience. We were hustled out of the building before the crowd could leave.

As we headed out the door we were met by Steps' manager, Bruce Davidsen, who I had previously met in Calgary. He thanked us for our efforts, acknowledged it must have been a difficult task, and realizing we had not eaten dinner, offered to treat us to a meal at the posh Privateers restaurant. We were joined by Steps, who proved to be gracious losers, even though there were some accusations of Tchukon being ringers.

We finally checked in at the Sheraton, and after depositing our bags in our rooms, noticed Tchukon were performing that night at the hotel across the street. By 10:30 we had caught our second wind and we crossed the street to catch the band. Brad Giffen was there (surrounded by local groupies) and the Tchukon members were naturally delighted to see us, acknowledging our presence from the stage.

All of this travel was taking its toll on yours truly. Luckily, the last show was in Toronto on Thursday, so the final stretch was in view. As CBC didn't have the plush studios they currently operate from, the show was filmed in a makeshift set-up at a warehouse on Jarvis Street. Even the crowd wasn't a regular studio audience, they were school kids who had been offered an afternoon off to attend the taping. The kids didn't know any of the three bands — London's The Waiting, Ottawa's Eight Seconds, and Toronto's Eye Eye — and exhibited an air of indifference during all three performances.

I recollect The Waiting made no impression on any of the judges. Ottawa's Eight Seconds were quite strong — their lead singer, Andres Del Castillo, was a ringer for Spandau Ballet's Tony Hadley. In the end Toronto's Eye Eye were just a shade more polished. Samantha voted for Eye Eye but David preferred Eight Seconds, so the final decision was left to me, and I opted for Eye Eye. David was so disinterested at this point he wasn't even fighting over the points spread.

Both Eight Seconds and Eye Eye eventually scored recording contracts, and Kings' manager Gary Pring co-managed Eye Eye. Eye Eye joined Peter Mann & the Lonely, Tchukon, and Vancouver's HB Concept in the finals, which Tchukon won convincingly. In reflection, it was a hectic experience, but great public relations for *Music Express,* and I seem to recollect the CBC paid well — something like fifteen hundred dollars to each of us for our three-day commitment.

Tchukon's win earned them a thirty-minute CBC special, and they used this tape as a demo for the U.S. show *Star Search* in 1986 — which they also won, receiving a prize of one hundred thousand dollars. They eventually recorded an album for Aquarius, *Here and Now,* but by the band's own admission it didn't contain their best material. Sadly, Tchukon broke up in 1990 when some of the members moved to Toronto to appear in *Dream of a Lifetime,* a musical based on the life of Motown star Marvin Gaye, produced by Donald K Donald's Donald Tarelton. As mentioned, guitarist Cat Dyson-Oliver successfully linked up with Prince before touring the planet with Cyndi Lauper and P!nk.

Music Express executed two massive contests in early 1985. The first one sent a grand-prize winner and friend to the Rock in Rio concert, January 10–22, in Rio De Janeiro, Brazil, to catch the likes of Iron Maiden, Queen, Rod Stewart, Ozzy Osbourne, and Def Leppard. Our L.A. correspondent, Ian Blair, tagged along and reported one of the girl winners had her bracelet snatched off her while lounging on the beach.

The second contest was a week in London, March 13–20, to catch Bryan Adams in concert at Wembley Stadium opening for Tina Turner. We joined forces with Samantha Taylor, who hosted CBC's *Video Hits,* and the two-week contest blitz produced over twenty thousand postcard entries. CBC took the contest one step further by agreeing to shoot a video of the winners attending the concert for future airing on the show.

The winner was nineteen-year-old Corinna Ienna, from Kingston, Ontario, who brought along her boyfriend. I wasn't sure what the protocol for sleeping arrangements were when we arrived at the London hotel, but they seemed eager to share the same room, so I trust I didn't get in trouble with her parents.

Turner's four sold out nights at Wembley Arena were London's hottest concert ticket. Her cover of "Ball of Confusion" with Heaven 17 had sparked enough interest on both sides of the Atlantic for her EMI label to fund Turner's *Private Dancer* comeback album. The architect of this comeback was her Australian manager, Roger Davies, who rescued the forty-five-year-old Turner from a routine of Vegas-type R&B revival shows and surrounded her with a slew of hip new writers and performers. It didn't hurt Adams that the nightly highlight of her encore numbers was their duet of "It's Only Love."

As the winner, her boyfriend, myself, and the London CBC correspondent headed north by taxi to Wembley. I tried to calm Corinna down, saying she had nothing to be nervous about as Bryan was just a really nice guy. We arrived at the venue just as Adams concluded his sound check. He was on stage, bedecked in his usual white T-shirt and jeans. Our winner walked straight past him thinking he was one of the roadies!

Having realized her faux pas, Corinna had a pleasant meeting with Bryan in his dressing room. She had her photo taken with Adams, was filmed for the CBC *Video Hits* segment, and received a stack of Bryan Adams merchandise. When we went out to find our seats for the show, our CBC rep reported the venue had slipped up and had not assigned us tickets for the show. As the crowd started to filter in for the gig, we were given seats in the first five rows on the understanding that they were for Tina Turner fans, and if any showed up before Adams finished, we'd have to move!

As we feared, the real owners of those front row seats arrived during the intermission, and we had to vacate our position. Aware that our dilemma was being filmed by the CBC crew, the Wembley public relations officer guided us to the side of the stage and found accommodation in the VIP section. Suddenly, our winner and her boyfriend were surrounded by the likes of Elton John, David Bowie, the Eurythmics, and Boy George.

Tina Turner live was an awesome spectacle, and her energetic dancing and powerful vocals totally belied her age. She closed her set by singing a duet with Elton John, Bruce Springsteen's "Dancing in the Dark," before bringing out Adams, whom she referred to as "Denis the Menace," to close with "It's Only Love." Our winner spent most of Turner's set mesmerized by the plethora of celebrities hanging around our booth. I even got Elton to say hi to her.

As she left the arena, Corinna was interviewed by the CBC correspondent. "So, how did you enjoy the show?" asked the interviewer?

"Oh, it was great," she responded. "We saw Elton John, David Bowie, the Eurythmics, Boy George."

"And how was Bryan Adams?" enquired our interviewer.

"Oh, he was alright too," she mumbled.

I had barely unpacked from my England trip when I was out the door again, this time Kerry Doole, photographer Phil Regandanz, and I flew down to Jamaica to cover Jamfest 1985, a musical adjunct to the UN's International Youth Year conference that was being staged in Kingston during the first ten days of April.

As the Canadian government had given us that hundred thousand dollars to stage our own Youth Year event, we felt the least we could do was return the favour and cover Jamfest. Jamaican senator Olivia Grange, who had developed strong cultural ties with Toronto's black music community, was instrumental in soliciting support from the bands Messenjah, The Parachute Club, Jane Siberry, Carlene Davis, and Bruce Cockburn. With MuchMusic also on board, and an offer of free airfare to *Music Express*, we were on our way. Truth is we had no idea what we were flying into.

The whole event turned out to be a fiasco. The conference was boycotted by communist elements, Kingston's National Stadium, which holds a capacity of fifty thousand spectators, only drew sparse crowds of under five thousand spectators, and even those numbers were reduced to a handful as the performances dragged into the early hours of the morning. By the end of the event, we were all happy to be heading home.

Meanwhile, on the domestic front, Canadian rock continued to grown in 1985 and *Music Express* was at full stretch monitoring all the developments. Following the success of Loverboy and Platinum Blonde, Gowan was Jeff Burns's latest signing to CBS, and *Strange Animal* was afforded a major PR push when launched in March. Former keyboardist for the band Rheingold, Gowan had seen his debut release fail out of the box and had taken four months off to rediscover his genetic roots in Scotland and Ireland. A call from top English producer David Tickle came with an offer to produce Gowan's next album. Tickle also was key in enlisting the services of two ace session musicians, drummer Jerry Marotta and bassist Tony Levin, to play on the album.

Recorded at Ringo Starr's Startling Studios in his Tittenhurst Park residence, the material for *Strange Animal* proved to be adventurous vignettes for a unique video treatment. Following the album's completion, Gowan engaged master videographer Rob Quarterly, and the two spent an additional two months creating a ground-breaking video for "A Criminal Mind," as well as an equally effective clip for "Strange Animal." "Videos can be powerful but they are so misused and so miscalculated," Gowan told *ME* writer Nick Krewen. "That's why I'm really happy with the way we portrayed 'A Criminal Mind.'"

Gowan proved to be an amazing live performer as well as an engaging personality. I had the pleasure of catching his headline gig at Ontario Place in May and was greatly impressed by his musical ability. In one memorable medley, he covered the entire history of the piano in popular music, starting off with Beethoven, then Scott Joplin, moving on to Jerry Lee Lewis and Little Richard, before finishing with Paul McCartney and then his own material. An outstanding showman!

To this day, Paul Hyde grimaces at the butchered job he perceives David Foster executed on the Payola$' *Here's the World for Ya* release. "David Foster wouldn't know a rock song if it bit him in the knee," fumed Hyde. "Bruce

Allen brought him in because he thought it would gain us credibility with A&M — but that whole idea backfired."

Hyde disclaimed the notion their Payola$ name was a problem in the States. Yet he conceded A&M dropped the album virtually from the moment it came out. "Bob and I heard that a relative of Allan Freed [who was found guilty of Payola charges in the late fifties] was on staff at A&M's publishing department and obviously had no sense of humour. At that time it was the perfect storm. Both Bob and I were going through personal problems. Everything was a swirling mess of shit." The release did not do well and the band rebranded itself as Rock and Hyde for their next record before disbanding.

Mid-June found yours truly in Montreal for a July front cover interview with Corey Hart, who was about to issue a new album, *Boy in the Box*. I was on the second floor of his Aquarius label's office one Saturday afternoon, chatting with the label's promo chief Keith Brown and wondering why Corey was late for the interrogation, when we heard this furtive banging coming from downstairs.

Moving to the window to investigate the disruption, we saw Hart stuck outside, desperately trying to attract our attention. Apparently, the security guard had locked up and left for the day, leaving our boy stuck outside his box. Resplendent in a brown T-shirt, faded blue jeans, and sneakers as battered as his Mazda, Hart nonetheless exhibited the same air of confidence which convinced Aquarius to sign him in the first place. Since debuting *First Offence*, Hart had connected on both sides of the border, with his "Sunglasses at Night" track enjoying mass radio and video exposure on both MTV and MuchMusic. That track earned Hart U.S. touring spots with Rick Springfield and Hall & Oates and a Grammy nomination for Best New Artist (which he lost to Cyndi Lauper).

Hart had recorded *Boy in the Box* at Le Studio at Morin Heights, and the album poised to spark a massive response, one that would eventually match Bryan Adams's *Reckless* with over one million records sold in Canada. Superficially, Hart had everything going for him. Handsome, pouty James Dean looks, sure-fire hit singles, and a riveting live performance tailor-made for video exposure. Like Platinum Blonde (who he totally upstaged as the opener during a New Year's Eve gig), Hart was triggering a new wave of fan mania. "Never Surrender" scored as a tremendous hit single, with the title track, "Everything in my Heart," and "Eurasian Eyes" all racking up heavy airplay.

Hart allowed that the sessions for *Boy in the Box* had been a lot more satisfying than his first album, which had been recorded in England over a three-month period. "This time out, I am working with my own band who knows how I write and how I like to hear things. It's much better having a rapport with the people who play your music on a daily basis."

While the Can-Aid controversy raged on, Platinum Blonde prepared to launch an ambitious headline national tour for *Alien Shores*, promoted by Hamilton's Jim Skerrit. The band had drafted Kenny MacLean, formerly of the Deserters, to play bass, supply backing vocals, and help free up front man Mark Holmes. Rumour had it that CBS U.S. had insisted their lineup be strengthened, and with much riding on the band's second album, produced by former Emerson, Lake & Palmer engineer, Eddie Offord, the band were anxious to comply. The one question on everyone's mind? How was MacLean going to get his strawberry red locks coloured peroxide blonde?

Platinum Blonde, in full makeup and sporting a decidedly preppy look, arrived at the upstairs patio at the Madison Pub to discuss their new release with yours truly for an interview that would be featured as the cover story of our August issue. Of course, they caused a commotion with local punters — mostly U of T students who constantly interrupted our chat and asked for autographs and snap photos, attention which Holmes, Galli, Steffler, and now, Kenny MacLean, thrived on.

MacLean, the amicable Glaswegian, brought a new dynamic to the band's collective personality. An easygoing jokester, always good for a quote, he definitely grounded a band previously described as somewhat aloof. "Platinum Blonde is everything I wanted the Deserters to be," he allowed. "The Deserters were never teenage heartthrobs but we were into the glitter and fashion a bit at one time until we got tired and sloppy."

Other notable Canadian acts ran into trouble as the year went on. Loverboy's stock had dipped when their 1983 *Keep it Up* release only sold two million copies, which was, nonetheless, not bad by most standards. Headline touring and solid video support produced two major singles, "Hot Girls in Love" and "Queen of the Broken Hearts," yet the sales were still a drop of two million from their 1981 *Get Lucky* LP.

Rejected in Europe and only marginally successful in Japan, Loverboy took one year off to regroup, employing Judas Priest producer Tom Allom on their third album, *Lovin' Every Minute of It*. Despite the title track being one of their most commercial radio songs to date and the album also containing a monster ballad with "This Could Be the Night," Loverboy's career began to slide. The album sold a further two million copies, yet only reached No. 13 on the *Billboard* charts.

The Headpins were in the midst of recording *Head Over Heels* at Little Mountain when they learned their label, Solid Gold, had gone bankrupt. Having survived a similar experience with his former band Chilliwack, lead guitarist Brian MacLeod instantly pulled the band out of the studios and instead continued the sessions on his Grand Marnier boat, anchored by the side of Vancouver's Bayshore Inn. "It was a real character builder," said MacLeod of the sessions. "We've become a band that's used to adversity. It seems twice a year, regular as clockwork; something comes along to fuck us up."

MCA, who had owned international rights to their last album, *Line of Fire*, bought out the band's contract and the Headpins returned to Little Mountain Sound to finish off the sessions. New drummer Mike Craney (formerly of Whitesnake) replaced Bernie Aubin, yet the band struggled to regain lost momentum despite embarking on a national tour opening for Helix. Same with formerly popular Saga, whose new *Behaviour* release also failed to connect with a Canadian audience. As well, Myles Goodwyn's April Wine–tagged *Walking through Fire* release wasn't fooling any of their former fans.

Triumph found a unique way to promote their live double-album, *Stages*. Bassist Mike Levine set off on a national one-day promotion marathon that saw him sell the album to eight key FM-radio stations in seven cities, starting with Q-104 in Halifax and finishing at Vancouver's CFOX. Pepsi Cola and MCA offered to donate a dollar for every mile Levine covered and we sent Lenny Stoute and photographer Phil Regendanz along to document the mayhem.

The fifteenth annual Juno Awards, tagged as the Bryan and Tina show, were staged Sunday, November 4, at the Harbour Castle Hilton. Hosted by SCTV's Andrea Martin and Martin Short, the Junos naturally honoured Canada's Northern Lights efforts, with David Foster winning Producer of the Year and Prime Minister Brian Mulroney receiving an honorary Juno … which instantly disappeared. An interesting side battle had been looming between Adams and Corey Hart, with *Reckless* and *Boy in the Box* albums zeroing in on diamond status (one million units sold), a level never previously reached domestically by a Canadian artist or group.

Adams won the TV skirmish, winning two Junos, Male Vocalist of the Year and Album of the Year for *Reckless*, and performing the show's climax, his duet with Tina Turner, "It's Only Love." Corey had to console himself with the Single of the Year Juno for "Never Surrender."

The Parachute Club won the Canadian Group of the Year award with Platinum Blonde not even nominated! Despite selling 150,000 copies of their debut album and engaging in a sell-out national tour, the Blondes were inexplicably left off the ballot entirely. CARAS's explanation was that *Alien Shores* had been released too late for voter consideration — yet didn't explain why they weren't nominated for Group of the Year? Which begs the question, if CARAS changed the Juno date to promote Christmas sales, why would they eliminate all products that were being released in the fall for that same Christmas sales period? Surely the biggest sales push any band or record could receive would come from winning a Juno award.

Survival was the key word to describe 1985. A year that started out so promising for *Music Express* was marred by the political infighting of our Can-Aid debacle. Yet we did learn one invaluable lessen: never mess around with Bruce Allen.

17

ATTACKING

THE U.S.

f 1985 had been a rough year for *Music Express*, 1986 would be an amazing year for *Rock Express*. Why the name change you ask? We had been aware for a while a conflict had been building with England's *New Musical Express*, as our magazine was being distributed around Britain and Australia. So we decided to mark our hundredth issue in March (with Honeymoon Suite on the cover) by changing the name and creating a sharper image.

A phone call from New York irreversibly changed the fortunes of *Rock Express* magazine. I took a call from Mark Greenberg, the vice president of Warner Publishing Services. He said his company was familiar with *Music Express* (he didn't know about the name change) and enquired if we were interested in launching our magazine in the States? He told me *Rolling Stone* was being targeted by a new magazine, *Spin* (circulated by rival Curtis Publishers), and that *Rolling Stone* was decreasing their music content. Warner thought *Music Express* would be a decent addition to their service.

I had no idea how Warner Publishing became aware of (what was now) *Rock Express*. We had sent a couple of bundles down to a wholesaler in Long Island (I presumed they were box-stuffing them, like Records on Wheels) and U.S. visitors had picked up copies and requested subscriptions. Yet for *Rock Express* to be invited to launch in the States was both flattering at the same time it was difficult to comprehend. After all, we were a tiny operation without the financial resources to possibly contemplate a U.S. expansion.

Conny and I ran the idea by Allan Gregg, and he was all for it, saying we should seize any opportunity to move forward. With Warner pushing for an April issue, we didn't have much time to organize ourselves. As a compromise, we agreed with Warner to launch *Rock Express* in a selection of key U.S. cities, including New York, Los Angeles, Boston, Atlanta, Houston, Minneapolis, Chicago, and San Francisco. To promote *Rock Express* in these markets, we recruited a network of writers similar to our "Regional Reports" staff in Canada. Many of these writers were radio station DJs, Carter Allen at WBCN in Boston, Dana Steele at KLOL in Houston, and Kelly Kincaid at 96 Rock in Atlanta, and all contributed to the book while also providing valuable radio exposure for *Rock Express* in their respective regions.

In planning our roll out into the States, Boston's Carter Allen called to suggest an ideal way for us to launch *Rock Express* in the Boston area would be to attend WBCN's Rock Expo, set for Saturday, April 21. The station offered us a free booth, said they would promote us at the Expo, and gave us a chance to meet rock fans in Boston and distribute copies of back issues. Our receptionist/public relations girl, Julia Owen, distributions person, Robert Kunz, and I packed my trusty Camaro full of back issues. We also brought a healthy supply of music videos; my intention was to rent a television for the expo and pull spectators in by airing the music videos. We had also pre-ordered a supply of *Rock Express* T-shirts from Bill Graham's Rock Express merchandise company (no relation) in San Francisco, and had arranged for Platinum Blonde (who were touring in the area at the time) and Wendy O. Williams to be at our booth and sign autographs.

On April 19, we headed southwest toward Buffalo, staying overnight in Fort Erie where we crossed the border that night to catch Honeymoon Suite open for Heart. Early Friday morning we headed to Boston, arriving there late in the afternoon. We somehow got a little disoriented on our way into Boston and instead ended up in Cambridge, north of the city, on the grounds of Harvard University. We went into a corner shop to ask for directions and were thrilled to see a copy of our April *Rock Express* (with Van Halen on the cover) in the store's magazine section.

Carter Allen made us welcome at the Expo and interviewed me on-air to plug our magazine. Both Platinum Blonde and Wendy O. Williams arrived and created chaos signing autographs. I can't recall how we obtained Wendy, but she proved to be a real doll and agreed to do the session for two hundred dollars in expense money plus her return plane ticket to New York.

Her sweet and demure behaviour totally belied her on stage punk image. It was tragic to learn she later committed suicide.

The Blondes were just getting noticed in the States, but the flurry of activity around Mark Holmes and Kenny MacLean indicated a positive response stateside to their *Alien Shores* album. They made such an impression with Carter Allen that WBCN agreed to sponsor a Boston date for the band on May 21. By combining back issues with the sale of T-shirts (two magazines plus a T-shirt for ten dollars) we enjoyed brisk business at our booth. Of course, all this activity generated major crowds in front of our unit, which blocked off traffic to the Strawberry Records' booth located directly behind us

The Strawberry people were initially upset when our autograph sessions blocked off entrance to their store, but when they noticed the buzz *Rock Express* created, their VP of sales asked if *Rock Express* would be interested in being distributed in their store chain, which extended down the U.S. East Coast. I explained our Warner Publishing deal to him and said I would have to enquire if this would be a conflict of interest. A rival store manager overheard the conversation and said to me, "You don't want to do business with Strawberry Records, they're owned by the Mafia!"

Driving back to Toronto on the Sunday, with Robert at the steering wheel, I perused the latest issue of *Billboard* and came across an item about Minneapolis based Musicland/Sam Goody retail chain expanding their network with a hostile takeover of California's Licorice Pizza, a chain of record stores. Bruce Jesse, Musicland's director of marketing, was quoted on his chain's intent on taking on Tower Records and Wherehouse, California's established retail powerhouses.

Monday I'm back at the office and my phone rings. "Hi, my name is Bruce Jesse, and I am calling from Musicland/Sam Goody, you probably don't know me."

"Well, actually, I was just reading about you in *Billboard* yesterday," I responded. Musicland/Sam Goody had been looking to establish an in-house music magazine similar to *Tower Pulse*, which had been successfully introduced into all Tower Records. Jesse had been unsuccessfully looking a magazine his chain could use to compete with Tower when he stumbled upon *Rock Express* in his local Minneapolis magazine rack. The fates were aligning in our favour.

He asked me questions about our organization. I informed him of our newsstand expansion into the U.S. via Warner, which impressed Bruce no end. I then told him I had just come back from Boston where Strawberry Records had just made a similar offer. "You don't want to do business with Strawberry Records, they're owned by the Mafia," he warned. Now where had I heard that before?

Strawberry Records were owned by Morris Levy, also owner of Roulette Records. Extensively detailed in Fredric Dannen's *Hit Men* book, Levy was a notorious New York music industry hustler with reported ties to the Genovese Family, enough to turn me off strawberries for life.

"So, how would *Rock Express* like to be the official in store magazine for Musicland/Sam Goody?" Jesse countered. "We can guarantee circulation in over 750 stores in the U.S." My head was swimming. I stammered yes, very much interested. I needed to touch base with Warner Publishers though.

"Tell you what, let's meet at your office, tomorrow!" offered Jesse. True to his word, Jesse flew into Toronto from Minneapolis, and the next day this tall chap with blonde hair and a thin moustache strolled into our office. There was something about Bruce's personality that instantly clicked with me. After showing him around and introducing him to everyone, we headed down to the Madison Pub to have lunch and discuss our agreement.

Shaking hands on a potential deal, we agreed the next step would be for Conny, Allan, and me to fly down to Minneapolis to meet with his boss, Jack Eugster. Conny and Allan were both enthused about the opportunity but were concerned whether Musicland/Sam Goody would sell enough advertising to fund this increased circulation. But to have little *Rock Express* expanding throughout North America was indeed a heady tonic.

Arrangements were made for the three of us to head to Minneapolis. We met Bruce, his boss Jack Eugster, and senior VP of marketing Gary Ross, and Allan succeeded in charming the collective pants off them, regaling them with stories of his connection to Prime Minister Brian Mulroney and his various chats with world leaders. By the end of our meeting, *Rock Express* had been brought into the Musicland/Sam Goody empire. We set the launch date for our October issue. We just needed to work out a budget that would see Musicland fund at least enough issues to execute a proper distribution.

Anticipating a potential backlash from Canadian readers, we agreed to publish a Canadian insert that would be absent from Musicland's U.S.

version. We also decided to occasionally switch covers to promote Canadian bands in our domestic issues. Canadian record companies seemed enthusiastic about our ability to promote domestic artists into the States, yet they didn't significantly increase their ad support.

One challenge was that although Musicland agreed to handle all record company advertising, we were responsible for additional corporate advertising, which potentially could be quite lucrative considering we were about to reach over six hundred thousand new readers in that key sixteen- to twenty-five-year-old age demographic. How to go about setting up a national sales force would be our next challenge.

An advertising representation house was touted as a solution, and the Chicago-based Pattis Group was suggested. They operated offices in Chicago, New York, and Los Angeles, and seemed, on the surface, to be an ideal solution. So I flew down to Chicago to meet their sales team, who seemed to be interested in doing business with Musicland via *Rock Express*. The cost was tagged at ten thousand dollars per month, but this would cover all three offices, and they would only need to sell two full-page ads per month for us to recoup our investment (or at least that was their sales pitch).

With all this U.S. activity going on, we still had to keep *Rock Express* on schedule. We featured the Rolling Stones on our May cover, Heart on our June issue, and David Lee Roth on a double-length summer issue. All this was a lead up to our October-issue premiere in Musicland. Warner Publishing saw the value of our additional circulation through Musicland and aggressively targeted *Rock Express* through their newsstand network.

A slew of new domestic talent emerged early in the year, led by Newmarket's Glass Tiger, whose Capitol/EMI *Thin Red Line* debut, produced by Jim Vallance, would score instant airplay with their "Don't Forget Me (When I'm Gone)" single, which included a much-hyped vocal contribution by Bryan Adams.

"We were supposed to sign with Island Records and Canadian label manager, Doug Chappell, was about to sign us. But label president Chris Blackwell wanted to check us out first so he caught one of our shows in Brantford but didn't like us and passed on the signing," explained band lead singer Alan Frew. "I knew by the way he shook my hand that he was going to pass. Apparently he told Doug we sounded too much like U2! Doug was devastated and he left the label shortly after to go to Virgin."

"One thing Doug did do for us was to put us in touch with Derek Sutton and suggest he co-manage us," continued Frew. "Derek had worked with Styx and had great contacts in the States. Even though we were unsigned at the time, he made one phone call and got us the opening gig in Toronto for Culture Club. He was the archetypical British upper-class music manager, his persona was parodied as the manager of Spinal Tap. He even got acknowledged in the movie's credits."

Kim Mitchell followed his *Akimbo Alogo* album with *Shakin' Like a Human Being*, which launched "Patio Lanterns" into the public's collective conscious. During his chat with Lenny Stoute, Mitchell proved to be in an irascible mood, trashing his American touring experience opening for Bryan Adams with shots at Americans who could only focus on "Go for Soda," which had been adopted as a new theme song by MADD (Mothers Against Drunk Driving).

"Radio jocks would ask me if 'Go for Soda' was about the perils of drinking and driving," fumed Mitchell. "I would tell them it wasn't but they'd report that's what it meant anyway. In America, if they decide you're round, you're round, no matter how many angles are sticking out of your head."

Tom Cochrane bounced back from his disastrous 1984 *Breaking Curfew* release, which had culminated with a concert blow-up in Halifax that saw Cochrane punch his bassist Jeff Jones and road manager Graham Lagden after Cochrane refused an encore request. A recalcitrant Cochrane, who subsequently fired manager Bruce Allen, returned with a new album *Tom Cochrane & Red Rider*, retaining just guitarist Kenny Greer. Radio acceptance of the album's debut single, "Boy Inside the Man," sparked a career revival.

Meanwhile Triumph encountered problems with their latest *Sport of Kings* release. A disastrous production liaison with Ron Nevison ended when Nevison walked out on the sessions, leaving the band to finish the project with recording assistant Mike Clink. "We'd already completed two-thirds of the album but Ron wanted to re-record everything," explained percussionist/lead vocalist Gil Moore. "We didn't want to, but we gave him the benefit of the doubt and went back to the drawing board. We worked with Ron until he quit in May. He just walked out. Apparently he then started to work on a Night Ranger album but lasted just two weeks. He's a weird guy!" *Sport of Kings* produced just one top-forty U.S. hit in Rik Emmett's "Somebody's Out There." The band added guitarist Rick Santers to their lineup for a major summer tour opening for Sweden's Yngwie Malmsteen, but sales started to slip considerably.

In settling on an ideal cover to launch *Rock Express* into Musicland/Sam Goody's 750-plus U.S. stores, it was felt Huey Lewis and the News provided a safe, wholesome target, whose feel-good R&B songs were well accepted throughout the States. MCA Canada, who had been faithful supporters of ours, informed of Huey setting up camp in St. John's, Newfoundland. The province's capital had occasionally served as the launching spot for major artists like Tina Turner and Corey Hart, but the arrival of Lewis to rehearse for a major tour and cap his stay with three nights of performances was unprecedented in the city's history.

Accompanied by MCA marketing VP Steve Tennant, I made my first (and so far only) visit to St. John's, booking into the opulent Hotel Newfoundland, located right on the harbour. The swank seventh-floor Silver Suite provided a magnificent panoramic view of the harbour and would serve as an ideal location for my scheduled interview with Mr. Lewis.

That night (Thursday), I attended the band's final rehearsal and met their affable road manager, Lowell Hallsy, who gave me full run of the backstage, taking me into the dressing room to meet Huey, his band, and the Tower of Power horn section. Huey remembered a previous phone chat and was pleased I was staying for at least two of his scheduled performances. To watch the News rehearse is a treat in itself, as the band launched into a recognizable song that evolved into an extended Grateful Dead–like jam.

Huey Lewis and the News in concert are like the best party you can imagine. Great songs, affable stage presence, and great American music that extends into lengthy jams, with Tower of Power being a dream support unit. Even then-new songs like "Jacob's Ladder," "Stuck with You," and "Hip to Be Square" slotted nicely into their set.

After their rehearsal, I just barely had time to race back to my suite and freshen up before meeting with Huey and his entourage in the lounge. Then it was off down the street, where we gate-crashed Dutch Mason's gig at the Fishing Admiral, a smoky little bar on George Street.

Inside, the locals nodded approvingly as Dutch Mason, a Maritimes Blues guitar wiz, smoked through his usual set. Then, a tall American with clean-cut good looks and an unmistakable cleft splitting his chin joined Mason on stage, wailing away on harmonica. Out of the shadows slipped a posse of other participants, and before you can say Newfie Screech, Mason was being supported by Huey Lewis and the News — with the Tower of Power horn section!

Chrysalis label chief Chris Wright joined us at the bar and seemed enthused when I explained *Rock Express*'s new affiliation with Musicland/ Sam Goody and our future Huey Lewis cover for our October issue. Wright gave me his London address and said he would make sure his New York office supported our book.

Saturday morning at 11:00 a.m., Huey joined me at the Silver Suite location and we both marvelled at the view of the harbour. Over the next two hours, Lewis discussed his early struggles in England, how the News broke through in the U.S. — with an English record label — the pitfalls of a follow up to *Sports*, and his recent successful lawsuit against Columbia Pictures, the producers of *Ghostbusters*, who had usurped "I Want a New Drug" and changed the lyrics to 'Ghostbusters' with Ray Parker Jr. getting the writer's credit.

"We had a very legitimate complaint and that was settled out of court — very handsomely I might add," explained Lewis. "The movie company wanted my song, 'I Want a New Drug.' The ethical question was who paid Ray Parker Jr. to write "Ghostbusters," which was an obvious rip-off of my song. There are people in Hollywood who think they can buy any damned thing — well they can't damn it! That song wasn't for sale."

When Lewis was asked what made his band such a unique entity, he responded by saying, "I think I've been successful because I do it not to be a star or make money or meet girls. I do it because I always wanted to be in a band. Because being in a band is the coolest thing in the world and the News is the coolest band in the world. When that feeling isn't there anymore — it's over!"

There was no denying Lewis's pull over the female population of St John's. Even the lowliest cleaning lady or waitress at the hotel earned a smile, a handshake, or even a peck on the cheek. "Did you see that one; she must have been about fifty," said Lewis scrambling from the grasp of one amorous female for the safety of the band van taking the News to the arena for their second gig.

"I'll bet her husband gets laid tonight," cracked guitarist Chris Hayes.

"She'll probably make him wear bags under his eyes," replied Lewis. "Yeah, Huey bags, we should sell them as a merchandising item at concerts."

18

SURVIVING THE
EASTERN BLOC

Before settling in for the mania I knew would be triggered by our pending Musicland launch, I allowed myself the luxury of a trip to Hungary and Poland to tour with Iron Maiden. They had broken ground in 1985 by being the first British rock band to headline in communist Poland, and the crowd response had been so fanatical that they had promised a return trip in 1986. Looking at road testing their new *Somewhere in Time* album, Maiden played one date in Budapest (Wednesday, September 17) and six dates in Poland. Manager Rod Smallwood thought it would present me with a unique story angle, and also asked if I would bring my soccer cleats along as I would need them for Maiden's annual tour match.

Flying into Budapest via Zurich on September 16, I took a cab from the airport and crossed the River Danube to pull up in front some impressive hotel digs, the Budapest Hilton. Imagine a ritzy five-star hotel surrounded by a thirteenth-century Gothic church, "the Fisherman's Bastion," and a thirteenth-century Dominican Monastery, which had been converted into a nightclub. Maiden had just driven in from Graz, Austria, and we quickly met before they disappeared for a brief press conference at the local EMI affiliate office.

Taxis were commandeered to take a group of us back across the river from Buda to Pest (the city is split into two communities) where Maiden met up with tour companions Waysted, who were to leave the tour after the next day's gig in Budapest. As the drinks flowed, Maiden vocalist Bruce Dickinson retold the horrors and exhaustion of their previous Powerslave tour. "I never want to do a tour like that again," allowed the Sheffield native. "Three months in America was fine but six was too bloody much. I got to the point where I hated music, I didn't want to listen to the radio or even hang out with other musicians. I was going to phone our manager [Rod Smallwood] and quit the band. I was so neurotic I couldn't even write new songs for the album. But Adrian [Smith] filled in the slack and I started to come around when the album was recorded."

Following a photo shoot at the hotel's thirteenth-century parapet walls, Maiden was joined by Waysted for a brief sightseeing tour before driving to the MTK Stadium for their only Hungarian date. A crowd of thirty thousand fans came for their first look at Maiden and did not leave disappointed as the band pulled out all the stops.

The constant highlight of Maiden's set was their "Iron Maiden" finale, which traditionally marked the appearance of super-ghoul Eddie. Maiden's mascot had evolved from a masked stage-hand to an elaborate Pharaoh mummy on their Powerslave tour, and the Somewhere in Time tour's version was even more elaborate. In mid-song, Nicko McBrain's drum kit started to levitate hydraulically, and out from under the kit appeared Eddie's head — this time as Arnold Schwarzenegger's Terminator, a giant ray gun projecting from his shoulder. Twin hydraulics also lifted Dickinson and bassist Steve Harris high above the crowd, with Eddie's monstrous two hands appearing to hold them aloft. The Hungarians erupted in disbelief. They'd never seen anything like it.

On the last tour, the Czech border guards had held up the bus for more than eight hours, searching the Maiden tour bus with a fine tooth comb while gazing incredulously at this army of mop tops. Fortunately, on this tour the sleek double-decker Volvo Starliner bus, the latest in touring luxury, passed through the Czech border near Kosice without much incident. The Czech customs officers proved to be a group of youthful army inductees who happily received autographed photos and T-shirts, and even stayed on board for a quick can of lager. Relations at the Czech–Polish border were more formal. A bulldog of a Polish officer, a prototype communist militia-man, strode onto the bus. It was 3:00 a.m. and our friend had obviously consumed a few vodkas on the job. His eyes sparkled when he spied a bottle of Stanley whisky, and a healthy glassful was donated to facilitate a smooth crossing into Poland. A few autographed pics later and we are heading to our first Polish destination, Katowice

Katowice is an industrial mining centre, boasting a population of some 350,000. It became a German city after the Treaty of Versailles in 1919, but rebelled against that decision and regained its Polish identity in 1922. It is situated close to the notorious Auschwitz death camps, where hundreds of thousands of prisoners were exterminated during the Second World War, a site the band had visited during their previous tour.

But it was rock music and not the city's troubled past that was the band's focus, and the six thousand fans at the Zabrze/Katowice Sport Hall were bursting at the seams. A series of rocket launchers were used to prop up the stage and made the military presence obvious. Yet manager Rod Smallwood was relieved that security wasn't as tight as it had been on the last trip when there had been more army personnel in attendance than actual ticket holders. "This actually feels like a normal gig," Smallwood said approvingly.

The pyramid-shaped spectacle of Wroclaw's Folk Hall loomed dark and foreboding for the September 21 gig. Constructed at the start of the Second World War in honour of Nazi Minister of Propaganda Josef Goebbels, the hall's roof features a massive swastika embedded into the ceiling. I was taken on a tour of the structure, which is cocooned with small rooms that were once used for interrogation purposes. "This place gives me the creeps," muttered Dickinson as he headed for the cafeteria.

By that point in the tour, things had settled into a steady rhythm. Concerts were going well and short hops between venues made for entertaining stints on the bus. One day, as we bounced along a narrow two-lane highway heading to the central industrial centre of Posnan, Dickinson and Harris took time out to discuss the current tour and circumstances behind their latest *Somewhere in Time* album. Both were in good spirits, claiming Maiden maintained its edge by being meticulous about their stage presentation. "I remember stuffing my monitor engineer in a bass bin because I thought he was messing around with my sound," recalled Dickinson. "Then we have 'Arry here who at one point kept jumping into the audience if he saw something wrong ... remember Memphis?"

"Oh yeah," laughed Harris. "This huge mountain of a guy was punching out this punter. I don't know what came over me but I just leaped off the stage and grabbed him around his neck. The roadies came and sorted him out. Good job they did because if he had gotten hold of me he would have killed me."

Recorded partially in their usual base of Compass Point, Nassau, but with guitars and vocals taped at Amsterdam's Wisseloord Studio, *Somewhere in Time* projected a more melodic sound, with Smith's two songs, "Wasted Years" and "Stranger in a Strange Land," shaping up as the band's strongest singles efforts since "Run to the Hills."

Both Dickinson and Harris were excited by the impact Maiden had caused in the Eastern Bloc, feeling the success they had already achieved in Poland, Hungary, and Yugoslavia would open the doors to further concerts in Czechoslovakia (as it was then called) and Russia. "I'd love to play Moscow," observed Dickinson. "Napoleon never made it there, but we might."

Poznan, a city of over five hundred thousand noted for its iron and steel manufacturing, was also receptive to the Maidens, whose set benefited from the exclusion of the lengthy "The Flight of Icarus." Passing on their Poznan hotel, a decision was made to head straight for the Baltic port of Gdansk.

Nowhere was the defiance that the Polish people had against the ruling Russian government more evident than in Gdansk. Out of bounds to Maiden on the last tour because Lech Walesa's Solidarity Movement was in the process of being dismantled, Gdansk is comparable to Hamburg or Liverpool in its feisty nature and aggressive outlook. Declared a "free city" by the Treaty of Versailles (access to both Germany and Poland), the city's importance is its geographical window to Western Europe (it sits directly across the Baltic from Sweden).

It was here that the first shots of the Second World War were fired when the German battleship *Schleswig-Holstein* opened fire on the Polish military depot. Briefly renamed Danzig during German occupation, the city was 55 percent destroyed, but by 1986 it had been totally rebuilt with many of its historic sites painstakingly reconstructed.

Our first day in the port was crew's day off, which meant Maiden's soccer team engaged in a friendly against a highly competitive Gdansk squad. Played at the city's pro stadium before a volatile crowd of over eight thousand fans (who donated product for a city food-bank drive), Maiden shocked their rivals, 4–2, with yours truly performing in goal for the Maidens. The opposition were so upset they demanded a rematch, but instead Maiden appeased them by taking the players back to our hotel where we engaged in a spirited contest called a "boat race," which is a relay race to see which side can down eight glasses of beer first. Of course, the Poles were no match for a team of beer-guzzling Brits. Yet they turned the tables by insisting on a repeat match involving Polish vodka — that stuff tasted like gasoline!

The September 22 concert was shaping up to be the best yet. Some four thousand kids had been shoehorned into Gdansk's Olivia Hall, and as Maiden returned for their first encore, Dickinson launched into the call-and-response routine of "Running Free" when, without warning, he interrupted the song to spew a mouthful of obscenities at some unknown culprit. Apparently, Dickinson had spotted some lug attacking another audience member. Dickinson assailed the miscreant and sent security guards Peter (Rambo) Lokrantz and Mark (Rangy) Williamson into the crowd after the assailant who quickly bolted the scene.

Maiden added "The Phantom of the Opera," from their self-titled debut, to the set for their concert in Lodz, Poland's second largest city. The main drama of the song played out behind the light board, where Dave Lights manfully remained in control, even though stricken with a debilitating stomach virus. Half slumped over, he hung in until the encores when he received relief.

Warsaw's Towar Hall had an official capacity of six thousand, but at least three thousand more had been crammed into the venue for Maiden's show there. Tickets had sold out well in advance, but kids gained entrance by slipping money to the corps of militia serving as security. "It's a common practice but what can you do," bemoaned Joe Mirowski, the organizer of the Polish tour. "You either let them do it or you don't have a concert." A contingent from the Soviet Embassy in Warsaw met Maiden prior to the gig. T-shirts and autographed pics were given in exchange for a verbal promise to help stage a future concert in Moscow.

This was the eighth date on the tour, and Maiden had honed their show to razor sharpness. The lights were in sync, the sound was perfect, and a fanatical crowd responded as the band attained peak performance. Mixing subtle dynamics with Teutonic power, Maiden were so far apart from your average thrash metal band, it's not even a contest. Suffice to say, Warsaw loved every minute of it.

Early on the morning of Friday, September 26, panic reigned at the Victoria Hotel lobby as band and crew scurried to make flights to various locales. With the British tour still a week away, Maiden took a brief vacation. Harris was off to his beloved Portugal (where he runs a pub); Dickinson was heading for Calais, France; Smith and Murray to the English Channel Island of Jersey; and McBrain was anticipating a pint in his local London pub. Smallwood joined me on a flight back to Toronto to talk shop with Maiden's Capitol Canada label, and had astutely switched flights so we headed out via Germany's Lufthansa Airline rather than Poland's dodgy LOT Polish Airlines.

En route through the customs check, Smallwood glanced at the piece of paper that constituted his visa and was struck by the significance of that document. "Stupid isn't it that a piece of paper should have so much value," mused Smallwood. "Something we take so much for granted, they can only dream about — God, I hate communism!"

19

PLANTING

OUR U.S. ROOTS

We finalized the editorial content of our debut–Musicland/Sam Goody issue aware of Musicland's mandate not to go heavy on Canadian content in their U.S. version. However, we decided we could justify a stateside push for Glass Tiger as both their new single, "Don't Forget Me (When I'm Gone)," and album, *The Thin Red Line,* had not only topped Canadian charts, but with help from Derek Sutton and Bruce Lundval's new Manhattan Records label, the single had gone to No. 2 on *Billboard* and was pushing serious unit sales at U.S. retail. Musicland supported our push behind Glass Tiger, and we even arranged for the band to visit Musicland's Minneapolis head office while on a tour stop opening for Journey, which made their album an even stronger priority for the chain.

"Manhattan's A&R chief Jack Satter told me, 'Okay Alan, kiss your family goodbye, pack your suitcase, you're moving to New York to break this record,'" reflected singer Alan Frew. "It was literally breakfast in Baltimore and lunch in Cincinnati, but I did everything to break that record. When the album came out we were on tour with Journey and Tina Turner before returning in triumph to headline Canada. Things couldn't have gone better at that time."

That debut Huey Lewis issue of *Rock Express,* now subtitled "The Pulse of World Rock," was well received by Musicland's customers. The retail chain alerted their U.S. label contacts that they should touch base with me, and by the end of October I was headed out for my first visit to Los Angeles. The trip was primarily to do some PR work with recalcitrant Licorice Pizza record stores and stage my first meeting with the L.A. branch of the Pattis Ad agency.

Lenny Stoute had tipped me off about this motel called the Park Sunset, almost at the corner of Sunset and La Cienega, where a lot of touring bands stayed. The Park Sunset served as my operations base for all my trips to L.A. Even though it was October, it was still warm and sunny when I arrived at LAX. Having heard all the horror stories about driving in L.A., I approached my Hertz rental car with severe trepidation, yet was pleasantly surprised to discover it was quite easy to navigate into Hollywood and was soon parked up at the motel.

A call through to the Pattis group gave me directions to their office on Highland, just north of the famed Capitol Records Tower, and I met my ad contact, George Henderson. Originally from Scotland, George took me out for lunch and described how Pattis did business. "The deal is, we work for you, but how much work we do for you depends on how much you pay us," he stated, matter-of-factly.

"But we pay your head office ten grand a month," protested I.

"Yeah but we don't see much of that. That's why we need a little incentive if you want to see results," he said, as though stating the obvious. And I thought payola was only confined to the record business!

Astrid Young, Neil Young's younger half-sister, had relocated to Los Angeles. A talented singer in her own right, we had met while she was in Toronto and Astrid was delighted to offer her services as my unofficial guide. She drove me out to some of the Licorice Pizza places where I was given a hostile reception by owners obviously not thrilled about Musicland's take over. That night I was invited to a local recording studio where I met Astrid's band, Sacred Child.

I had purposely not set up meetings with L.A. record companies. I wanted to wait until they had become more familiar with the magazine, figuring I would save that task for my next visit. I did put one call into the Levine-Schneider Public Relations Group. They handled press for some of America's biggest names — Heart, Aerosmith, Tom Petty, and Ozzy Osborne, to name a few — and I was anxious to make contact with them.

Back in Toronto, we got together our second Musicland issue (with Tina Turner on the cover). We were getting ready to launch our February issue, which featured Duran Duran on the cover, when Musicland's Bruce Jesse invited me to attend the 1987 NARM (North American Retail Merchandisers Association) meeting in Miami. NARM is a major convention that brings together all the major record labels and national retailers. It's a star-studded affair, with mundane policy meetings offset by guest appearances by major acts and presentations by all the majors of their scheduled product releases. Bruce convinced me this provided an ideal forum to spread word of Musicland's association with *Rock Express* as well as a perfect opportunity to meet all the record company bigwigs.

February 13 found me flying into Miami to attend the conference being staged at Miami Beach's famous Fontainebleau Hotel. I was booked next door at the equally famous Eden Roc. I met up with Jesse at reception in the Fontainebleau and he informed me a reservation screw-up meant he didn't have a room that night at the Fontainebleau. "No worries," said I. "You can bunk with me tonight."

Jesse thankfully accepted my offer and we spent a great evening chatting about Musicland, their mandate to expand into California via Licorice Pizza, and he provided tips in dealing with U.S. record labels. Jesse checked into the Fontainebleau the following day and paid for my entire three-night stay at the Eden Roc.

NARM in Miami was everything Jesse said it would be. As a member of the media, I received a full pass to the event, which kicked-off with an industry breakfast where I started to make invaluable contacts. Just to mention *Rock Express* was the official magazine of Musicland opened many doors and produced a plethora of business cards. It seemed every record-promo contact at the function was clamouring to meet me and set up future meetings.

Split over three mornings, the record company product presentations were amazing. Of course, most major labels were affiliated to movie companies (MCA-Universal, Warner Films–Warner Music, Columbia Pictures–CBS Records), so the presentations were first rate, star-studded, and provided me with valuable information on which new releases ranked as the label's top priorities. I also received plenty of advance releases to plot future issues.

I soon found out just how powerful Musicland was at that time. Although all major U.S. retail chains were present at NARM, only Musicland possessed the clout to be feted by all the major labels at one function. I soon found myself being introduced by Musicland's president, Jack Eugster, to PolyGram's president, Dick Asher. Yes, the same Dick Asher who, as CBS International Records president, had been embroiled in that payola scandal. He was impressed I knew all about Loverboy. I also met key personnel with all three major Warner labels, Warner, Elektra, and Atlantic, all amicable to our new position with Musicland.

Present at this soiree were Bee Gees Barry, Maurice, and Robin Gibb, who resided and recorded in the Miami area. I was asked to pose for a photo with them and they, realizing I was from their home city of Manchester, were quite animated. I bit my lip, but finally rebuked them about that incident in Vancouver with PolyGram president Tim Harrold. I told them I didn't think it was right that they dumped on their Canadian label that had worked so hard on their *Saturday Night Fever* album. Barry claimed ignorance saying he knew nothing about the snub and that it must have been a management problem. "No worries," said I, but I did feel a sense of justice in unloading on them; I thought Ken Graydon would be proud.

The dinners also featured great star entertainment with Gloria Estefan and the Miami Sound Machine performing to a mainly disinterested industry crowd. To wind up the night, all the majors had their own VIP suites. Stick your head through the door of the PolyGram suite and you might find yourself chatting with Bon Jovi, who was there to plug their mega selling *Slippery When Wet* release, or Runaway's Lita Ford in the RCA suite, or Michael Bolton in the Columbia suite. It was an absolutely ideal way to chat with important artists and record personnel without the usual media hysteria.

Back in Toronto we were intent on making up for the disastrous 1985 Rock Express Awards at the Copa. Having been unable to schedule a 1986 awards with all the Musicland activity, we set about scheduling the 1987 awards with a major ceremony to be staged mid-March at Toronto's Diamond Club. With MuchMusic now established and organizing their own awards show, complete TV coverage was out of the question, yet we still wanted to execute a classy show.

Since we knew the winners in advance, and considering our growing stature in the U.S., we had no problem luring the likes of Glass Tiger (triple winners for Top Canadian Single, Top Canadian Group, and Top Canadian Album), Luba (Top Canadian Female), Triumph (Working Class Hero Award — for their United Way concert), and Honeymoon Suite (Top Canadian Live Group) to the show.

Prince Edward Island's Haywire was there to receive Most Promising Group honours for their album, *Bad Boys*. Fair compensation for being shafted by the Junos, who bypassed their sales achievements for the New Group Award, even though Haywire's debut had reached gold-record status and proved to be one of the year's great success stories. The only major Canuck artist not in attendance was Bryan Adams (who won Top Canadian Male Vocalist).

Our surprise guest was Robert Palmer, who had won Top International Single for "Addicted to Love." He was in Toronto for two days to record with Hugh Marsh. Stuart Raven-Hill, Marsh's manager, lured Palmer to the event. But we had a problem.

To get Palmer to the show and also to accommodate Glass Tiger's plans, there was only one date (a Thursday) that worked for everyone. Unfortunately, a new artist, Zeke Rivers and Davoom, had already secured that date for a showcase performance. In discussing this problem with club manager Randy Charlton, he suggested, "Why don't you book Zeke for your show — and nick his date!" So we made contact with his manager and suggested Zeke could either showcase to an empty room or he could perform on our show to a capacity crowd in front of the industry's elite. Suffice to say Zeke made the right decision.

We also added New Regime, a hot new local band *Rock Express* had just profiled in our February issue (and who were about to release their debut LP, *Terminal City*), as well as the hysterical Montreal comedy act George Bowser and Ricky Blue. As an added twist, the Laserlite Company asked if they could be involved. Their speciality was laser effects that could spell out award winners and performing artists in mid-air.

Brad Giffen and Lee Aaron were recruited as hosts, and I tried to make the procedure simple for them. I sequenced a bunch of index cards, cueing them on which awards to present and which bands were performing, and let them fill in the blanks, a procedure that had been successful in the past for Long John Baldry.

We had an all-star cast of Canadian recipients, but it was obvious Madonna (Top International Female Vocalist), Genesis (Top International Group), and Peter Gabriel (Top International Male) would not be in attendance to collect their awards. So we arranged for Warner Music's affable Roger Desjardins to accept all the awards for them. But before he went on stage, I asked Roger if he could, in his acceptance speeches, spin a story on how *he* discovered them all. At first Roger was reluctant, but going on stage to accept for Madonna, he goes into this diatribe taking full credit for her discovery. Now warming to the task, he repeated his stories with Genesis and Peter Gabriel. It was totally hilarious.

Of course when it came to the Top International Single Award, Giffen announced, "And now accepting for Robert Palmer ... is ... Robert Palmer," and the club erupted when the man himself walked on stage. Up until that point, we had hidden Robert away in a VIP cubicle located above and to the left of the stage, and only Stuart, his label, and I knew Palmer was there. He was awarded a triple-platinum album for *Addicted to Love,* and photos of him adorned the following day's *Star* and *Sun* front pages — great press for *Rock Express* and our awards.

The end of March found me back in L.A. I had set up a number of meetings with U.S. record companies and made my introductions to Capitol, A&M, Atlantic, and MCA, who all put *Rock Express* on their direct mailing lists. One memorable meeting was with Geffen VP of Marketing Eddie Gilreath. I asked him how *Rock Express* could be an effective medium for Geffen. His answer was, "To respond to our key projects when we need you."

Asked to clarify, he mentioned Guns N' Roses. "Now all the media are all over Guns N' Roses, but where were they five months ago when we couldn't get arrested with them. It's one thing for *Rolling Stone* and *Spin* to run features and covers now, but we needed their help months ago. Where *Rock Express* could be invaluable to us is for you to be there when we are trying to break a record — not after it's already broken!"

This was advice I took to heart, and I assured Gilreath we were willing to respond to his priority releases. Again, I thought I was getting invaluable advice from top people which could only strengthen our publication. Another piece of advice I received from Hale Milgrim, the VP of marketing at Elektra. When asked how his label prioritized their releases, he grabbed a stack of cassettes. "Now, these are all our releases for the month," he said. Then he took away all but six cassettes. "And these are *our* priorities," he pointed to the surviving six releases. I thought it was too bad if your release wasn't amongst those six cassettes.

A couple of weeks later a *Rock Express* contingent comprising of Conny, Dianne Collins, and I flew to L.A. to join forces with Musicland/Sam Goody to launch their takeover of the Licorice Pizza outlets and to help launch *Rock Express* there. The party was staged at the Palace Theatre (now called the Avalon), right across the street from Capitol's head office and gave me a feeling of what a real Hollywood party is like.

Klieg lights tracked the sky and a who's who of the music industry attended. Diane Collins had succeeded in convincing Crowded House to headline the live entertainment, and upstairs a sumptuous feast was laid out for celebrities, including Pink Floyd's David Gilmour, Bob Dylan, Tom Petty, Jon Anderson from Yes, John Waite, Steve Van Zandt, Night Court actor Richard Moll (Bull), Lou Diamond Phillips, and Miami Vice's Olivia Brown, to name a few.

On the afternoon of the gig, Conny and I were booked into the swank Mondrian Hotel, when we received a phone call to our suite. It was Burton Cummings on the phone. He and Randy Bachman were in L.A. and wanted to know if we can add them to our guest list. Of course we said yes, and Burton, Randy, and his wife, Denise McCann, sat at our table in the VIP lounge.

It was amusing for both Randy and Burton to continually ask, "Hey Keith, can you introduce us to David Gilmour or Tom Petty?" like I knew them and they didn't! Still, using my clout as party host, I approached both David Gilmour and Tom Petty, introduced myself and indicated that two of the biggest names in Canadian rock music history wanted to say hi.

Sam Goody had a catch phrase "Goody Got the Best Deals," and to stand on stage that night, face a room full of top U.S. record people and say, "And Goody's got *Rock Express*," showed what a massive achievement this partnership was for our magazine. By this point we had secured Roy Trakin, a highly respected music trade writer, as our L.A. contact, and his inclusion gave us instant credibility with the West Coast industry.

Surprisingly, for all the attention our Musicland/Sam Goody partnership generated in Canada, the reception from our domestic retail partners was cool to say the least. It had been our intention to continue stocking *Rock Express* in a network of retailers — including A&A, Music Word, Discus, plus independents like Records on Wheels — to supplement our newsstand and subscription circulation. Despite all the positive press and accolades *Rock Express* generated, Sam Sniderman's Sam the Record Man (who remained loyal to *RPM*) still wouldn't touch our mag.

The A&A sales group, headed by Terry Stevens, noticed the attention *Rock Express* generated with Musicland/Sam Goody and offered to do a similar partnership in Canada. A&A would be recognized as our official Canadian retailer, support domestic ad sales with co-op dollars, increase circulation at retail, and also execute key promotional activities with us. It was a decision we later lived to regret, yet a viable decision at the time understanding we were committed to focusing our marketing activities in the States.

Business aside, promoting bands was still our primary focus, and 1987 saw the birth of one of Canada's most popular groups. After a ten-year career in industry/commercial real estate, John Caton had done well enough to retire to a farm in Owen Sound. But before he could don his first pair of overalls, Caton received a phone call from old friend, Dean McTaggart, who had just started up a new group, The Arrows, and wanted to enlist Caton's help.

"Dean had been out of the music business for about eight years," Caton told *Rock Express* writer Roman Mitz. "Since I had been a salesman, he figured I could help him contact a few record labels. I asked him what this would entail and he said, 'Just a couple of phone calls.'" Just a couple of calls ended with Caton contacting Daniel Lanois at Grant Avenue Studios in Hamilton and spending a bundle on a six-song EP which received attention from A&M. "Next thing you know, I am forming a production and management company and signing a deal with Dean's Arrows that lasted over four years."

A falling out with Caton's business partner ended that relationship and left a bitter taste in Caton's mouth. But the industry bug had bitten him. He set up office downstairs at The Horseshoe Tavern, which he called "The Dungeon," with support from club manager X-Ray MacRae. About a month later, Caton was standing at the back of The Horseshoe watching a band play that, he said, "Hit me right between the eyes." He introduced himself, hauled the band down to the Dungeon, and signed them to a management contact. That band was Blue Rodeo.

"I liked the fact he wasn't that much of a fast talker," noted vocalist/guitarist Greg Keelor. "He had just been through the break-up of that other management company so his ideas seemed completely accessible."

The original plan was for Caton to put a record deal together, find them new management, and then bow out. As their relationship progressed though, he found it increasingly difficult to separate himself from the group, so he assumed management duties and targeted former Rush producer Terry Brown to record the initial demos. A born entrepreneur, Caton decided to form his own indie record company, Risque Disque. To initiate the plan, Caton formed ACT (Artist Consulting Team) with MacRae, Tony Neilson, and Peter Lloyd, in order to provide tactical support.

After some initial reluctance from WEA A&R chief Bob Roper, the label bit and Risque Disque signed a distribution deal, the result being a world-wide release for Blue Rodeo's *Outskirts* record. Having spent the past four years attracting favourable comparisons to R.E.M. with their precise vocal harmonies and jangly guitar sound, Keelor and his vocalist/guitarist/writing buddy Jim Cuddy had served their apprenticeship.

With bassist Basil Donovan and drummer Cleve Anderson, WEA launched the album with great fanfare. The only problem was that nobody could settle on the right single. The title track was issued as a lead-off single, but when that choice met with radio resistance the band reluctantly agreed to Jim Cuddy's 'Try,' even though they didn't feel that song was illustrative of the band's overall sound. 'Try' would prove to be *the* monster single of 1987.

Not one to rest on his laurels, Caton also signed Prairie Oyster, who had just won a 1986 Juno as Canada's top country music group. Their first album, *Oyster Tracks*, released in 1986, attracted critical acclaim when released on Holger Peterson's Stony Plain label. And with WEA having first right of refusal on all Risque Disque releases, band leader Russell DeCarte and his band were hoping to follow Blue Rodeo and cross over into the mainstream charts.

Truth was, though, that Canadian product had hit a dry spell in the U.S. Bryan Adams's *Into the Fire* encountered huge resistance despite constant U.S. touring. Corey Hart's *Fields of Fire* bombed badly on both sides of the forty-ninth parallel, and neither Gowan nor The Parachute Club sparked any airplay stateside. Hart was doing so badly in Canada that he pulled the plug on his Canadian tour, complaining of feeling ill after his Sudbury date. Ticket sales for the rest of his national jaunt had been depressingly bad.

A sad downside to the music business is when you witness the careers of bands or artists, who have become your friends, suddenly starting to crash and burn. Virtually back-to-back this happened to Helix, Loverboy, and Platinum Blonde. When bands start talking about new directions and how they have to win back the U.S. market, you know they have problems.

Helix lead vocalist Brian Vollmer and I met on the Madison Pub patio and swilled pints with writer Lenny Stoute. It's a scenario both Lenny and I had played out with Vollmer previously. I had remained friends with Helix after the European trip, and Lenny had been with the band to both Texas and Sweden (even crossing the Arctic Circle with them). Superficially, Vollmer fronted a brave face, along with guitarist Paul Hackman, in chatting with Stoute about the band's new release, *Wild in the Streets*.

Vollmer and Hackman waxed enthusiastically about the album being a return to their rock roots, boasting songs like "Never Gonna Stop" and "High Voltage." Yet the reality was their previous release, *Long Way to Heaven*, had failed to connect in the States. Considering *Walking the Razor's Edge* had been such a huge hit stateside, a sense of desperation had kicked in and the band were trying to relocate that missing formula. Suddenly, the airplay wasn't there, lucrative tours had disappeared, and the band members began to implode internally.

The stigma of living off former glories usually becomes too much to deal with, and inevitably these bands or artists become just another statistic. In Helix's case, they carried on, hampered by constant lineup changes, but still chasing a fading dream that their next release could recapture former glories. "In retrospect, our Canadian record company never could decide what kind of a band we should be," reflected Vollmer, now a vocal instructor who still keeps a version of Helix on the road. "We'd tour Europe and they would want a hard rock band like Iron Maiden or Metallica, but in North America the labels wanted a power pop band which could attract radio airplay. That's why we kept putting out ballads for singles. We couldn't please everyone and we should have just worried about pleasing ourselves."

Loverboy also witnessed a dip in fortunes, with a lack of international appeal for their 1985 album, *Lovin' Every Minute of It*, starting to erode what had been a strong American base. By the time they recorded their fifth album, *Wildside*, lead vocalist Mike Reno and guitarist Paul Dean were suffering from a collective case of writer's block. The album's lone single, "Notorious," was co-written with Jon Bon Jovi and Ritchie Sambora, and all but three tracks were written by a core of professional writers.

After scoring two multi-million-selling albums, with *Loverboy* and *Get Lucky*, Loverboy started to receive critical scorn from fans and critics alike suggesting they should try something different. "So we did," responded Reno in an interview with Brad Kruger. "And then people started looking at us and saying, those songs like 'Working for the Weekend' had so much more energy ... why did you change? Because you bloody well asked us to." *Wildside* tanked dramatically and Loverboy disappeared from major U.S. concert venues just as quickly as they had arrived.

↗ Helix (with Queen's Brian May) on their 1983 tour with KISS.
Photo courtesy of Brian Vollmer.

↘ Marquee shot of Spectrum before the first Music Express Awards.
Photo courtesy of Phil Regendanz.

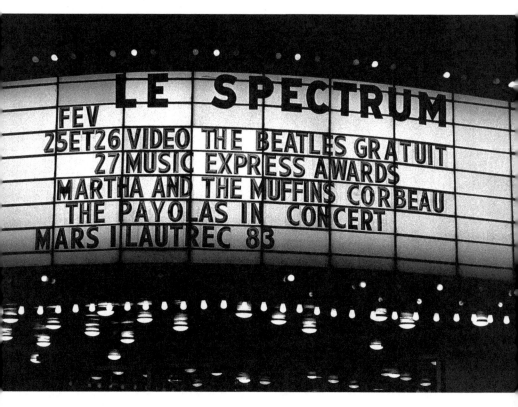

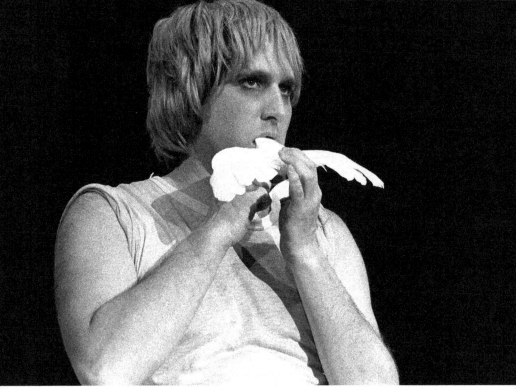

↖ Comedian Steve (Ozzy Osbourne) Brinder biting the head off an (ornamental) snowbird.
Photo courtesy of Phil Regendanz.

↙ Lee Aaron getting cozy with Krokus front man Marc Storace at the second Music Express Awards.
Photo courtesy of Dimo Safari.

↗ Prism's Ron Tabak was a powerful vocalist who died too young.
Photo courtesy of Charles Hope.

↖ Bryan Adams (centre) with Sergio Galli and Mark Holmes of Platinum Blonde at the 1984 Music Express Awards.
Photo courtesy of Dimo Safari.

↙ Sir Bob Geldof, the Live Aid spark plug.
Photo courtesy of David Plastik.

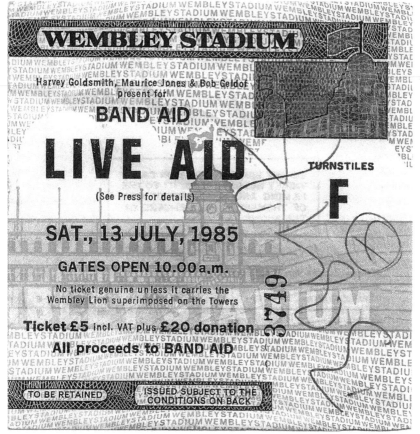

↗ My Live Aid ticket, autographed by Sir Bob Geldof.

↖ Montreal's Tchukon stole the show on CBC's Rock Wars in 1985.
Photo courtesy of Warren "Slim" Williams.

↗ I first met Hugh Dillon after Live Aid in 1985. He'd later return to Canada and form the Headstones.
Photo courtesy of Bernie Breen Management.

↖ Musicland's Bruce Jesse, one of the biggest supporters of our magazine. Pictured here with Vanessa Williams.
Photo courtesy of Bruce Jesse.

WARNER PUBLISHER SERVICES

News Release

Mark Greenberg
Vice President
666 Fifth Avenue
New York, New York 10103
(212) 484-2946

WARNER TO DISTRIBUTE 2 CANADIAN
ROCK MUSIC MAGAZINES IN U.S.

NEW YORK, Feb. 26--Canadian publisher Rock Music Communications, Inc., has signed an agreement to have Warner Publisher Services distribute two of its successful rock music titles in the U.S. market. Plans call for initial distribution of issues on sale between April and August to approximately 20 major U.S. cities, followed by a complete rollout across the country in the succeeding months.

The magazines, Rock Express and Metallion, have maintained a strong, steady sales pace in Canada and will be editorially tailored for the U.S. marketplace with forthcoming issues. Rock Express, a monthly, will enter the American market with issue No. 101, on sale April 10th. Its primary focus is on "contemporary" rock music. The cover price is $1.75.

Metallion, a bi-monthly, joins WPS with issue No. 10, on sale April 17th. Metallion spotlights "heavy metal" sounds and also carries a $1.75 cover price.

Though the 20 cities to be included in the initial phase of distribution have not yet been finalized, they are likely to include such music-oriented cities as New York, Boston, Detroit, Atlanta, Houston and Memphis.

Connie Kunz, President and Publisher of Rock Express Communications, is planning a major advertising and promotion campaign in a number of major markets to stimulate sales.

Rock Express Communications' distributor, Warner Publisher Services, is the world's foremost distributor of magazines, comics and paperback books.

#

A Warner Communications Company

↗ Our U.S. distribution announcement from Warner Distributing.

David Bowie performing in Australia on his Glass Spider tour, 1987.
Photo courtesy of David Plastik.

↗ (top) The *Music Express* staff in 1987.
Photo courtesy of Phil Regendanz.

↗ (bottom) Helix front man Brian Vollmer cheers up a young patient during the *Music Express* celebrity Christmas visit to Toronto Sick Kids Hospital.
Photo courtesy of *Music Express*.

↖ (top) Allan Gregg (back row, far right) with his band the Tragically Hip and their manager Jake Gold (back row, far left).
Photo courtesy of Management Trust Entertainment.

↖ (bottom) *Music Express*'s swank new Jefferson Avenue address, 1988.
Photo courtesy of *Music Express*.

↗ Conny takes a bite out of Robert Plant's hair during the Led Zeppelin singer's visit to officially launch our Jefferson Avenue office.
Photo courtesy of *Music Express*.

↖ Blue Rodeo circa mid-eighties.
Photo courtesy of Blue Rodeo.

↙ The 2012 Trooper concert at the CNE that helped spark a Music Express digital revival.
Photo courtesy of Ted Van Boort.

20

BOWIE'S

OZ ADVENTURE

Asked by Columbia to execute a massive promotional push for Michael Jackson's new *Bad* release, Musicland's Bruce Jesse called me to book the front cover for the October/November 1987 issue. "We want to go BIG on this issue; we want to double the circulation. We want to flood our stores with the magazine," hyped Bruce. Okay, Bruce, let me stop you there. First of all, to put Michael Jackson on the cover, we need a feature story and we all know Michael doesn't do interviews. Second, that bit about doubling our print run for the issue ... that would mean we would be printing about 1.3 million copies?

A man with an answer for everything, Bruce's response was, "Okay, we can't guarantee an interview, but Columbia wants to send one of your writers to Japan to cover one of Michael's scheduled Tokyo concerts. That should work for the cover. Secondly, Musicland will hike our ad revenue for that press run." In the immortal words of Monty Python, "Say no more."

Vancouver's Brad Kruger was given the Michael Jackson assignment. Brad is a gifted writer who promised he would produce a cover story, even if he couldn't arrange a meeting with the Sequined Gloved One. Also, there was a convenience factor in flying Brad out of Vancouver to Tokyo at a time when direct flights from Toronto to Tokyo were not feasible. Brad's story was a masterpiece of creative journalism, even if the closest he got to Michael was a brief press conference with album producer Quincy Jones.

One Wednesday in early October 1987, Conny and I had joined Allan Gregg at his swanky Forest Hill home for a party that featured some of his political cronies (including Conservative MP Larry Grossman), when a van pulled up outside his house. "Right everyone, we're going on a brief road trip," Allan announced, shepherding everyone out of the door and into the van.

Like the Beatles' proverbial Magical Mystery Tour, we headed out into the night and soon found ourselves parked outside the dodgy Hotel Isabella, right across from the notorious Jamestown housing complex. Still mystified, we trudged into the bar where we were greeted by Jake Gold, manager of New Regime, who had just formed a talent management agency with Allan.

This scruffy band ambled on stage and started to play. I wasn't familiar with their material until the lead vocalist, Gord Downie, delivered a riveting cover of "House of the Rising Sun." This was my introduction to The Tragically Hip. Following their brief set, I had a chat with Downie, who told me the band was from Kingston and they had come to Allan's attention via contact from one of his political cohorts.

"Allan had received this tape, from one of his political contacts, Hugh Segal," explained former co-manager Jake Gold, who now heads the Management Trust talent agency. "Allan and I went to a Blue Jays game and he played the band's demo tape for me in his car. I could hear their potential. To check them out, we set up an audition gig for them at Larry's Hideaway, opening for a Rolling Stones clone band. They only played a forty-minute set of their own material, but got a standing ovation from the people in the room. Allan and I decided after one song we were going to sign them. So we took them to the Pilot Tavern and agreed terms."

Gold informed me their strategy had been to "just bring them into Toronto one night a month [on Wednesday] at the Club Isabella and build up a following." Soon they had crowds queuing down the street. It was the lyrical uniqueness of Downie that attracted Gold and Gregg's interest. "Gord had this lyrical perception that was totally Canadian, yet totally unique. When people heard them they knew there was something entirely different about the band. Our goal right away was to record a mini LP and get them on the road as soon as possible."

The 1987 Juno Awards, staged at Toronto's O'Keefe Centre on November 1, continued to shoot itself in the foot. The Guess Who were in the midst of accepting their Hall Of Fame award when host broadcasters CBC went to a commercial break right in the middle of Burton Cummings's acceptance speech. CARAS finally got the message that their November telecasts weren't working, and announced they were returning to their spring format in 1989 — which meant there would be no awards presented in 1988.

It was good to see CARAS honour some decent new talent in awarding Most Promising Group to Frozen Ghost, and Edmonton's Tim Feehan received the Most Promising New Male Vocalist Award. Yet the evening's big surprise was the recognition of Rita MacNeil, from Big Pond, Cape Breton, as Most Promising Female Vocalist — beating out Celine Dion. At forty-two years old, MacNeil, finally hit pay dirt when her *Flying on Your Own* album and title track became the year's sleeper hit. MacNeil had toiled in obscurity for more than two decades, yet manager Brookes Diamond maintained faith in her talents and Virgin Records president Doug Chappell took a gamble on a project which paid dividends.

As we completed preparations for our monster October/November issue, I prepared to embark on my first visit to Australia. The pretence of the trip was to accompany winners of a contest Musicland had executed with one of our U.S. advertisers, Chess King. The grand prize was a week in Sydney to catch David Bowie's Glass Spider tour at the city's Entertainment Centre.

The contest winners and I arrived at Sydney Airport around 4:00 p.m. on Thursday November 5. We emerged into a torrential cloudburst. I commandeered a cab and we drove to our hotel, the Sheraton Potts Point, which is located in the supposedly notorious King's Cross area of Sydney. I checked the girls into their room, staggered into mine, and collapsed into the deepest sleep I had ever experienced.

Intent on maximizing this trip, I phoned Grant Thomas, co-manager of Crowded House. I had met Grant when he toured through Ontario with his band, and, of course, we had got Crowded House that Musicland launch party gig in L.A. His parting words to me in L.A. were: "And if you're ever in the neighbourhood, please say hi." So I was in his neighbourhood and calling to say hi. Of course, I had made Grant aware of my pending trip and he promised to show me the sights on arrival. True to his word, Grant drove by the Sheraton, scooped me up in his car, and forty-five minutes later, we were at famed Bondi Beach enjoying a meal of Orange Roughy in this superb restaurant overlooking the Tasman Sea.

Grant filled me in on the latest Crowded House news, was complimentary of the work *Rock Express* had executed in helping to break the band in North America, and offered his services for the week. I didn't want to use too much of his time, but did agree to allow him to take me to one of the City's top clubs on Saturday, and he insisted on me meeting his family for a 'barbie on the beach' Sunday at Bondi.

It was late afternoon when Grant dropped by the hotel. First he insisted on a run across the Sydney Harbour Bridge into Manley where we then took a brief run along the Northern Beaches, which were less populated than Bondi. The first thing that struck me (aside from a bevy of topless Aussie girls) was the "Beware of Sharks" signs and the nets which were laid out to protect swimmers and surfers alike from being separated from various body parts.

Our destination Saturday night was the Parramatta Social Club where Mental as Anything were performing. As many sporting clubs are run as amateur operations, the clubs generate revenue through their social clubs, which are generally impressive operations. The Parramatta Club, which operated rugby, soccer, cricket, and Aussie Rules football teams, boasted a multilevel complex that featured a major restaurant, casino, gymnasium, swimming pool, and on the top level, a massive bar that was full to capacity when we arrived around 10:00 p.m.

Aussies are notorious for showing their displeasure at any bands not generating sufficient energy, often greeting less-than-satisfactory bands with a few well-aimed beer bottles to the head, but not the Mentals. They were a finely tuned Aussie group and well received by the locals. Grant introduced me to the band in their dressing room. They had been interviewed previously by Kerry Doole and were happy I was seeing them on their home turf.

An obvious obstacle for any Oz band is to establish themselves outside of Australia. A local band can complete a domestic tour in two weeks, and Australia's small population restricts the amount of product you can sell locally. "Yet to tour in Europe or North America you have to commit to being on the road for months on end, and that's not easy for guys who have families or girlfriends," explained Thomas. "Neil [Finn, Crowded House lead vocalist] absolutely hated touring and I always have my fingers crossed hoping he's going to meet us at the airport. So far, so good."

Tuesday night saw me join up with the two contest winners backstage at the Sydney Entertainment Centre. Bowie's eight Australian concerts in eleven days were to be followed by a solitary date in Auckland, New Zealand, on November 28. That would be the final show of an eighty-six-date tour, which had started in Rotterdam on May 30 and travelled across North America, with the Canadian dates occurring through September.

Bowie was well settled into his residency at the Sydney Entertainment Centre when the two winners and I were hustled backstage for the meet and greet. The winners were told they would only get five minutes with him, and sure enough, David hustled into the room, smiled, signed autographs, posed for photos, and chatted briefly with them about the previous shows they had caught, and then was out of the room in exactly five minutes!

I was led into another room where Bowie, guitarist Peter Frampton, and the rest of his band were preparing to go on stage. I managed to get a quick five-minute chat with Bowie about the success of his tour. I also got an additional five minutes with Frampton, who said he was experiencing a buzz touring as a sidekick and loved the idea of playing someone else's music without the pressures of carrying his own show. As I headed back to the lounge, I was verbally attacked by the two winners who claimed I hijacked Bowie before their five minutes were up. Note to self, stay clear of these two!

Rock Express had reviewed Bowie's Rotterdam concert, so I had an idea what to expect. I ended up having mixed feelings about the concert. No question it was visually quite stunning. Bowie and his band entered on the claws of a giant spider. Musically, the band was stripped down to the basics, with the dual guitar threat of Frampton and Carlos Alomar giving Bowie a strong rock sound reminiscent of Ziggy Stardust and the Spiders from Mars. Bowie also incorporated Montreal's La La La Human Steps dance troupe.

The problem with the show was its pacing. Many people were not familiar with his latest album, yet material from *Never Let Me Down* dominated almost the entire first half of the show. It was only during the second section that Bowie hit his stride, with classics like "Fame," "Blue Jean," "Let's Dance," "China Girl," and "Scary Monsters" the venue came alive. For his first encore, Bowie stood on a platform above the stage and started to sing "Time" as black wings spread out behind him and he was lowered to the stage. Performance-wise, Bowie's show was quite ambitious with a strong marriage of music and theatre. Overall, the packed house seemed content as they streamed out of the complex — yet I had to admit, I'd seen him play better.

The last full day in Sydney was spent shopping for souvenirs, although I did pay a visit to INXS manager Chris Murphy, whose MMA Talent Agency was located in the Kings Cross area. He brought me up to speed on his band — *Rock Express* had just run a front-cover feature on them — and also raved about Icehouse, who were just about to break in North America with their new album *Man of Colours*.

I met briefly with the two winners, reminded them to make sure they had their plane tickets and to be at the airport well before our 2:00 p.m. departure. Since it was our last night in Sydney, I offered to take them both to dinner but they declined as they had scored another pair of tickets to see Bowie. Flying back took eighteen hours from Sydney to Los Angeles, all the way in bright sunshine. In L.A., I immediately boarded a connecting flight from LAX to Chicago, and then straight on to Toronto, meaning I had flown almost consistently for twenty-five hours. I can't imagine making that trip on a regular basis — any band from Australia or New Zealand has my greatest respect!

I had mentioned my Oz trip to Gary Slaight at Q-107 and he invited me to drop by and chat about my experience. As part of the interview I played a couple of tracks from Australian bands I thought Toronto listeners might be interested in. I played one track from Jimmy Barnes's new album *Freight Train Heart* ("Too Much Ain't Enough"), one from Icehouse's *Man of Colours* LP ("Electric Blue"), and then, for the final track, I played Midnight Oil's "Beds are Burning" from their *Diesel and Dust* release, explaining Garrett was reluctant to release this song in North America because the whole album's theme was "too Australian."

I was told the following day that the airing of "Beds are Burning" virtually stopped traffic. Q was swamped with phone calls asking about that song and requested repeat spins. Kim Zayac from Columbia's Toronto office called to ask how Q obtained the track. About a week later, I received a phone call from Oil's manager Gary Morris demanding to know why I aired the song. I told him of the interview and pointed out that, based on the excitement that one listen created, maybe the Midnight Oil should reconsider releasing *Diesel and Dust* in North America.

All of this had gone down in November, yet it took until April of 1988 for Canada to release the album domestically, and a further month before the U.S. followed suit. I like to think I had something to do with sparking that initial interest — but I am sure they would have eventually released it.

That album is an absolute classic and meant so much in establishing the Oils worldwide. I did re-acquaint myself with Peter backstage at the CNE later that summer during Midnight Oils' headline concert, and he acknowledged my support and awarded *Rock Express* a *Diesel and Dust* platinum album for our promotional efforts.

21

A BEATLE, ZEPPELIN, AND OTHER STUFF!

Areflection of our magazine's growth came in early 1988 with the launch of the *Rock Express* radio syndication program. The show debuted in March on seventeen major Canadian FM stations. Created by Alan Lysaght of Lysonic Productions in conjunction with Doug Thompson of Telemedia Entertainment Radio Network, this one-hour weekly show allowed the magazine to promote current magazine issues as well as run timely news updates, live interviews, and high-profile contests. It also gave us a great promotional link with key stations like Q-107 Toronto, CHOM-Montreal, CFOX Vancouver, K-97 Edmonton, C-100 Halifax, and CITI-FM Winnipeg. The program's host was MuchMusic's J.D. Roberts.

"Initially, Doug and I were bidding against each other to secure the syndication rights and I think Conny (Kunz) liked me more because she decided Sonic Workshop should get the rights," reflected Lysaght. "Then Doug called me and suggested we join forces, citing Telemedia's ability to sell the show to corporate advertisers and create a viable network."

J.D. Roberts was selected as host because Lysaght didn't want an over-bearing Toronto presence to the show. Roberts had worked nationally on *The NewMusic* and MuchMusic shows and had come from CHUM so he had a radio background. "J.D. was a delight to work with," enthused Lysaght. "He wasn't viewed as a Toronto DJ; he knew how to read radio scripts. He was warm, intelligent, and well received by our other partner stations."

Rock Express was the first nationally syndicated music magazine of its kind to link key stations, utilize DJs as regional reporters, and actively promote new music and new artists. "It was our policy, rarely to mention the word Toronto in our broadcast," noted Lysaght, who also created major syndicated programs on The Beatles and the Rolling Stones. "It was so important to make our show feel national that we avoided any Toronto reference whenever possible but we would go out of our way to mention events in Vancouver or Montreal or other places in Canada."

"The show's format was designed as a magazine to complement *Rock Express* but to also react to newsworthy events on a weekly basis," said Lysaght. "It was great when the magazine could pass along interview opportunities like the one we did with Paul McCartney (December 7, 1989). It gave the show so much more credibility."

We also utilized J.D. and his MuchMusic sidekick, Erica Ehm, to host our 1987 Rock Express Awards, which were staged March 1 at the Diamond Club. It was hard to top the previous year's surprise appearance of Robert Palmer, yet we went all out. We hired Stuart Raven-Hill to secure the talent, and ultimately finished with a lineup of new artists who went on to dominate Canadian music over the next decade. To say we presented The Tragically Hip, Blue Rodeo, and the Jeff Healey Band, along with Platinum Blonde and April Wine's Brian Greenway, for a combined talent budget of four thousand dollars was impressive.

Rock Express was fortunate because our U.S. circulation pulled some clout with the bands. But more importantly, Blue Rodeo (*Outskirts*), The Tragically Hip (*The Tragically Hip*), and Greenway (*Serious Business*) were all promoting debut albums.

As usual, the results of our annual fan ballot fairly reflected consumer trends, with Montreal's The Box winning Top Canadian Group and Top Canadian Album (*Closer Together*) gold microphones; Glass Tiger won Top Canadian Live Act; Bryan Adams retained his Top Canadian Male Vocalist and also won Top Canadian Single ("Heat of the Night"); Luba won as Top Canadian Female Vocalist; the New Artist Awards went to Blue Rodeo (New Group), Rita MacNeil (New Female), and Jeff Healey (New Male). International awards went to U2 for Top Group and Top Album (*The Joshua Tree*), Bon Jovi for Top Single "Living on a Prayer," John Cougar Mellencamp for Top Male, and Madonna for Top Female. We also awarded gold microphones to Tom Cochrane (Working Class Hero award) and to Rock and Hyde (Top Canadian Songwriters).

Most domestic winners were in attendance (Glass Tiger, Luba, The Box's Jean-Marc Pisapia, Bob Rock, Blue Rodeo, Jeff Healey, and Tom Cochrane). Bryan Adams sent a video acceptance, and Virgin's Doug Chappell apologized in saying Rita MacNeil was too shy to attend — but was genuinely thrilled to be acknowledged by our readers. The evening's talking point though was the talent. To have such amazing bands together for one night was a jewel in our magazine's crown. Musicland's Bruce Jesse flew in to attend our awards, and even he was impressed by artists he was not previously familiar with.

The buzz band of the night was The Tragically Hip. They had created a massive local following their appearances at Club Isabella and had recorded what they called a "Mini-LP," which was produced by Red Rider's Kenny Greer. "We had agreed on a seven-year production deal with BMG," noted co-manager Jake Gold. "And BMG released the first record. But the label's new A&R chief, David Bendeth, refused to accept our deal saying all agreements had to be direct signings. So we took our record and walked away."

Watching The Tragically Hip live defied description; they were similar to R.E.M., but more intense, with Downie's lyrical prose uniquely Canadian in content. Songs like "Small Town Bringdown" and "Last American Exit" provoked a hometown intensity that would later become a band trademark on future releases. On stage, Downie's almost Jim Morrisonesque persona was stoked by dual guitarists Bobby Baker and Paul Langlois and a watertight rhythm section in drummer Johnnie Fay and bassist Gord Sinclair. Even their covers were unusual, with "Baby Please Don't Go" and "I'm a Werewolf Baby" — complete with trademark Downie histrionics — melding well with their original songs.

The evening's wild card was blind guitarist Jeff Healey who, along with bassist Joe Rockman and drummer Tom Stephens, tore up the club with a spectacular display of Blues and R&B instrumentation. Born Norman Jeffrey Healey, he contracted retinoblastoma (a rare cancer) at the age of eight months and had both eyes removed and optical replacements inserted. Playing guitar from the age of three, Healey developed a unique style of playing with his instrument on his lap. By the age of seventeen, he was performing in a local band Blues Direction, becoming a staple at clubs like The Brunswick's Albert's Hall and Grossman's Tavern.

Healey's jam sessions with the likes of Stevie Ray Vaughan and Albert Collins became legendary, yet despite linking up with Rockman and Stephens to front his own band, Healey couldn't find a local label interested in signing him. One industry wag was reported to have observed, "The kid needs a gimmick." As if being a blind teenage guitar phenom wasn't gimmick enough?

Healey was popular enough to win our Most Promising Male Vocalist Award, but it took a trip to New York by drummer/manager Tom Stephens to convince Arista's Jimmy Iovine to sign Healey to their U.S. label. This resulted in the release of *See the Light* on September 13. Fuelled by a major single, "Angel Eyes," *See the Light* achieved platinum sales in Canada, which came as a collective slap in the face to all Canadian A&R types who failed to recognize such obvious talent.

As our awards show wound down, I stood next to Jeff backstage when suddenly the whole room was plunged into darkness. A power failure had drained all electricity from the downtown core. Panic enveloped the club as patrons try to find their way out into the street. Someone even drove their car right up to the front door to direct the car's headlights into the building.

"What's wrong?" enquired Healey, obviously aware something wasn't right.

"It's pitch black and I can't see a thing," noted I, floundering around behind all the monitors and other gear used during the performances.

"No problem, follow me," smiled Healey as he deftly manoeuvred through the equipment and out into the club's corridor with me holding on to him and his handler Joe Rockman. The irony of that situation has always stayed with me.

I was preparing to head out to Los Angeles and eagerly anticipating my second NARM convention, staged at the Century Plaza Hotel on March 11–14, when I received a phone call from Gary Ross at Musicland informing me Bruce Jesse had been relieved of his position. "Not to worry, though, we love the magazine," reassured Ross. "Jack [Eugster] and I will meet with you in Los Angeles to discuss future plans."

"I was fired," reflected Jesse, tracked down for this book in his suburban Minneapolis residence where he now works as a realtor. "They said there had been some corporate restructuring, but the reality was my boss, Gary Ross, and I didn't operate in the same social circles, I didn't drink, didn't womanize, didn't party ... and didn't play golf. I focused on being professional at all times. Yet Gary was a known womanizer and party animal who like to booze with the boys. I guess our personalities didn't mesh."

Bruce's dismissal made no sense. He had been the driving force behind introducing *Rock Express* to Musicland, seemed to be involved in much of their promotional activities (including arranging our launch party), and from what I had observed at the NARM convention, he was well respected of by his peers. Yet Musicland cast him aside like yesterday's newspaper.

The first morning at the convention Conny and I met with Gary Ross. Superficially, the meeting went well. Gary assured us Musicland was committed to their support of our magazine and that we should formalize an agreement at a future date. He even introduced us to members of MTV's marketing team and suggested a working relationship with the network — which did show some forward progress at their end. One thing was evident though: Conny and Gary didn't like each other. Nothing offensive was said between the two, yet Conny's strong persona was the exact opposite of the subservient attitude Ross was accustomed to in dealing with women in the industry. For her part, Conny barely succeeded in masking her scorn at Ross's chauvinistic personality. I spent the rest of the conference trying the keep them apart, which was relatively easy as Conny came down with the flu and spent most of the convention in our hotel suite.

Attempting to put on a brave face, I did the rounds at NARM, promoted *Rock Express* at the product displays, and even bumped into Iron Maiden manager Rod Smallwood, who had just started managing Poison. Rod introduced me to lead vocalist Brett Michaels and guitarist C.C. DeVille, who were hustling their debut album *Look what the Cat Dragged In*. Unlike the friendly Maiden boys, these two struck me as surly characters — they barely uttered a friendly response. Smallwood must have felt the same way as he dumped them shortly afterwards.

NARM's product presentations were as informative as ever but I did note something obvious. If you are an artist and your product is included in your label's presentation, it's a good sign they are behind it. Yet if your release is not mentioned, I suggest you have a problem. I say this because I was aware Blue Rodeo's *Outskirts* was supposed to be getting a push from Atlantic, but they weren't mentioned in the label's presentation. Ditto for Glass Tiger, whose *Thin Red Line* album had scored them Grammy attention in 1987, but their proposed new release, *Diamond Sun*, didn't rate a mention with Capitol-EMI, which had just absorbed Glass Tiger's Manhattan label.

I bumped into Dick Clark in one of the suites and even managed a brief chat with Robbie Robertson. Yet one of the most significant events occurred outside of the convention. In agreeing to work with *Rock Express*, Ron Hartenbaum and Gary Schonfeld at Media America (the Pattis Group's replacement) were anxious that I not talk to their competitors Westwood One. Yet all the news in the U.S. trades indicated Westwood were in full expansion mode. They owned the trade tip sheet, *Radio & Records*, and were buying a number of major radio stations, but still had a problem alerting potential listeners to key programming broadcasts. If you weren't listening to a particular station on a particular date, you probably missed their broadcast. I believed Musicland and *Rock Express* could be an answer to their problems.

I had mailed out copies of *Rock Express* to Norm Pattiz (no relation to the Pattis Group!) at Westwood One and followed up with a call to their Culver City head office during my visit to NARM. Pattiz's response was to invite me over to meet him. Located adjacent to a Harley Davidson garage, Westwood One was comprised of a series of loft-type offices. I met his marketing guy whose brother was drummer for REO Speedwagon, and I was brought in to their conference room located in the middle of a maze of cubicles.

I detailed the history of *Rock Express* to Pattiz, explained how I thought there was an obvious synergy between Westwood One, Musicland, and *Rock Express,* and suggested I would be open to some kind of formal relationship, and could probably convince Musicland to come on board. Pattiz warmed to the idea, suggesting a relationship would be a favourable arrangement. I left his office with a promise he would give my proposal his strongest consideration.

While *Rock Express* was growing in the States, our ability to communicate with the U.S. labels meant we had inside information on key Canadian bands that were running into difficulty stateside. One such band was Glass Tiger.

The collective members of Glass Tiger were decidedly nervous about the pending release of their sophomore *Diamond Sun* record. Their reluctance to debut the new material was only broken down by our promise of a Canadian cover for the April issue (Robert Plant got the U.S. cover).

Dianne Collins was selected to pen the feature, and her exploits in accessing a listening session at Capitol's Toronto rivalled protocol in cracking The Pentagon. "I feel very apprehensive," admitted drummer Michael Hanson. "It's just like starting over again for me. You can't really look back and say okay, now we've had success so everything is just going to fall into place. You have to work just as hard or harder to make it continue. It's going to be tough."

Hanson's comments proved to be very perceptive. Although Jim Vallance was back behind the console and the band enjoyed strong success with "I'm Still Standing" and "My Song," a Celtic flavoured track which also featured the Chieftains, certain developments occurred stateside which would limit the band's future U.S. endeavours. Success for their debut, *Thin Red Line*, was generated in part by the efforts of Bruce Lundval's Manhattan Records, who had launched his Capitol-distributed label with Glass Tiger and Richard Marx as the label's principal two acts. But in the time between the launch of *The Thin Red Line* and *Diamond Sun*, Lundval's label had been rolled into Capitol-EMI and Glass Tiger were no longer a priority.

I learned this first hand when visiting New York. In discussing Capitol-EMI's 1988 priorities with the label's marketing director, I noticed Glass Tiger's new title wasn't listed. When I asked about Glass Tiger, the marketing contact enquired, "Who is Glass Tiger?"

I pointed to a photo of the band on the wall, and said "Those guys. I think they sold over a million copies for you guys last year. I think they were also up for a Grammy."

"Not on my list," snorted the marketing lady, obviously not impressed by my rebuke.

At the Canadian launch party for *Diamond Sun*, staged at a Richmond Street West disco, I recalled my EMI meeting with the band's co-manager Gary Pring, saying, "Gary, I think you have a problem with the States!"

Blue Rodeo suffered the same U.S. fate with their *Outskirts* record. I was in Los Angeles when the band was slated for a preview performance, to be staged at noon at a Sunset Boulevard bar called Club Lingerie. It was about 105 degrees outside and what few journalists Blue Rodeo did attract were probably there because of the free Corona beer. Still, the band gave it the old college try and received a smattering of applause before being whisked off to New York for a similar performance.

The following day, I went to the office of Atlantic Records and the marketing girl is going through her list of new titles they wanted *Rock Express* to plug. "So we have Mr. Big, Robert Plant, INXS," she informed me.

"What about Blue Rodeo?" asked I.

"Who is Blue Rodeo?"

"Er, the band you showcased yesterday," noted I.

"So that's who they were? No, can't say we have them listed as a priority," responded the marketing contact, again not impressed I had questioned her judgement.

The highlight of 1988, for me, was getting to interview George Harrison for *Rock Express*. Before I could meet Harrison, though, I had to get by Pete the security guard, who cut an impressive figure as he stood in full military position, legs astride, hands behind back, totally controlling access to the eleventh floor of Toronto's prestigious Sutton Place Hotel in Toronto. The fact that a Beatle held court a few doors down the corridor didn't faze him. As one of the chief celebrity protectors at the hotel, foiling the frenzied efforts of fans and groupies was all in a day's work.

"You should have been here when Tom Selleck, Steve Guttenberg, and Ted Danson were here shooting *Three Men and a Baby*. They all decided to go for dinner at the same time and the place went crazy," he explained.

By comparison, the atmosphere around the hotel for Harrison's promo visit to push his new *Cloud Nine* record was comparatively mundane. Aside from a scheduled press conference at the hotel later that afternoon, Nicholas Jennings and myself had been selected to do an exclusive one-on-one with the former Beatle in his suite.

To make sure we maximized our time with George, Nicholas and I went over our questions prior to the interview and agreed I would ask the music questions and Nicholas, aware Harrison was joint-head of Handmade Films, would ask the movie questions. I was trembling with nerves when I stepped into Harrison's suite. The ex-Beatle to emerged from the washroom and greeted us with a firm handshake. Casually attired in jeans and a floral T-shirt, Harrison proved to be a dream interview. Humorous, articulate, but so disarming you forgot you were chatting with a music legend.

In the thirty minutes or so we had with Harrison, we chatted about his *Cloud Nine* comeback album, his adventures with Handmade Films (particularly with *Shanghai Surprise*), and the enduring legacy of being a surviving

Beatle. Harrison had seemingly run out of creativity when his 1983, *Gone Troppo* album was universally panned, and it took him five years to summon up the initiative to go back into the studio. The resulting success of *Cloud Nine* was attributed to Harrison's new partnership with former Electric Light Orchestra lead man Jeff Lynne.

I mentioned to him that Paul McCartney had gone on record as saying that he didn't work well with co-collaborators because they were so intimidated by him they were afraid to offer constructive criticism. "Paul tends to think, 'Now who's made good records with people?' He tends to pick them out of a hat without having any basic relationship with people," noted Harrison. "So with Jeff, that was the point. I got his opinion long before we entered the studio so it worked well both ways. He made me sing much higher. Knowing that he was standing there and that he was such a good vocalist, he made me want to try harder. Because Jeff was there, the standard was much better. He'd say 'Well that's okay but that note was a little too flat and that was a little sharp. I think you can do better.'"

Harrison explained Handmade Films was created initially to bail out his Monty Python mates after funding for their *Life of Brian* movie was pulled from them. "I think Sir Lew Grade must have read the script and deemed the film too controversial," noted Harrison. "So I asked my business manager, Dennis O'Brien, if he thought we should help and he came back with this idea of us producing the movie. *Life of Brian* did well enough that Handmade sunk their profits into another Python project, Terry Gilliam's *Time Bandits*. And when that made money, we kept on sinking the funds back into future projects." That philosophy almost came to an abrupt ending when Handmade decided to fund Sean Penn and his then wife Madonna in *Shanghai Surprise*, an enterprise which proved to be a financial disaster for Handmade.

"We were one day away from deciding not to bother when we get this phone call saying Sean Penn and Madonna want to be involved," explained Harrison. "Anybody in that situation would think, 'that can't be bad because Sean Penn is reputed to be good and Madonna was pretty good in *Desperately Seeking Susan*.' So it didn't look like too much of an outrageous idea. The end result reminded me of that Mel Brooks's line about *Springtime for Hitler* [from *The Producers*] — 'I picked the wrong actors, the wrong director, the wrong producers, where did I go right?' Only our situation was the exact reverse."

Of the number of Beatles questions I managed to pitch to George, his most poignant response came when I asked him how his own children felt about their famous dad and his Beatles legacy. "Well I've never told them about The Beatles but I think every kid finds out about us by watching *Yellow Submarine* when they're four or five," responded Harrison. "My son has just started to learn the piano and he says 'How does that piano lick go in "Hey Bulldog."' I go. '"Hey Bulldog"? How do you know about that?' Then you think, right 'Yellow Submarine.' It's great that as each generation grows up, they still like Beatles records. It's reassuring to know that what we've done actually has some value."

A few weeks after the interview with Harrison, I was invited to cover a concert which rivalled both Live Aid and Woodstock in sheer star power. Atlantic Records chose to celebrate their fortieth anniversary with a thirteen-hour extravaganza on May 14, at New York's Madison Square Garden, which featured a dazzling array of former and current Atlantic talent capped by a one-off reunion appearance of Led Zeppelin. President Ahmet Ertegun presented a lineup which melded the label's classic black R&B artists with the best of their rock acts from Britain and the U.S. All this meant that in one amazing day (and night) I was entertained by the likes of Genesis, Yes, Emerson Lake & Palmer, Crosby, Stills, & Nash, Robert Plant, The Coasters, Ben E. King, Wilson Pickett, The Bee Gees, Foreigner, Phil Collins, The Rascals, Vanilla Fudge, Iron Butterfly, Roberta Flack, and a seventeen-year-old Debbie Gibson, all prior to Zeppelin's grand finale.

Phil Collins kicked off the extravaganza at noon with his typically cheery, "Hello New York," and from that point on talent was on and off the stage with head spinning regularity. I was able to secure an all-access pass that enabled me to watch the show from the Garden's press box and also gave me access to the interview room, which hosted a steady stream of mega talent.

The whole event was a blur of one major act after another. I finally got to see my favs, ELP, perform an abbreviated set, and I even enjoyed R&B artists like Ben E. King and Wilson Pickett, and of course Booker T playing with Duck Dunn. Foreigner had just broken up, but they reunited to perform a killer set including "Juke Box Hero," "Urgent," and their classic "I Want to Know What Love Is." I remembered chatting with bassist Rick Wills, praising the band's performance, and encouraging them to stick together.

"Thanks, but you're talking to the wrong guy," remarked Wills. "It's Lou [Gramm] and Mick [Jones] you should be talking to. They are the ones busting up the band."

Robert Plant proved to be the day's star, plugging his *Now and Zen* album by performing a solo spot in mid-afternoon, featuring "Heaven Knows," "Ship of Fools," and "Tall Cool One," before returning to close the show with his old band mates. As time ticked away, and Zep's turn loomed on the program, the packed crowd became more and more excited. The act on before Led Zeppelin, Rufus Thomas, didn't stand a chance. His "Walking the Dog" hit was met with cat whistles and boos.

It was like a thousand volts of electricity simultaneously hit the crowd when, at 1:05 Sunday morning, Led Zeppelin hit the stage for the first time in eight years. Deceased-percussionist John Bonham's son, Jason, launched into the hypnotic beat of "Kashmir," and it was just like old times. "Heartbreaker," "Whole Lotta Love," and "Misty Mountain Hop" were all delivered with faithful precision, although it must be noted Jimmy Page's guitar solo on "Whole Lotta Love" was a little sloppy.

Then came "Stairway to Heaven," and it was as though time stood still, an opportunity to reflect on one's lost youth, a chapter in one's life that had been reopened for one quick flashback. Zeppelin's rendition of what had become *the* rock classic was faithful to the note. The crowd sang as one, the smoke cleared and it was over, an amazing climax to an amazing evening.

Phil Collins summarized the evening by saying he was there "to honour a label which made black American music accessible to white English kids." That being the case, if the first two generations of Atlantic Records gave black music to white kids, by the third generation it was those same white English kids giving back as good as they got.

The biggest development at this time was the change back of our magazine from *Rock Express* back to *Music Express*. We were quite happy with our *Rock Express* image when Gary Ross at Musicland called me in late May to tell me Bill Graham (the San Francisco concert promoter) had already registered the name Rock Express for his merchandise line and was threatening to sue us if we didn't change our name.

This came as a surprise to me because Graham's people had known for ages our magazine was called *Rock Express*. We had bought T-shirts of him for our Boston WBCN party, and we had always sent out magazines to his office. Still, Graham had belatedly decided this was an issue, and as his company sold that Rock Express product line to Musicland/Sam Goody, I guess he felt he had an argument.

Not one to rock the boat, we decided to redesign our *Music Express* logo and present our new-look magazine for our July 1988 issue. The name change also caused problems with Lysonic Productions, which now had to change the name of our radio show. Still, most Canadian readers still knew us from our original *Music Express* handle so it wasn't too much of a hassle — and we had determined to keep Musicland happy at all costs!

But try as we did to keep Musicland happy, events began to unfold that would eventually mark the end of our relationship. It all started innocently enough. By May 1988, things couldn't have been better for our magazine. My backstage pass to the Atlantic Records concert was proof to me of our acceptance by the U.S. music industry. Our North American distribution was up to seven hundred thousand copies per issue, we were being well received by our retail customers, the record industry recognized we were willing to support and promote new artists, and we had that deal with Westwood One pending that would really establish *Music Express* as a major media force.

Understanding that we had yet to sign off on a long-term agreement between Musicland and our company, Wembley Productions, Jack Eugster and his VP of marketing, Gary Ross, agreed to meet me in New York where I was scheduled to interview Daryl Hall and John Oates.

I met with Eugster and Ross at the famous Park Plaza Hotel. Both were complimentary about the acceptance of *Music Express* in the Musicland/Sam Goody chain. They said they wanted to establish a long-term commitment to *ME*, but added that they wanted a piece of our company. The figure they requested was 35 percent of our entire operation. Considering they represented the bulk of our distribution and their record company advertising provided the majority of our funding, I didn't think this was unduly out of line. Yet I couldn't agree to their request on the spot as I had two other shareholders, Allan Gregg and Conny Kunz, to consult with.

If I really needed a trump card in the negotiations, I could tell Eugster and Ross about my Westwood One negotiations, but I wanted to firm up our deal first before telling them about the third-party interest of Westwood

One, which represented a sizeable financial investment. With the opportunity of both us and Musicland to make money off Westwood One, it seemed like a win-win situation for both everyone.

They agreed to give me time to respond to their offer, and I flew out of New York's La Guardia Airport confident we could come to terms on a long-term agreement. I thought I had handled things correctly — yet so many times since, I wished I could replay that meeting.

22

ADAMS IN

EAST BERLIN

The neat row of white crosses told a stark grisly tale: *Marienetta Jirkowski 20.11.1983, Unknown 22.11.1986.* While Glasnost may have been the in word in political jargon, in 1988, a swim across the River Spree from East Berlin to the nearby western bank was almost certain to draw a deadly hail of machine-gun fire ... and your own personal epitaph on the Reichstag wall.

Despite Soviet General Secretary Mikhail Gorbachev's congenial PR gestures and an obvious thawing of the Cold War, the East German government's concrete bastion, which encircled three million West Berliners, stood as a cold cruel barrier between conflicting cultures. To his credit, East German President Dr. Erich Honecker had tried to pacify the surging hormones of East Germany's youth by allowing the FDJ, the Communist party's official youth organization, to host an International Meeting for Nuclear Free Zones in Europe convention that was also to feature three nights of concert activity. Bryan Adams had been tabbed for the third night, Sunday June 19, following James Brown and Marillion on the preceding days.

A chance meeting between Adams and Katrina Witt, the East German Olympic-gold-medal champion, prompted Adams's invitation. Adams had executed a free concert for the athletes at the 1988 Calgary Winter Olympic Games, and Witt was impressed enough to offer Adams the chance to play in her country. Adams had scheduled a brief European tour in support of his *Into the Fire* album. Since he had a West Berlin date on the itinerary, he agreed to pop over the wall and perform in East Berlin also.

I flew into West Berlin on Saturday, June 18 and met up with Adams's entourage, who had just flown in from Portugal and were camped out at the swank Kempinski Hotel on West Berlin's trendy Kurfurstendamm. I was greeted by Bruce Allen, who seemed to have forgotten about our Can-Aid run in, along with Adams's tour manager, Randy Berswick, and their European tour agent, England's Carl Leighton-Pope.

Bryan introduced me to his girlfriend, Vicky Russell, daughter of famed movie producer Ken Russell, when we all met to discuss the protocol of the following day's trip through Checkpoint Charlie to East Berlin. "Whatever you do," warned Leighton-Pope, "don't tell them you are a journalist. As far as they are concerned, you're a member of our crew."

I had a chance for a brief stroll down the Kurfurstendamm and was very surprised how modern and vibrant West Berlin was. This stood in stark contrast to my exposure to East Berlin. Entering East Berlin through Checkpoint Charlie was like being in an episode of *The Twilight Zone*. The graffiti-emblazoned wall, the armed guards, the anti-tank traps, the barricaded security stops, and the vacant sprawl of no-man's land between the cities were enough to make anyone feel uncomfortable.

Getting from West Berlin was a minor, if irritating, formality. Exchange twenty-five dollars for useless East German marks, survive the scrutiny of your passport, and you too could obtain a day pass to the other side of the wall. As we waited in the Volkswagen for our turn at the crossing, driver Peter Dolle, a freelance TV reporter, told us of a couple of the more daring escapes made through the checkpoint.

"One guy escaped by contorting his body around the inside of a hollowed out truck tire," noted Dolle. "But the best one was this skinny girl who got through by sitting inside the car's passenger seat. They cut out the interior of the seat, she sat inside and someone else sat on top of her. The guards were so busy checking the interior and exterior of the car, they never thought of asking the passenger to move."

An interesting observation came when Bryan flashed his British passport to the East German guards. "Busted!" said I. "Someone has some explaining to do to CARAS when you get back to Canada." Adams just smiled at getting caught with a foreign passport.

The transformation between the two Berlins was startling. Uniform slabs of concrete stood in stark contrast to West Berlin's cheery, colourful architecture. Mercedes were replaced by Skodas and Ladas, and the people themselves seemed dour and introverted.

After checking into the bleak units of the Stadt Berlin hotel and sharing a quick beer with Big Country's sound engineer (they were opening for Adams), we were back in the van for a twenty-minute drive to the Ander rad Rennbahn racecourse, site of the concert.

Word was a crowd of over 120,000 were in attendance, about 25 percent more than what Marillion pulled the previous night and about 80 percent more than the woeful crowd attracted to James Brown's Friday gyrations. Backstage, things were surprisingly organized. The twin stage setup looked decidedly rickety and the lighting grids were hardly Showco quality, yet everything was sturdy and functional and there was even a huge video screen to project onstage images to the back of the crowd. Tour manager Berswick's only concern was the large expanse between the stage and the barrier holding back the crowd. "Bryan isn't going to like that; he likes to be in touch with his audience."

Two East German groups plodded through their amateurish but enthusiastic sets while Adams and his band arrived backstage and were greeted by Katarina Witt. Attired fashionably in a denim outfit and looking every inch a Western teenager, Witt was quickly brought into an impromptu press conference by yours truly. "I'm here because I like Bryan and because we are all here to promote world peace. The fact that music is playing such an important role is of great significance," she stated in flawless English. Asked if she saw herself as a role model for East German youth, Witt responded by saying, "I like to do what I can for my country but I'd rather skate than talk." Probably the only person not thrilled with Witt's presence was Vicky Russell. Adam's live-in girlfriend settled into a slow burn while Adams and Witt posed for the local paparazzi.

An item of media speculation was that the Adams concert has been staged to create a diversion for kids who would otherwise have massed at the Wall to eavesdrop on a Michael Jackson concert that was happening in West Berlin at exactly the same time. Adams ended up winning the numbers count, with an estimated 120,000 in attendance at his event compared to just thirty thousand at Jackson's concert. However, more than five hundred eavesdropping East German youths were dispersed from the Wall in violent fashion by plainclothes security officers wielding electrified cattle prods.

West German TV camera crews there to film the event were also attacked and many had their equipment destroyed.

To say Adams could do no wrong sounded like pure hype from some publicity flak. Yet by the midway point of his concert, he had the exuberant masses swaying and singing phonetically to the likes of "Heat of the Night," "Kids Wanna Rock," "Straight from the Heart," and "Cuts like a Knife." Maple Leaf flags and banners flew euphorically in the breeze.

The concert had a midnight curfew, but it was obvious Adams was going to play this to the hilt. He concluded his regular set with "Somebody" and beamed from ear to ear as he towelled off backstage. Manager Bruce Allen nodded approvingly as he launched into a three-song encore. East German military types looked nervously at their watches and seemed tense, it was 12:30 and the kids didn't want to go home.

Behind the curtain Witt gave Adams a nod and he went back on stage again, launching into Bobby Fuller's "I Fought the Law" and "Dancing." "Somebody had better watch this guy," cracked Allen. "He's so out of control, he doesn't know what he's doing." Adams was finally bundled off stage and into his trailer. "A career highlight," bubbled Allen.

"A great experience," concurred Adams.

The following day as our bus weaved down the Unter den Linden en route to our border crossing back into West Berlin, Adams talked about his latest album, *Into the Fire*, and how it could be considered his East Berlin album. "Jim Vallance and I wrote two songs during my previous visit here: 'Heat Of The Night' and 'Another Day.' It's not so much that East Berlin is a bad place to live. It's just that there's no choice here. They can't buy any records or even go to shows. I just wish the government would be more lenient and give them more of want they want. Then things wouldn't be half bad."

Bryan's appearance in West Berlin on the Tuesday was a contrast of the sublime to the ridiculous. His gig was scheduled for the city's Summergarten outdoor venue. A torrential downpour had kept the turnout to less than a thousand hardy souls, and there were serious doubts the gig could go ahead. While waiting for the rain to ease off, Adams played a spirited game of darts with Carl Leighton-Pope. Adams hit the winning target; Leighton-Pope feigned disgust, executed a well-acted mock rage, but paid up before storming out of the room. Adams checked the bills to make sure Leighton-Pope hasn't slipped him any of those worthless East German marks. "There's only one worse loser than Carl and that's Bruce," grinned Adams. "We played foosball at Bruce's house and I beat him so badly he punched a big hole in his pop machine. It's a wonder he didn't break his hand."

The rain subsided, and since there was a crowd, however small, the green light is given for the band to take to the soggy stage which looks like a gazebo in the middle of a swamp. Playing off the situation, Adams opened with Anne Peebles "I Can't Stop the Rain" and followed through with a playfully energetic set which avoided his usual greatest-hits set list to instead feature Patsy Cline's "Walkin' After Midnight" and, again, Bobby Fuller's "I Fought the Law." The band left the stage to set up for an encore, but realized everyone could see them through the sheer plastic design of the stage, so they turned around and went back on to wrap up the gig with "Somebody."

History showed the Berlin Wall collapsed just over twelve months later (November 9, 1989), when the ruling GDR government opened up the wall and watched both East and West Berliners tear it apart. Adams is probably the only artist who can claim to have played East Berlin, West Berlin, and Middle Berlin, as he posted a guest appearance in Roger Water's The Wall concert July 21, 1990, which was staged in no-man's land between both cities.

23

A CONCERT

FOR JOEY

I had just returned from Berlin when I received the phone call from Musicland saying that they wanted to meet me in Minneapolis to conclude our negotiations. Conny and Allan's position, knowing that Westwood One wanted to make a sizeable investment in our partnership, was that we were reluctant to give up 35 percent ownership of our entire company (which included Canada). As our Canadian operation (which published independently of the U.S. version) was subsidizing their publication, Conny and Allan felt Musicland were playing hardball and that they could be convinced to lessen their request. Yet when I began to plan my trip to the meeting neither Conny nor Allan were prepared to travel with me.

I began to feel a sense of foreboding when I flew out to Minneapolis that November, and that sense of dread was soon realized. Eugster came straight to the point. Musicland wanted 65 percent of the entire operation (not the 35 percent previously discussed), they wanted all bookkeeping and financial dealings redirected to their head office, and they wanted the printing of both the Canadian and U.S. books to be handled by their Chicago-based printer, Donnelly & Sons. This was a deal-killer, as the exchange rate between the Canadian and U.S. dollars was seventy-four cents, so we made twenty-six cents per dollar on the exchange by printing both magazines in Canada.

I protested that Musicland was virtually taking the magazine away from us, but they wouldn't budge. Even my revelation about Westwood One's interest made no impression on them.

The meeting concluded with me saying I would have to confer with my partners and that I would table a response in writing, but I knew there was no way Allan and Conny were going to agree to what seemed to be Musicland's extortionate demands.

At this time, *Music Express* was on the move again. The lease had expired on our Madison Avenue headquarters, and Conny had found our new home. It was a former garage on Jefferson Avenue (in what is now known as Liberty Village) that had been converted into an office complex. The place was huge, seven thousand square feet, and was painted in hip-hop pink and blue colours, with a main office for Conny at one end of the building and another one for me at the other end. In between was a haven of cubicles, a wide area for graphic layout, two large washrooms, and a separate, glassed-off conference room and reception area.

We moved into 47 Jefferson Avenue in mid-October and set up the place as a real showcase for the music industry. A central feature was a giant Lado electric guitar that the Toronto-based manufacturers had loaned us. The guitar had been designed as an exhibit in many musical-instrument shows around North America, but for the most part sat at the back of their Scarborough warehouse. My selling point was musicians would see the guitar displayed at our office and might wish to enquire about Lado's guitars, which were been utilized by the likes of Iron Maiden, Honeymoon Suite, and Coney Hatch.

I was watching CTV one night in November when a news item aired about this brave fifteen-year-old Orillia boy named Joey Philion who had been badly burned in a house fire on March 10. He had been flown to the world famous Shriners Hospital in Boston where he survived two critical pneumonia attacks, and it was only his great fortitude and will to live pulled him through. The TV broadcast informed me that Joey had been transferred to Toronto's Sick Kids Hospital where he was to undergo further intensive treatment and rehabilitation. Although his prognosis was favourable, Philion still faced years of skin grafts and therapy before he could regain a certain level of mobility and speech.

Watching this moving broadcast, I felt a charity fundraiser for Joey would be the ideal motivation for our 1988 Music Express Awards. I called the news editor at the *Orillia Packet* newspaper, and he forwarded to me clippings of the fire and informed me that fund raising efforts were under-way to build a special wheelchair accessible house for Joey and his family.

Having learned from my Can-Aid experience that I could not pull this fundraiser off alone, I contacted Glass Tiger's Alan Frew and explained my intentions of turning the 1988 award show into a fundraiser for Philion. I invited Glass Tiger to headline the show and asked if Alan would join forces with me to promote the concert. Alan was also aware of Joey's heroics and pledged his time and support to promote the concert. As well, I had just interviewed Gil Moore and Mike Levine about the current state of Triumph, so when I called back to ask if they would be prepared to join forces with Alan, both readily agreed.

The next step was to locate an appropriate venue. We had used the Diamond Club for the past two years but wanted a space with a larger capacity. I was notified that a "super club" was currently being constructed at Dixie Road and Courtney Park Road in Mississauga. I contacted owners Scott McLean and Dale Murray about possibly opening their club with our charity concert, and they invited me to inspect their budding venue, Superstars Niteclub.

I arrived to find a mass of construction. I doubted the club would be ready for the mid-February event. Both owners assured me their club would be ready on time and that their 32,000-square-foot space would be ideal. The capacity would be 2,300 in a multi-level construction featuring an upstairs VIP area with private boxes and a state of the art sound and light system. I told them we were planning on a mid-December press conference to announce the show and could provide their club with a massive amount of positive publicity, but they had to commit to a February date. "Not a problem," said they.

Aired at the press conference were special videos by superstars Rod Stewart, Phil Collins, and Robert Plant. The conference generated mass media attention and we used the occasion to launch ticket sales at all BASS outlets for the February 15 Gala at a cost of $17.50 per ticket. CMG, our hired press agency, organized a raft of radio and print interviews which were split between Alan, Gil, and me, and we benefited from several PSA ads from our radio and print partners. Then the *Toronto Star* dropped a bombshell on us.

Some bright spark at the paper uncovered the fact that, contrary to the story Linda Hawkins told of Joey returning to the flaming house to rescue his brother Danny, it was actually Danny who had rescued Joey. This was of no consequence to us, yet the *Star* was shedding some doubt about the authenticity of our fundraising events. This meant Alan and I had to do another round of interviews, stating the sole reason for the concert was to acknowledge Joey's bravery. Still it was an aggravation we could have done without.

Talent-wise, Glass Tiger were there at the beginning, Candi fit our demographic, and we were also solicited by Big Bang, a hot new A&M act who sounded just like U2. We tried for another major act, settling on the Jeff Healey Band. We also decided to replicate our Vancouver Music Express show by executing an all-star finale. Domenic Troiano and Ian Thomas were drafted to organize the all-star team, and we invited a host of talent to join forces in the group. Suffice to say, with all the publicity we generated the two thousand available tickets were snapped up within days.

With the holidays approaching, we decided it would be great if we could launch our new office with a major Christmas party. We pulled favours from all our brewery contacts and Molson, Labatt, Carling, and Budweiser all came through with crates of beer. Warner act The Razorbacks were booked to perform, and invites went out to about three hundred industry types for the December 11 party. On top of all this, I was about to pull a major coup!

While chatting with Warner's Roger Desjardins about our launch party he informed me Robert Plant was appearing in concert in Hamilton on the Friday before and was hanging around until Saturday (to visit with his then girlfriend, Canadian Alannah Myles). I jokingly suggested it would be great if Robert could drop by our office and cut the ribbon on our new offices. "Hey, you never know, I'll ask him," responded Desjardins.

Two days before the party, Roger called me and said, "Robert loves the idea of dropping by your party." He asked for directions but warned anything could happen so he would appreciate it if I didn't say anything. I kept my word, but on the off-chance Plant did put in an appearance, I grabbed a gold-microphone award that had been left over from our last show and had a thank you Robert Plant engraved on the faceplate.

On the night of the party, hundreds of people flooded into our office. The Razorbacks were playing when I received a phone call. "It's Roger with Robert," informed Desjardins. "We are about five minutes away." I notified Conny and then went to The Razorbacks' microphone (they were on a break) and made the announcement we were about to be visited by a very special guest ... Robert Plant.

The place went berserk. I asked everyone to be cool in the hope that we could get him to stick around. Five minutes later, Robert Plant arrived. I met him at our conference room and we guided him into the main area of the office where he posed in front of the Lado guitar, made a brief speech saying he was happy to be at our office, and cut the blue ribbon attached to the guitar. I handed him his gold microphone award and I was hoping he would stay in the centre of the office and circulate through our other guests.

But the crush became so intense that his security guard escorted him into Conny's office. Once safely out of the crowd he posed for photos (including a classic one of Conny biting his hair) and had a beer. Whilst talking to us, he spied the Glass Tiger cover issue that included a major feature of him promoting his *Now and Zen* release. "Hang on," he muttered. "I thought I was on the cover of that issue." He was — but on the U.S. cover! I explained how we did the split covers and did show him the U.S. cover that featured him, which seemed to placate him. I was hoping he would agree to stay for a while, but the crush from our guests eventually forced Robert to be smuggled out by Conny's entrance. It was a shame really, because had everyone been a bit more self-controlled, I am sure he would have stayed and maybe even jammed with The Razorbacks.

Robert's visit capped a year of success and made me think about how much we had accomplished with the mag. It was hard to comprehend Musicland was prepared to pull the plug just because they wanted total control. Surely they would realize the value we brought to the table and would be willing to build on that value. Yet going into the New Year, I had a bad feeling about the whole situation.

As we prepared for our big awards concert, first on the agenda was our execution of the Q-107 Rock Stop autograph sessions at the Speedorama automotive show scheduled to go at Toronto's CNE Automotive Building from January 27–29. In our agreement with the event organizers, we arranged for major Canadian bands and artists to attend autograph sessions in return for them donating ten thousand dollars to the Joey Philion fund. We had executed similar events with Speedorama in previous years, and this year would be a no-brainer as everyone had heard of Joey's story, and of our up-coming, now sold-out concert.

On top of all the positives, YTV, stationed directly across from our Jefferson Avenue address, asked if they could televise the awards for a two-hour special, which they would air nationally March 4. It took me about three seconds to approve that commitment. Then Wardair came on board and offered to fly in any talent we needed for the show. This allowed us to bring Candi in from Los Angeles, Colin James and Boulevard's Mark Holden in from Vancouver, and Luba in from Montreal at no cost to the fund.

As February 15 grew closer, I started to panic. Numerous visits to the club revealed the building was still under construction. I couldn't possibly see how they were going to have this place finished on time. And it wasn't like we had an alternate 2,300-capacity venue available to us. If we had to call off the gig and return the tickets, *Music Express* would be hit with a sizeable bill. Something I didn't want to contemplate.

Early on the evening of the fourteenth, Domenic Troiano and Ian Thomas organized our all-star-jam rehearsals at the venue. Fortunately, the club was rounding into shape. A few signs on the bathroom doors were missing, but the overall venue looked spectacular. Attending the rehearsal was an excellent gathering of talent, including Triumph's Mike Levine, Gil Moore and Rick Santers, Colin James, Dan Hill, Honeymoon Suite's Derry Grehan, Johnnie Dee and Rob Preuss, Frozen Ghost's Arnold Lanni, Lee Aaron, Alan Frew of Glass Tiger, Sass Jordan, Liberty Silver, Blair Packham from The Jitters, Paul McCann from Big Bang, Eria Fachin, Hugh Marsh, Sascha Turkash from Platinum Blonde, and Boulevard's Mark Holden.

The original plan was to rehearse two songs: The Traveling Wilbury's "Handle with Care" and The Beatles' "With a Little Help from My Friends," but the session was a little chaotic so it was decided just to go with the Beatles' nugget, which went down well during the run-through.

On the day of show, I was at our Jefferson Avenue office entertaining my brother Robert and his wife Monique, who had travelled down from Elliot Lake for the show, when we were hit by a bombshell. Despite Molson being a corporate sponsor and Scott McLean having months to organize it, the Liquor Control Board had rejected a liquor license for that night's gig. Citing an absence of a fire inspection, Mississauga Mayor Hazel McCallion's office made the decision. Great! We've got 2,300 people arriving for the opening of Ontario's largest nightclub, and the club can't sell them any booze!

Don Antle called to confirm McCallion's decision. But instead of admitting Molson might have dropped the ball in not working with the club to secure its liquor license, he blamed me for scheduling the event too early! I tried to calm him down. We agreed Molson could service the dressing rooms with product, and Antle agreed to donate a number of cases of beer for an after-party *Music Express* had scheduled for our guests.

Arriving at the venue late that afternoon, I immediately noted areas of concern. One big problem was a lack of parking spaces. Superstars was located at an industrial mall and shared parking space with a number of other companies. Yet the space designated for Superstars could only hold about two hundred vehicles, and we had over two thousand people arriving, the majority of them by car! As a result, vehicles would end up being abandoned up and down Dixie Road and ticket holders were forced to walk, in some cases a considerable distance, to the venue.

Inside the venue, it was obvious the place wasn't quite ready for business. There were still no designated signs on the washrooms, so we decided to make them unisex facilities for the evening. But more importantly, the Superstars staff looked lost and bewildered. We had asked for two people to service the main entrance when the flood of spectators began to arrive. Yet by 7:00 p.m., no one from Superstars was in position and Carole Marx George had to use her own people until we could convince Murray and McLean to provide staff for the door.

Our next problem was our VIPs, who entered the building from a side entrance. CMG had solicited a VIP list of fifty-six people, *Music Express* had kept our list down to a minimum and we had a list of talent and award presenters. Again, understanding we were limited to a strict maximum of 2,300 by the Fire Department, we told the Superstars people to keep their list down to a bare minimum. By 7:30, only thirty minutes before the start of the show, CMG had not received a list from Superstars. Then Carole was handed a list containing some forty names! And sure enough, all these people started pouring through the VIP entrance.

The YTV crew were there, and show host Laurie Hibberd (now Laurie Gelman, wife of *Regis and Kelly* producer Michael Gelman) asked for an event schedule, which I was in the process of completing while putting out sundry other fires. I had decided to use the same index card system I had used in all four previous award shows. Yet the evening's four hosts, Mike Levine, Gil Moore, Ian Thomas, and Q-107 radio DJ John Derringer, weren't quite in sync with this procedure.

I was set to go on first. I thanked everyone for supporting Joey Philion, apologized for the lack of booze, and then introduced Moore and Thomas, who greeted the night's first performers, Big Bang. Levine and Derringer then introduced Candi and her band to perform "Dancing under a Latin Moon." I was very impressed with their on-stage presence.

After a sizzling live performance from Jeff Healey, I went back on stage with Mike Levine and John Derringer. We presented the celebrity clips for Joey from Phil Collins, Robert Plant, Rod Stewart, and Bryan Adams. Joey Philion's parents and brother, Danny, were presented, and I was able to announce the event had raised forty thousand dollars for Joey's fund. Then the whole venue fell into total silence as we aired a special taped message from Joey himself, recorded from Sick Kid's hospital. Just to hear Joey's fragile voice brought home the true meaning of the evening's event and there wasn't a dry eye in the building.

Glass Tiger turned in a storming performance before we wrapped up the awards, with the Newmarket band winning two gold microphones. A problem arose when Cheap Trick's Robin Zander and Tom Peterson arrived backstage. We wanted to get them on the show, but all the presenters had been assigned. Jeff Healey, Tom Stephens, and Joe Rockman were meant to present Glass Tiger with their awards. I asked them if they would mind surrendering their spot to the Cheap Trick boys. Tom Stephens started to protest, but I pointed to his band on the cover of our current issue, and he understood I meant no disrespect. So in a surprise appearance, Zander and Peterson from Cheap Trick made the final presentations.

Then came the climax of our all-star band tearing into "With a Little Help from My Friends." Blair Packham took the lead as the stage filled with celebrities. DJ John Derringer took centre stage, obviously playing out one of his fantasies. Despite all the horrors and hardships, the end result was a classy show, a classy television broadcast (courtesy of YTV), forty thousand dollars in the bank for Joey Philion, and another triumph for *Music Express* magazine. And, although I didn't realize it at the time the show would be our last, it was a fitting way to end our years of staging the awards.

Of course, the Mississauga police did their best to put a damper on the night. They towed away a number of vehicles from around the club, including Domenic Troiano's car, and set up spot-checks on both sides of Dixie Road. Couldn't have had much luck though as no one at the club had been drinking! The Molson rep with the beer for our post-concert party almost drove off with it in his trunk, only for Robert Kunz to flag him down. For the record, Molson blamed us for the club not getting their liquor license and refused to pay eight thousand dollars to Joey's fund. Nice guys!

I finally mustered up the courage to send my response letter to Musicland. We backed off and offered them 65 percent of the U.S. operation, but we insisted that we retail 100 percent of the Canadian operation (rationalizing that Canada had no value to them). We also wanted to continue to print the Canadian version with our Toronto printers, but they could print the U.S. version with Donnelly. I also reminded them of the potential of our still-standing offer with Westwood One. I sensed something else was going on with them when I submitted the written proposal.

I was met both Eugster and Ross in New Orleans for the 1989 NARM convention that February. Ross acknowledged he had received my counter-offer and said that it was under consideration, but their demeanour to me was decidedly frosty, and I just knew something negative was brewing.

One positive occurrence at the conference was a re-acquaintance with Bruce Jesse, who had moved on to Los Angeles–based Wherehouse Records. His new company was being lauded by NARM as 1988 retail chain of the year. On hearing of my dilemma with Musicland, Jesse responded by saying, "If you ever lose Musicland, you can always come and work with us." An offer that would eventually prove necessary.

24

THE JUNOS

GET AN INSIGHT

The 1989 Juno Awards had returned to the more sensible date of Sunday, March 12, at Toronto's O'Keefe Centre. Having been forced to skip 1988 to facilitate the switch from that absurd November/December time slot, CARAS finally got with the times and hired John Brunton's Insight Productions to produce the first Junos in which artists would perform live. Brunton had established himself as a savvy producer of independent television documentaries with the ambitious *Heart of Gold* documentary to his credit.

I had been heavily critical of previous shows, but the 1989 telecast was pure magic. CARAS finally employed a charismatic host in Montreal's André-Philippe Gagnon, and the show's highlight was the induction of The Band into Canada's Rock And Roll Hall of Fame. The show was capped off with a performance by Band members Robbie Robertson, Rick Danko, and Garth Hudson, appropriately supported by Blue Rodeo.

You could sense by that performance The Band were passing their musical torch to Blue Rodeo, who also won three Junos that night for Band of the Year, Single of the Year ("Try"), and the Canadian Video of the Year, also for "Try." Robertson himself won three Junos, for Male Vocalist, Album, and Producer of the Year (shared with Daniel Lanois).

Unlike other years, it was hard to criticize other winners. k.d. Lang was acknowledged as Female Vocalist of the Year, ending Luba's three-year run, Glass Tiger were Entertainers of the Year, Sass Jordan was recognized as Most Promising Female Vocalist, Colin James took Most Promising

Male Vocalist, and Barney Bentall and the Legendary Hearts clinched Most Promising New Group.

Insight's revamping of the telecast was what made the show truly great. Even though the O'Keefe had been the venue of many previous Juno disasters, Brunton transformed the place. The sets and lighting were more professional, but the most exciting development was how he executed the live performances. To add tension, a huge clock counted down the seconds to the live broadcast as stage crew scurried around Colin James's gear. As the clock hit one second, the crew magically disappeared and Colin James launched into "Voodoo Thing," a raucous track which set a positive tone for the entire night.

"I only agreed to handle the production because one of my all time favourite bands, The Band, were being inducted into the Hall of Fame and I wanted to do them justice in the broadcast," noted Brunton, now a seasoned broadcasting vet whose credits include *Canadian Idol*, *Battle of the Blades*, Canada's *Amazing Race*, and Canadian productions of *Who Wants to be a Millionaire* and Howie Mandel's *Deal Or No Deal*.

"Up until 1989, the Junos' broadcast was like some bad game show. Ugly sets, badly lit, lip-synching talent. All played out before a couple of thousand industry types who sat on their hands and created no atmosphere," noted Brunton. "I wanted to create a rock 'n' roll feel with live performances and real fans in the building. I think we achieved that in 1989."

Brunton's big challenge was how to work the equipment switches in a confined space with limited breaks between sets. "There had been no precedence on previous shows. We had to figure out how to mic situations like The Men of the Deeps coming on stage from different entry points for Rita McNeil's 'Working Man' song and execute quick equipment turnarounds. We had the perfect host in Andre-Philippe Gagnon, whose whole shtick was music parody so he could fill in the gaps between acts." However, one technical glitch almost ruined Brunton's grand finale.

"It was all set for The Band to perform 'The Weight' as the show's finale with Blue Rodeo joining them," recalled Brunton. "I am at the back of the stage, André-Philippe is winding up is final dialogue when I noticed Robbie Robertson is executing a sound check and no sound is coming out of his guitar. We are into that twenty second countdown and we had a problem. I sprint over to the side of the stage and frantically signalled to André-Philippe to stretch his dialogue but it was too late as he had turned his back on me and was walking off.

"I thought 'Oh no!' The show had gone so well but now, for the grand finale, my icon, the guy who wrote all those great songs was going to get hung out to dry. Magically, right at the last second, some technician found the right input, the curtain parted, the lights went on, Robbie struck his guitar ... and sound came out! I was so overwhelmed, I started to cry."

Brunton passed on the next two Junos, but returned in 1992 when the Junos decided to expand the size of the venue to Hamilton's Copps Coliseum. "I missed the buzz of doing the show and I felt there was so much potential in taking the show to the people by staging it in Hamilton. Suddenly The Junos was a rock concert rather than an awards show. We had twelve thousand fans and three thousand industry delegates and the fans were at the front of the stage." The format was so successful Brunton's Insight Productions has continued to stage the Junos to this day.

The inevitable phone call finally came on Monday, March 26. It was Gary Ross on the line from Thailand saying that after further consideration, Musicland had declined our offer and were going in another direction. It would take me a few more weeks to find out what Ross meant by "another direction." It seemed that one of his golfing buddies was also a magazine publisher who agreed to publish a vanity magazine for Musicland and give them 100-percent ownership. Suffice to say, this guy apparently knew nothing about music and did not have the contacts we had developed over some twelve years of being in the business, yet this did not seem to matter to Musicland.

"I was shocked to hear Musicland had ended their relationship with *Music Express*, bringing the magazine into Musicland was one of my proudest achievements," acknowledged Bruce Jesse. "All my industry contacts were highly supportive of *Music Express*. They all felt the magazine provided a valuable marketing vehicle for them and for Musicland/Sam Goody customers. But you have to know that Musicland were totally arrogant. In retrospect it doesn't surprise me they wanted full control. At that time, they really thought the owned the entire music industry."

Conny and Allan were understandably shocked, but I wasted no time in calling Jesse. I told him the news, reminded him of his offer, and was soon en route to Los Angeles to reposition the magazine with Wherehouse.

Unfortunately, things got worse before they got better. That April, after I returned from L.A., I was greeted with the news *Music Express* had been rocked by the death of our copy editor, Dean Haynes.

Dean, aged thirty-six, had been employed by Conny to handle the stream of copy that came into our office for each issue and had helped in the stylistic evolution of the magazine. Everything seemed fine on Thursday, April 8 when Dean left our Jefferson Avenue office. Yet the following morning, he failed to show for work. That wasn't like Dean, and when Conny didn't receive a phone call from him she started to get worried. She called his apartment and didn't receive a response, so she went over to his place and banged on the door. Still no response! Conny spotted a police officer nearby and told him she was concerned about Dean's lack of communication. The officer told her Dean would have to be missing for twenty-four hours before anything could be done by the police.

Conny returned to the office and phoned Dean's brother Brent, who had briefly worked in advertising for us, and expressed her concern over Dean's absence. Brent didn't seem too worried until Saturday, when he dropped by Dean's apartment and found him unconscious on the floor. Dean was rushed to St. Michael's hospital, but died a week later. The cause of death was reported to be the accidental consumption of a diabetic pill that triggered a diabetic seizure in Haynes, who was not a diabetic.

A month before Dean Haynes died, he asked Conny if he she would hire an assistant editor to work with him. He needed someone with computer skills and had suggested Perry Stern. Stern is the first person to admit he and I were not friends prior to his employment at *Music Express*. Matter of fact, in researching this book, neither I nor Conny had any recollection on how Perry actually ended up with the job. I know Perry attended our opening ceremonies with Robert Plant, but I had seen Perry as a rival, having worked with our competition *Graffiti*. In the chaos around losing our Musicland deal and chasing Wherehouse as a replacement, I wasn't able to stay focused on our domestic operation and had left running things in our editorial department up to Dean.

Perry had pitched Dean on a couple of story ideas and had shown a prowess for computers. He had begun helping out informally before Dean's untimely death. Stuck for someone to take over Dean's job, and with a May deadline looming, Perry found himself dropped into the job. Kerry Doole had been working as associate editor and technically should have been promoted to Dean's position, but admitted he wasn't the most computer-savvy person around. As well, he was heading out on his annual jaunt back home to New Zealand at the time of Dean's death, so wasn't available for the position.

Stern's initial impact with *Music Express* was quite positive. Under his tenure, we started to feature bands like Lou Reed, The Cult, and David Bowie's Tin Machine on the covers as well as provide editorial coverage on the likes of Depeche Mode, Concrete Blonde, 10,000 Maniacs, and The Replacements, features that were well received by our readers. But what was sacrificed in the editorial department was a tight bond between the writers. I had always got along personally with the staff, Kerry Doole and Roman Mitz had been with us ever since we moved to Toronto some nine years before, and Tarin Elbert, Dianne Collins, and Lenny Stoute had always worked well together.

But with Stern assuming the editor's position, this environment changed dramatically. First off, let me say it wasn't Perry's fault. I should have been more focused on the editorial department and we should have taken some time out after Dean's death to appoint a new editor whose personality fit with the overall feel of the magazine. Instead, we panicked at the sudden loss of Dean and Perry was there to instantly fill that void. In taking up the position, Perry showed a disdain for Kerry and soon fell out with Roman Mitz, who had been a long-time *ME* servant and was overseeing our Budweiser Country Music section.

Haynes's death, coupled with our Musicland loss, had a major effect on my relationship with Conny. When the Musicland deal fell through, *Music Express*, which had set itself up as a major international magazine, lost our distribution base, causing much internal strain on Conny who blamed me for losing our Musicland deal. We broke up, and she eventually quit her position and sold me her shares.

Despite all this going on, we still had articles to write. My annual jaunt to interview Rush saw me head up Bayview Avenue to chat with guitarist Alex Lifeson at his Oak Ridges enclave. Lifeson was facing a crisis. He had to shed seven pounds in five days to win a bet with a friend. "We bet each other that we could lose twenty pounds in ten weeks, the loser buying the winner a suit of his choice. But that's not all," revealed Lifeson. "The loser has to pose in a skimpy Speedo swimsuit and pay for the winner to place the offending photo in the magazine or newspaper of the winner's choice with an appropriate caption. He didn't show up for our tennis match last night, so I think I'm in good shape."

The genesis for *A Show of Hands*, the band's two-disc live release they were promoting in this interview, was a decision to close off a chapter in the band's discography and also fulfill a record company obligation. "It either had to be a greatest hits or a live album, and since we had been taping dates during the Grace Under Pressure, Power Windows, and Hold Your Fire tours, we had a good cross section of different shows and different stages of playing to choose from."

Paul Dean marked the end of his tenure with Loverboy by releasing a solo album, *Hardcore,* on Columbia Records. Co-produced with the Headpins' Brian MacLeod, Dean decided to go solo after being replaced as co-producer on Loverboy's less-than-successful *Wildside* album. It didn't help matters when he dissed lead vocalist Mike Reno during a radio interview. "I said that radio needed a break from Mike Reno's voice," noted Dean. "I didn't mean to say it in a negative sense but I guess he took it the wrong way."

Kim Mitchell was about to release *Rockland,* his first album in almost three years. The first track is "Rocklandwonderland," an ode to Canada Wonderland's Kingswood Theatre, scene of several standing room only performances that had earned Mitchell the venue's coveted Gold Ticket Award. I first heard the song when Tom Berry, president of Mitchell's label, Alert Records, slipped a cassette into his high-tech Bose stereo unit and peered across the room with the furtive look of an expectant father to gauge my reaction. The song was a catchy, mid-tempo tune and Berry murmured something about this being the album's debut single. Next up though was "Rock 'n' Roll Duty," a sonic thrust of pure energy on which Mitchell and guitarist Peter Fredette chant in unison, "I'm just doing my rock 'n' roll duty, creating a buzz, buzz, buzz."

"That's the single," I said. "That's what Kim Mitchell is all about."

"Sounds a bit too hard for AOR radio," countered Berry. "It's not exactly 'Patio Lanterns,' is it?"

"Have you heard AOR lately," said I defensively. "The Cult, Queen, Great White. Radio rocks again."

Berry pondered the quandary for a moment, and then reached for the phone. "Hey, you know that video script for 'Rocklandwonderland?'" he asked the disembodied voice on the other end of the line. "Can we change it to 'Rock 'n' Roll Duty'?" Eventually both tracks proved to be huge hits for the album.

Kim Mitchell ambled into our office as though he was paying a social visit. In truth, he was set to adorn our August cover, and he anticipated my line of questioning about why he had not succeeded in cracking the U.S. market. He had come close when "Go for Soda," off *Akimbo Alogo,* had been adopted as an anthem for MADD (Mothers Against Drunk Driving) in the U.S. That had triggered a number of guest appearances on the morning chat show TV circuit. Yet true to Mitchell's honesty he refuted that the song had anything to do with drunk driving.

"Kim's too honest for his own good," reflected Berry. "He goes on *Good Morning America* in front of millions of people and says it *really* isn't an anti-drunk driving song. He could have milked it for all it was worth but he didn't."

"I was flattered," countered Mitchell. "And I did go along with that organization's sentiments. But I'd be lying if I said it was an anti-drunk driving song."

Recorded at L.A.'s One on One Studios, and produced by Paul Devilliers, who had just produced Mr. Mister's chart-topping debut, Mitchell had to work around Devilliers's busy schedule, but felt the final result was well worthwhile. As for his hopes of cracking the U.S. with "Rockland," Mitchell joked, "I feel like a sperm cell trying to penetrate an ovary. There's me and a half million other bands out there trying to achieve the same thing." Mitchell concluded our chat on a philosophical note. "If people like the songs, buy the records and the concert tickets, and play me on the radio, then great that's all I ask for. But when the audience is gone and I have to go and pump gas, then fine. I'll do that too."

Through the summer of 1989, the buzz had been about Tragically Hip's pending full-length debut. Capitalizing on MCA's heavy financial commit-ment, The Hip had been holed up at Ardent Studios in Memphis working with ace producer Don Smith, whose previous clients had been The Traveling Wilburys, Tom Petty, Keith Richards, and Roy Orbison. Released in September, *Up To Here* had critics and fans alike raving about tracks like "New Orleans Is Sinking," "Blow at High Dough," "Boots and Hearts," and "38 Years Old," with favourable comparisons to early Rolling Stones, R.E.M., and Georgia Satellites. Allan Gregg called me into his spacious Decima Research office on several occasions just so I could hear some of those early tracks

With MCA set to stage an album launch party for The Hip in Los Angeles, I agreed to fly out to attend the function and also join forces with

Allan to meet with Bruce Jesse at Wherehouse to try to resolve the impasse over introducing *Music Express* into their retail chain. In trying to replicate our Musicland distribution with other retailers, I had run into resistance with Wherehouse initially. I did find another outlet in Texas-based Sound Warehouse Records, who agreed to carry the mag in their stores. Wherehouse Entertainment eventually got on board and we then had a good chunk of the south and western U.S. covered.

"I had always retained an interest in launching *ME* into our stores but we needed a few months to sort out co-op advertising and how we could utilize the book," noted Jesse. "I recall meeting Keith and Allan at our Torrance head office, I believe the meeting was positive and I am sure we were able to structure an agreement. It would have taken us a few more months to get things together at our end."

Thursday, September 21, The Hip debuted their album at the famed Roxy nightclub on Sunset Strip. The club was packed with key media, retail types, and sundry mix and match hair-band members off MCA's roster, along with label president Irving Azoff. The Hip ripped through a brief set and tore the place apart. Punters in attendance were making comparisons like, "Just imagine if The Doors' Jim Morrison fronted the Rolling Stones?" Gord Downie's vocal presence was that mesmerizing, even Azoff was on his feet cheering. But you could tell those in attendance were as much puzzled as they were impressed by the band's live persona.

The Tragically Hip were performing that Saturday night at a club called Bogarts in Long Beach, and Allan and co-manager Jake Gold had invited my new wife Karen and me to catch the show and have dinner with them in advance of the concert. The club itself was unusual in that it was located right by the ocean and contained multiple boat slips to accommodate customers who simply sailed their boats into the club. The Hip themselves appeared lost as the middle act on a three-band bill and, over dinner, Allan and Jake both agreed there might be problems sending them out as an opening act. "If I was a headliner, I wouldn't want The Hip opening for me," observed Gold.

Both also realized *Up to Here* contained great tracks but were also aware that "Blow at High Dough" and "New Orleans Is Sinking" were not your typical U.S. AOR-radio fare. "Gord [Downie] couldn't write a hit single if his life depended on it," Gregg had told me earlier in the week. "He just doesn't write like that. There is nothing formula about his material. How well this plays in America, we'll just have to see."

Back in Toronto, Paul McCartney was in the midst of his first tour in thirteen years in support of his *Flowers in the Dirt* CD, with December 7 (my thirty-sixth birthday) set as his date at Toronto's Skydome. *Music Express* was executing a contest to send winners to his London, England, concert on January 19, and I was offered an opportunity to interview Paul before his Skydome concert. This was one of my dream interviews ... but I passed on it because Allan Lysaght also wanted an interview for our radio syndication and we only had one shot for the magazine.

So, being magnanimous, I turned my slot over to Allan and contented myself with attending McCartney's press conference, where I did ask him one question. As a consolation, I was offered an interview with his guitarist, Hamish Stuart, formerly with The Average White Band. Stuart proved to be a very colourful character. He informed McCartney had indeed organized a proper band, not just a bunch of studio drop-ins. Word at the time was how Linda McCartney was imposing a vegan regime on the rest of the band. "She tries," cracked the affable Scot. "But we sneak hamburgers when she's not watching."

With my accountant wife Karen's Ernst & Young boss, Kerry Gray, currently working as a tax consultant for McCartney's North American tour, we were given prime front row tickets — or so we thought. Though the seats were in the front row, we didn't realize until we got to the show that the front row extended from one side of the Skydome to the other, but McCartney's stage only took up the centre one third. From our vantage point to the left of the stage, we had a great view point of Linda McCartney plonking one finger on to obviously pre-programmed keyboards — with the occasional flash of the man himself.

Still he sang a number of hits, spanning from The Beatles to his solo career, mixed in the odd 50s classic ("20 Flight Rock"), and finished with the final medley on Abbey Road before the inevitable encore finale of "Hey Jude." Wife aside, McCartney recruited a great band and produced a totally memorable concert.

25

SAILING THROUGH
CHOPPY WATERS

John Brunton's refusal to produce the 1990 Juno Awards at the O'Keefe Centre Sunday, March 18 meant a return to CARAS's old lip-synch format, which that year was a good thing because one of the featured performers were Milli Vanilli, who were later busted for lip-synching their entire debut album. Also on the show was Rod Stewart, who created his own controversy by performing "Downtown Train," a song he had hijacked from Tom Waits.

Hosted by Rick Moranis, the 1990 awards were dominated by Alannah Myles who won Most Promising Female Vocalist, Album of the Year for her self-titled debut, Single of the Year for "Black Velvet," and Chris Ward took Best Composer plaudits for writing "Black Velvet." Other notable awards went to Kim Mitchell, Best Male Vocalist; Rita MacNeil, Best Female Vocalist, Blue Rodeo for Group of the Year, and The Tragically Hip for Most Promising Group.

The night's big event was the after-show party staged by Warner Music Canada at the top of the Sutton Place Hotel. I had scored a pair of invites, so my wife Karen and I cut out of the awards early to occupy a prime table at the party. A number of people had the same idea and we shared the elevator to the reception with SCTV's Eugene Levy.

Finding a table at the back of the room, but on an angle to the other tables, we sat down and waited. Before long, the place was full and our table selection proved to be astute. To our far right, Aerosmith's Steve Tyler and Joe Perry were seated with their group. To our left was a table occupied by famed producer

Quincy Jones, and literally right behind us sat Rod Stewart. Being a true Cape Bretoner, Karen pushed all protocol aside and quickly bounded over to chat fashion with Steve Tyler and get Rod Stewart to autograph a piece of paper for her mate Kim Meade. I was weighing up how I could introduce myself to Rod Stewart when Glass Tiger's Alan Frew plonked himself down at Rod's table. I strolled over to them and said, "Now there's a sight, a Celtic supporter [Stewart] talking to a Rangers supporter [Frew]," — the Glasgow Scotland teams I referenced were deadly enemies. Both laughed and Alan introduced me to Rod. So I sat down and we talked soccer for about thirty minutes with the 1990 World Cup about to be played in Italy as a point of conversation.

During this chat, Alan and Rod got talking about the Skydome and its notoriously bad acoustics. Rod was surprised to find out Alan's Glass Tiger had opened the building June 3, as he had been awarded a special plaque for staging the first concert June 8. While their conversation was in progress, Stewart sent one of his assistants back to his hotel suite who returned with the plaque which he presented to Frew. A firm friendship between Stewart and Frew was established which culminated with Stewart's management team (Arnold Stiefel and Randy Philips) briefly managing Glass Tiger, and Stewart making a vocal appearance on a Glass Tiger track "My Town."

Canadian rock bands who had been successful through the eighties found the changing musical scene difficult to adjust to. Platinum Blonde had shortened their handle to just The Blondes, and had seemingly shortened the band, with just guitarist Sergio Galli and drummer Sascha Tukatsch appearing at *Music Express* for an interview to promote their new *Yeah, Yeah, Yeah* release on Jeff Burns's Justin indie label. Lead vocalist Mark Holmes had moved out to L.A., where he was currently involved in a romantic relationship with *Facts of Life* TV star Nancy McKeon (who played Jo) and was also hanging out with *The Young and the Restless* soap star Michael Damien. Guitarist Kenny MacLean was enjoying success with his own solo album, *Don't Look Back,* with the title-track single generating decent airplay and winning MacLean a Most Promising Male Artist Juno nomination

Both Holmes and MacLean claimed they were committed to promoting this new Blondes release, but their absence from this interview spoke volumes to discount any such enthusiasm. Written and recorded in a small sixteen-track Toronto studio, with long-time sound man Michael "Spike" Barlow serving as producer, *Yeah, Yeah, Yeah* was definitely a budget affair.

"We didn't spend a million dollars like we did on the last one, but to my mind the results are just as good as *Standing in the Dark* and *Alien Shores*," muttered Galli, somehow keeping a straight face.

"There's no makeup, no hairstyles, no fashion statements — just a band called The Blondes," added Tukatsch, effectively summarizing the fatal flaw in their project. Without all the trendiest fashion that had made Platinum Blonde so special, they were perceived as just another pop band, one that soon faded into obscurity.

That summer's biggest domestic release followed a call from CBS inviting us to attend a press launch in the Laurentian Mountains north of Montreal where they were about to release the English debut record of a young Quebec talent called Celine Dion. Diane Collins attended the launch for *Unison,* which was produced by David Foster and featured a Laura Brannigan cover, "If You Asked Me To," as the key single.

Dion had been a teenage sensation in Quebec, recording eight top-selling Francophone albums in a span of eleven years. She even won the Eurovision Song Contest representing Switzerland. Under the Svengali-like direction of manager Rene Angelil, whose previous client was Ginette Reno, Dion mastered English and released her debut English-language album to overwhelmingly positive reviews.

Collins reported back that Celine was very shy and her ability to conduct English-language interviews was restrictive. Yet she possessed obvious talent and her debut was a major priority for CBS. So much so that the U.S. got on board and pushed the album to No. 4 on the *Billboard* charts, while it reached No. 6 on the Canadian charts.

Our annual January year-end-review issue featured our first interview with Celine Dion, who chatted with our New York bureau chief Tina Clarke about the events which led to her first English release, *Unison.* "In English, you can use one word and it means so many different things," allowed the twenty-three-year-old Dion in her thick French accent. "It's another experience singing in English. When I started working on the album, it was hard for me because I didn't understand every word. I said to the people that worked with me [including Grammy-award winning producer David Foster] to explain each word to me ten times, because the most important thing to me is to understand what I'm singing. I like to sing things that I feel."

Celine built up toward her *Unison* launch, by releasing two singles: her Aldo Nova–written "Have a Heart" and her duet with Billy Newton-Davis on Dan Hill's "Can't Live Without You." The album itself came out on April 2, 1990, and was preceded by a third single "(If There Was) Any Other Way." By the time Dion got around to covering "Where Does My Heart Beat Now" (originally recorded in 1988 by Laura Brannigan), released in October 1990, the album's momentum was building.

Our first year of the nineties was shaping up to be a great one when right out of the blue, *Music Express* was rocked by a bombshell. The VP of A&A Records called to inform that A&A had declared bankruptcy and they could no longer carry *Music Express* in their stores. We had just printed our February 1991 issue, which was full of A&A tagged ads. A&A represented our largest domestic distribution and we had initiated a highly successful Music in Motion program with them that allowed us to provide special promotion for new Canadian releases. The labels advertised new releases, A&A tagged these releases and provided special store display areas at a discounted rate, and we provided editorial coverage — a highly successful program now in jeopardy.

With the deadline for our March issue fast approaching, I was stumped as to how to cover for the loss of A&A. The most logical chain to approach was HMV, but we already had them covered with their own book! As I called around to sound out my options, a suggestion was made that I contact Saturn Distributors. Saturn was a product wholesaler, or rack jobber as they are known in the trade. Saturn orders product wholesale from the record companies and then redistributes them to accounts like Zellers and The Bay, and to smaller mom-and-pop stores nationally.

I made contact with Saturn president Leonard Kennedy, who invited me to meet with himself and VP Sal Zagorsky at their Markham head office. Kennedy, a burly gregarious character, was aware of *Music Express* and immediately offered to position *ME* with his accounts. "Instead of just A&A, we can position *Music Express* with a wide range of accounts, nationally," boasted Kennedy. "I don't think you will have problems securing ad support, working with us."

I had always thought of *Music Express* as being a trend-oriented vehicle, but there was nothing trend-oriented about being circulated through retail outlets like Zellers! Still with the deadline fast approaching, I reluctantly agreed to give Saturn a one-issue trial. Our resulting March issue, with Gloria Estefan on the cover, was tagged "Compliments of Zellers," and distributed as a giveaway in their stores with a number of record-company ads featuring the Zellers tag.

The book itself looked classy enough, it was one-fifth colour and sported a gold logo on the cover. Inside, aside from a feature on Gloria Estefan, we interviewed movie producer Oliver Stone on his forthcoming *The Doors* movie, ran a report from correspondent Jeffrey Jolson-Colburn on the ten-day debauchery that was the Rock In Rio Festival, and celebrated The Tragically Hip's sophomore *Road Apples* release by sending writer Tim Powis on a European jaunt with the boys where he caught them in small clubs in Berlin and Hamburg Germany plus a triumphant performance at a sold out Marquee Night Club in London.

Produced again by Don Smith, this time in New Orleans, *Road Apples* sold six hundred thousand units in Canada, produced two decent singles in "Little Bones" and "Twist my Arm," but made little impression on the U.S. The band wanted to title the album *Saskadelphia* (as in where the hell are we now?), but were convinced to change the title to *Road Apples*.

I invited the now pregnant Karen (with my son Kyle) to accompany me to the Junos in Vancouver, her first visit to the city, and I was also scheduled to head up a conference panel on. It was to be some on the pros and cons of signing in Canada. We arrived in Vancouver on Thursday, February 29, to be greeted by a blanket of fog and rain. Friday night a reception was held by the Canadian Country Music Association, and we engaged in a great chat with both Michelle Wright and George Fox. On the strength of Garth Brooks and the Urban Country Music in the States, country was attracting serious attention in Canada with Wright and Fox leading a charge that also included Prairie Oyster, The Good Brothers, and Charlie Major. The oddity was that year's female country music Juno winner was Rita MacNeil, who is a lot of things — but not country!

Saturday morning, I attended the Record conference and Bruce Allen was giving his General Patton state of the union address to the assembled delegates. At one point he said, "Success in Canada is not just being interviewed by Keith Sharp at *Music Express*!" which I thought was quite flattering. Then he went on to praise Allan Gregg and Jake Gold at Management Trust for staging a Tragically Hip concert the previous evening at The Town Pump, saying that by limiting the size of the venue and the amount of tickets available (four hundred and fifty), they created such a buzz that scalpers were asking for a hundred and fifty dollars a ticket outside. This compared to Celine Dion's performance the same night at the Queen Elizabeth Theatre, which played out to a half empty venue. According to Allen, Gregg and Gold got it right but Celine's people had gotten it wrong.

Instantly, Donald Tarleton (of Donald K Donald) bounded out of his seat and marched to the front of the stage to confront Allen. He identified himself as the promoter of Celine's concert, stated it was important that she play in the right venue (not some smoky bar), and that, in the end, their strategy would eventually pay off. Compare the future successes of Celine Dion and The Tragically Hip and it's pretty obvious who won that argument!

Paul Shaffer, David Letterman's band leader and a native of Thunder Bay, was that year's Juno host. Staged at the Queen Elizabeth Theatre, the show went down without any spectacular performances. Local boy Colin James won Best Male Vocalist and Best Album (*Just Came Back*), Celine Dion was recognized for her *Unison* breakthrough by winning Best Female plaudits, while Blue Rodeo christened their new *Casino* album by taking Group of the Year honours. Sue Medley, Andy Curran, and The Leslie Spit Treeo took the Most Promising awards, Leonard Cohen was inducted into the Hall Of Fame, and a big cheer went up for The Tragically Hip taking the publicly voted Entertainer of the Year award.

"We feel kinda like Carrie on prom night," cracked Hip guitarist Robby Baker on accepting the award — alluding to a perceived industry resistance to the band who had been bumped off playing the 1980 Junos by the late inclusion of Milli Vanilli and who weren't even offered a spot in the Vancouver show.

The next best line of the night came from Alias guitarist Steve DeMarchi. Making one of their few appearances in Canada, Alias were introduced on stage by Aerosmith's Steve Tyler, who butchered their intro calling them Ally-as! When it came turn for DeMarchi and Freddy Curci to present a Juno, DeMarchi cracked, "And we'd like to thank our new best friends, Aerosmyth!"

The spring of 1991 saw the release of Blue Rodeo's third album, *Casino*, as well as releases by promising new bands, The Reostatics (*Melville*) and Montreal's The Doughboys (*Happy Accidents*). Murray McLauchlan released his first album in three years (*The Modern Age*), and a much-talked-about debut by Winnipeg's Crash Test Dummies (*The Ghosts That Haunt Me*) came out as well. But the most anticipated new release was by Glass Tiger, and it launched in March.

Titled *Simple Mission*, the band's intent was to record a more rock-oriented album, with new producer Tom Werman (Poison, Cheap Trick, Ted Nugent) stripping down the band's sound and eliminating some of the keyboard arrangements that had been established by previous producer Jim Vallance.

Behind the scenes, things weren't going that well for the band. Drummer Michael Hanson had quit during the touring behind *Diamond Sun*, and U.S. co-manager Derek Sutton felt he had taken the band as far as he could. Many of the band's problems were due to the merger between Manhattan and EMI. The latter, not being familiar with the band's debut *Thin Red Line* exploits (despite their Grammy nomination as Top New Group), gave *Diamond Sun* limited support.

In preparing to release *Simple Mission*, speculation was that Capitol Canada president Deane Cameron was not satisfied with the treatment they had received from EMI and was forging plans to form his own U.S. label (tentatively titled Thunderbird Records). He also wanted the band to be more energetic and had his VP of A&R Tim Trombley work with the band to write more aggressive tracks.

"Not quite true," responded Cameron via his director of media communications, Anastasia Saradoc. "Dick Williams, former EMI U.S. employee, was planning to launch a new record label and Deane had targeted the new Glass Tiger album as the debut release. Unfortunately, Williams couldn't raise the necessary funds and the label didn't materialize." Cameron conceded Glass Tiger's album did get lost in the backlash.

"The whole mess was a real dog's dinner," snapped a disgusted lead vocalist Alan Frew. "Deane passed on a bunch of U.S. labels to release the album on his own label. And then when that fell through, none of the U.S. labels would touch it."

"I wanted 'My Town' to be the lead single," added Frew. "I had gotten to know John Candy, who did a great impersonation of Rod Stewart, and he wanted to direct the video and get Rod involved. I remember a confrontation with Tim Trombley when I said 'You can't be serious! We've got Rod Stewart to sing on "My Town" and you want to lead with "Animal Heart?"'"

"Of course, 'Animal Heart' stiffed and 'My Town' never got the exposure it deserved," reflected Frew. "It did go to No. 5 in the U.K. and it's still one of our most requested songs. I think Deane [Cameron] dropped the ball on that album. If he had allowed Manhattan to invest as much as they wanted to, we could have been huge in the U.S. But I believe Deane was afraid of losing us. And by the time his own record deal collapsed, the momentum behind *Simple Mission* was lost." Rod Stewart's manager, Randy Phillips, was brought in to try to salvage the project but even he found things too messed up and *Simple Mission* never did receive a U.S. release.

Internally, it hadn't helped that guitarist Al Connolly and bassist Wayne Parker had supported Tremblay's more rock-oriented stance, and this caused a major rift in the band. So much so that by 1992, Frew decided to leave Glass Tiger. "I was so upset with what had happened to 'My Town' I felt if I wanted to write a good pop song, I would have to do it on my own solo album," explained Frew. "Just before a gig at the Ottawa Civic Centre, I told the band I was leaving. As I walked out on stage for the final time [prior to the band's reunion], manager Gary Pring was right beside me and he said 'I'm coming too!'"

So how did Glass Tiger persuade Rod Stewart to sing on "My Town"? "Since Rod is my idol, I was just happy just to get to know him personally, have a few pints and talk about soccer," explained Frew. "But Paul Rafferty, who sang back-up vocals on *Simple Mission*, told Rod we had this great Scottish song that was perfect for him. So he turned to me and said, 'So when are you going to invite me to sing on it?'"

"We're in [Hollywood's] A&M Studios with Rod, Sam [Reid, band keyboardist] is working the console and I'm walking Rod through the lyrics. We get to this point where I look at Sam through the studio window, and it was like the realization hit us both at the same time. Here was the voice of 'Maggie May,' 'Gasoline Alley,' and all those great songs, singing one of our songs! It's the kind of magic money can't buy."

I made a trip to Los Angeles in May and squeezed in a visit to Morgan Creek Pictures' Burbank head office. Their publicity department was hyping up Kevin Costner's new *Robin Hood, Prince of Thieves* movie and they had something they wanted to play for me. Settled into their boardroom, I heard the distinctive voice of Bryan Adams singing the movie's theme song "(Everything I Do) I Do it for You." Great, melodic track, I thought. It reminded me of "Heaven."

Released June 10, 1991, "(Everything I Do) I Do it for You" quickly conquered the planet, topping the singles charts in sixteen different countries, spending fifteen weeks atop the U.K. charts, seven weeks on top of the U.S. *Billboard* charts, and nine weeks as No. 1 in Canada. All of which set the stage for the long anticipated release of Adams's new CD, *Waking up the Neighbourhood.*

A call from Bruce Allen signalled it was time for an audience with Adams to promote his new disc. I flew out to Vancouver mid-August and arrived at Bruce's Gastown head office where his publicist Kim Blake provided me with my first listen to Bryan's newly completed album and to view the video from Bryan's second single, "Can't Stop This Thing We Started." Pinned prominently on the office wall was a list of all the countries "(Everything I Do) I Do it for You" had charted in and it looked like a United Nations roll call. It had gone to No. 1 in a total of sixteen countries, plus numerous others where it was top ten. I can't think of any other song in memory that had taken the world so completely.

We went to a hotel on Robson Street and Bryan bounded enthusiastically into the boardroom. Having witnessed his rise to fame since his Sweeney Todd days, it was always a buzz to chat with Bryan and I do believe he appreciated the efforts I had contributed to promoting his career. Either way, there has always been a good rapport between myself and "The Adams." Certainly, he couldn't have asked for a better launching pad than the *Robin Hood* movie for his album's debut single, but he admitted things weren't all rosy between himself and co-writer Michael Kamen.

Kamen had originally wanted Chicago's Peter Cetera to sing the vocals, but when he experienced problems with the arrangement, he pitched the composition to Bryan and his current producer, Robert "Mutt" Lange, who wrote the lyrics and injected a more contemporary feel to the track. "Initially, Michael wasn't too thrilled with the results but we held our ground and said we either do it our way or forget it," reflected Bryan. "So Michael let it stand and I don't think he's complaining too much right now."

Kamen indirectly got his own back on Adams by arranging to bury Bryan's video appearance about five minutes into the closing credits of the movie. The video shoot itself, helmed by Julien Temple, wasn't a particularly pleasant experience. "It was shot first thing in the morning, on location on the coast of England and it was freezing cold," reflected Adams. "Just the band, standing by some river, lip-synching. I said to Julien, 'You're going to do something with this aren't you?' 'Sure,' he says. But he didn't. Wasn't my video so I couldn't say much."

Waking up the Neighbourhood marked a new relationship with producer Mutt Lange, who was famous for his efforts with Def Leppard, though equally famous for taking his time on projects. "There is no question, Mutt has a different style, but after what I went through on *Into the Fire* I had to do something different. Jim Vallance has been great [he co-wrote four tracks on the album] but I think he had hit his sell-by date. I needed a fresh approach."

Adams conceded *Into the Fire* might have been too radical a departure from his singles-laden *Reckless* release and did allow that touring with The Police, Peter Gabriel, and U2 on the 1990 Amnesty Tour affected his mind-set in writing new material. "When Peter Gabriel is singing stuff like 'Biko' and I'm singing 'Kids Wanna Rock' there's obviously a disconnection. So my response was songs like 'Heat of the Night,' which wasn't a big single, but it allowed me to say something political in a song. The album might not have sold as well as *Reckless,* but I look at it as a transitional album. I was proud of that record."

Entering September I had to be careful as Karen was due to deliver our baby sometime in the middle of the month, but I did opt for another quick trip out to Vancouver, courtesy of Capitol Canada. They had arranged for a showcase for Kelowna's Grapes of Wrath, who were debuting their new album *These Days* at a club on Granville Island. Magazine editor Mary Dickie and I flew out with the Capitol contingent and we settled into the luxurious Bayshore Inn, right by Stanley Park. The itinerary included a boat ride on the Burrard Inlet where we listened to some of Capitol's fall releases before the boat sailed to Granville Island where we disembarked to catch The Grapes' gig.

We were on board the boat, cruising around Vancouver's scenic harbour on a sunny September day, partying away. The new songs started playing, and there's a single by Tina Turner, "Love Thing," not bad, followed by one from Richard Marx, "Keep Coming Back," which was okay. But then they started playing this new track by Tom Cochrane, "Life Is a Highway." Wow — what the hell was that?! The boat was rocking, people were dancing. As soon as it finished, I asked them to play it again, which they did. I thought to myself, "Tom me old son, you just hit the jackpot."

The Grapes of Wrath were pleasant enough in a Byrdsish kind of way, and we all went to an Indonesian restaurant somewhere in mid-town. But over dinner the conversation was still dominated by Cochrane's new single and his upcoming album, *Mad, Mad World*, which had been recorded in Memphis with producer Joe Hardy and finished at Mississauga's Metalworks.

In talking to Kerry Doole, Cochrane noted that the chief inspiration for *Mad, Mad World* came from a World Vision trip to Africa on a fact-finding mission for the Thirty-Hour Famine cause. "Before, I'd been very critical of Live Aid, as I thought there would be a backlash, but my opinion changed with this trip. I found out from missionaries in Ethopia that at least four million lives were saved in that one year, basically through Bob Geldof."

Working in Memphis with Producer Joe Hardy was a revitalizing experience for Cochrane, who found himself free of the last of Red Rider with the departure of long-time collaborator Ken Greer. "Memphis is just a great place to make a record," buzzed Cochrane. "And the bluesy, southern R&B feel of some of my songs sounded as though they should be recorded there. For a producer, I wanted someone who could get a great guitar sound and I liked the sound Joe got on Colin James and ZZ Top records."

With other tracks like "No Regrets" and Annette Ducharme's "Sinking Like a Sunset," and new U.S. management with Danny Goldberg (also in charge of Blue Rodeo), *Mad, Mad World* eventually hit one million copies. "Life Is a Highway" reached No. 1 in Canada and the album would enjoy similar success when released in the States the following February.

Promotion for Rush's new album, *Roll the Bones*, was in danger of being put on hold in fall of 1991 when the Toronto Blue Jays made (and eventually won) the World Series. Baseball fanatic Geddy Lee was not one to miss games, and his team's success came at potential cost of his band's.

Like other releases, *Roll the Bones* reflected a specific conceptual theme, that of chance and how it plays a role in people's lives. But, as Lee pointed out, "There's many layers and twists to that theme. It's about those unsolicited appearances. About the best laid plans gone to hell because of a strange twist of fate. It has a lot to do with the random equation of life. You think your life is organized but there's always that random element which will continually change things, the elements which separate the winners from the losers."

Roll the Bones immediately hit No. 3 on the *Billboard* charts which triggered talk within the band of a major North American tour followed by potential European dates. Like *Presto*, *Roll the Bones* was produced with English studio wiz Rupert Hine, who Lee says has helped create some artistic tension in the trio's performance to loosen up their natural tightness. "When you've played together for seventeen years, that tightness of performance comes naturally to us," noted Lee. "What Rupert has helped us do is become more relaxed and casual without being sloppy. He's pushed us to get a good live sound before we start applying the technology."

By the end of 1991 I felt like the circus guy who is juggling balls. I battled to continue making *Music Express* relevant in the U.S. by trying to expand our circulation to a number of regional American outlets. But even though the American labels still supported our mag, it was getting increasingly difficult to maintain our circulation.

26

STILL

SURVIVING!

A&A Records were back in business due to refinancing, and *Music Express* resumed our relationship with them for our August 1991 issue. We had been doing okay after establishing a relationship with Music World and Sunrise record stores, but neither chain was aggressively supporting our book. When A&A came back, they promised to re-establish their previously level of support. I had originally hoped we could slip *ME* back into A&A and still maintain circulation with Music World and Sunrise. But as soon as the November issue of *Music Express* appeared in A&A stores, Terry Stevens, who was now at Music World, called to complain about a conflict with the book and informed they would be pulling *Music Express* from their stores with Sunrise following suit soon afterwards.

To further complicate matters, I was visited by the building owner of 47 Jefferson Avenue who informed me he was in the process of selling the building, so our lease would be terminated and we should start looking for alternative space. Fine by me, as our present location was too big and we were paying too much in rent. I started scouring the neighbourhood and located an ideal option in a block of office space located at the corner of Dufferin and Liberty. The complication occurred when the owner of our Jefferson building informed me he had sold the building on condition that we agree to continue with our existing lease, something I flatly refused to do; he had presented us with the perfect out to our lease, so we had decided to take it.

Saturday, January 25, I gathered our staff at Jefferson, rented a truck and did a "moonlight flit," moving our 47 Jefferson Avenue office to our new location at 219 Dufferin Street. We knew that there would be some objection from the Jefferson's new owner but my opinion (supported by legal counsel) was that it wasn't our problem.

Indeed, the new owner, realizing we had vacated the premise, went absolutely ballistic. He reached me on the phone, started to scream at me and threatened lawsuits at me, Conny, Allan Gregg, and anyone connected with the company. I stayed firm on our decision and eventually the guy realized he didn't have a legal leg to stand on and, eventually, gave up on any claim against us.

As the 1992 Juno Awards approached at the end of March, a major controversy broke out. CARAS determined that Bryan Adams's *Waking up the Neighbourhood* release did not meet Canadian content regulations due to the involvement of British-based producer Mutt Lange. This meant Canadian radio couldn't include tracks off the album in their 30 percent Canadian quota. Both Adams and his manager, Bruce Allen, went ballistic and generated plenty of negative press against CARAS, calling it an affront to even suggest Adams wasn't Canadian.

CARAS got their own back during the Juno telecast. The show itself (back under the direction of John Brunton's Sound Insight Productions) was billed as a battle between Bryan Adams and Tom Cochrane. Each boasted No. 1 singles and diamond-selling albums, and neither particularly liked the other. Certainly there was no love lost between Cochrane and former manager Bruce Allen. Cochrane had written a song ("Citizen Kane") about Allen and had famously brawled with his tour manager, Graeme Lagden, in Halifax before pulling the plug on his relationship with Allen.

In reality though, there should have been no contest between Adams's "(Everything I Do) I Do it for You" single and Cochrane's "Life is a Highway" for the Single of the Year. Adams's song went to No. 1 in sixteen different countries, including seven weeks at No. 1 in the States, fifteen weeks No. 1 in the U.K., and nine weeks at No. 1 in Canada. For the life of me, I cannot think of one other song in the history of modern music which achieved such complete global domination. Certainly The Beatles, for all their success, never recorded a single which commanded the charts in so many countries at the same time. By comparison, "Life Is a Highway" only briefly topped the Canadian charts and had only just been released in the States (top position, No. 6).

Yet CARAS, in their infinite wisdom, gave the Single of the Year Juno to Cochrane's "Life Is a Highway," along with Best Male Vocalist, Best Album for *Mad, Mad World,* and the Songwriter of the Year, basically telling Adams to fuck off in the process! Adams did win Entertainer of the Year (which CARAS doesn't control) and co-producer of the year (with Mutt Lange). To top it off, CARAS invented a bogus "International Achievement Award," which basically recognized Adams's global achievements ... but not in Canada!

Personally, I was happy Tom's achievements had been recognized, yet it was so evident CARAS had played politics to stick it to Adams and Allen. When you consider the global success Adams's album and single achieved that year, it cheapens the awards when they're presented to someone else. But as I have chronicled in the past, CARAS had a history of questionable decisions and this was just another one that was par for the course.

Another band seemingly in CARAS's doghouse was The Tragically Hip, who lost the Group of the Year Juno to newcomers the Crash Test Dummies despite racking up platinum sales for their second album, *Road Apples.*

Someone appearing on the scene for the first time was Ottawa teenager Alanis Morissette, who won the Most Promising Female Vocalist Juno and whose "Too Hot" track was nominated in both Single of the Year and Best Dance Recording categories. Morissette had originally come to the attention of MCA's A&R chief John Alexander at the age of nine. He kept her under his radar, and Alanis became a protégé of One to One artist Lesley Howe, who helped Alanis in developing her own writing and performing prowess. At the age of eleven, Morissette appeared on the CTV/Nickelodeon show *You Can't Do That on Television* and was a regular singer of the national anthem at Ottawa Senators NHL hockey games and other major sporting and cultural events around the Ottawa area

It was during such a performance at the World Figure Skating Championships that Morissette drew the attention of local entertainment manager Stephen Klovan, who took Morissette under his wing, funded an expensive video in Paris of one of her tracks, "Walk Away," and encouraged her development with Howe. After all this, Alexander thought the time was right for MCA to step in. Debbie Gibson and Tiffany had already established themselves as teen stars in the States, and in April 1991, MCA released Morissette's debut *Alanis* album, which featured future Friends star Matt LeBlanc in the video for the "Too Hot."

Sadly, right after the Junos our relationship with Alan Lysaght and our *Music Express* radio syndication program came to an end. J.D. Roberts had hosted the first year, and when he left to pursue a news-casting career, Chris Ward took over briefly. When he didn't work out, John Derringer assumed control for the last two years. Unfortunately, Q-107 had started to develop their own Rock Radio Network syndication and felt our show represented competition so they eliminated the *Music Express* show from their station list. Without Q-107 we lost our credibility and Lysaght felt he couldn't maintain the sponsorship needed to continue the show.

The end of April brought the sad news of Brian "Too Loud" MacLeod's death. Formerly of Chilliwack and the Headpins, MacLeod succumbed to cancer on April 25, at the age of thirty-nine. A battler to the end, MacLeod produced and played on Chrissy Steele's *Magnet to Steele* record in his final months, preferring to go out with a bang rather than a whimper.

Late spring marked the release of Celine Dion's self-titled second album. Celine had established herself as the Queen of the Canadian Music Industry with two back-to-back Juno wins for Best Female Vocalist. She started the year singing her "Beauty and the Beast" duet with Peabo Bryson at the Academy Awards (where it won Best Song), and when our Tim Powiss caught up with her, Dion was buzzed that her latest LP contained a track written especially for her by Prince ("With this Tear").

For the July issue, one of our U.S. correspondents, Bert Van De Camp, tracked down U2's Bono. The band were about to start their Zoo TV Tour, a highly ambitious multi-media concert presentation that feature multiple video screens, upside down Trabant automobiles, fake satellite towers, sub-liminal messages, and bogus phone calls to the White House.

"Most times we're sick of the album by the time it's released, but this time it was different," said Bono of *Achtung Baby*. "I don't know what it is. You can put a band like U2 on automatic pilot and it will fly by itself for awhile. Success is not a problem for this band, but working constantly, that's almost impossible. This band is so elusive that I think we would quit if we no longer had the impression we were giving it our best. That day will probably come. As of yet, however, that is a long way off."

On July 5, Canada lost another top musician. Helix guitarist Paul Hackman was killed when the band's equipment van swerved off the road near Merritt, B.C., and rolled down a forty-foot embankment. Paul was asleep in a seat behind the driver at the time of the accident and was not wearing a seat belt, causing him to be thrown clear of the vehicle. He was forty years old.

For the August issue, I was determined to pull out all the stops. We introduced a new columnist, former *Partridge Family* TV show member, Danny Bonaduce. Bonaduce had been on one of those where-are-they-now-themed chat shows with a collection of former child stars, and I was taken aback by his knowledge of present music culture. He mentioned on the show he was short of cash, so when I found out he was appearing at the Toronto Yuk Yuk's comedy club, I arranged to meet him.

We met in the foyer of the Sutton Place Hotel. He seemed to be quite an affable character so I pitched him the opportunity to write a freelance column about any topic he wanted pertaining to entertainment culture. He asked for six hundred dollars U.S., which was a bit steep for us, but I gambled the celebrity status he brought to *Music Express* would solidify some of the U.S. retail targets I was pursuing. Bonaduce's column created quite a stir with our readers — some positive, some negative — but it did spark write-ups in both New York's *Village Voice* and in *Billboard* magazine.

Toronto's Barenaked Ladies was a band I *never* thought would catch on in the States. Initially a novelty act, they recorded an indie cassette in guitarist Ed Robertson's basement. A track off that cassette, "Be My Yoko Ono," was picked up by CFNY's Hal Harbour and quickly became one of the most requested songs on the station's rotation. They had earlier come to the attention of Ultrasound club agent Yvonne Matsell who booked them every Monday from October to December. At first, the Ladies busked outside the club to draw an audience, but by December they were busking between sets to people standing four deep in line to get into the club.

Having established a reputation at CFNY and had their Yoko song featured on the station's *Music Search* compilation CD, BNL members

Stephen Page, Ed Robertson, Tyler Stewart, and the Creegan brothers, Jim and Andy, then came to the attention of CBC Radio's Peter Gzowski who championed them on his *Morningside* morning show. In August 1991, they recorded a seven-song CD with producer Danny Greenspoon, funded by CBC Variety Recordings, which distributed the disc to CBC affiliates for airplay.

At the same time, WEA Canada publicist Nigel Best was driving home from work when he heard BNL being interviewed on CFNY. "I laughed so hard I had to pull my car over to the side of the road," Best told *ME* writer Howard Druckman. As publicist for WEA Canada, any involvement with BNL would be construed as a conflict of interest. However, that was resolved when WEA fired Best in the fall of 1990. March of 1991 saw Barenaked Ladies at the South By Southwest Festival in Austin Texas, where they earned a standing ovation, and at the New Music Seminar in New York that June, where they offered a free busking wake-up service for drowsing delegates, drew a crowd of over three hundred spectators whilst busking in Central Park, and even met Sean Ono Lennon, who said he liked that song about is mom.

November 1991 saw the band win three CFNY CASBY Awards and also a cheque for one hundred thousand dollars as winners of the station's Discovery-to-Disc record grant. This money was used to record their debut *Gordon* disc with no debt and no interference from any record company. The Barenaked Ladies also recorded "Lovers in a Dangerous Time" for Intrepid Records' *Kick at the Darkness,* a Bruce Cockburn tribute record, and the accompanying video went on heavy rotation at MuchMusic.

More publicity followed when then Toronto mayor June Rowland banned BNL from the city-sponsored New Year's Eve party because of the band's sexist name. All of which sparked further publicity for the band which by this time had sold over 75,000 copies of their indie cassette — the first indie cassette to reach gold.

I first met the band when they performed at the YTV Awards, which honoured young people for various achievements. The Barenaked Ladies performed "Be My Yoko Ono" and were hilarious. After their show I wandered over to the bar just as lead vocalist Stephen Page was buying a drink. "Excuse me sir, but I'll need to see ID for you to buy that drink," said I in the most officious tone possible. Page turned around, white as a sheet, and started to stammer an excuse and I burst out laughing, introduced myself, and congratulated him on the band's performance.

The grant from CFNY allowed the Barenaked Ladies to spend three weeks in March recording their debut album at Le Studio in Morin Heights. "It let us make a real record, instead of saying, we can't afford to do that," explained drummer Tyler Stewart to an *ME* interviewer. "Just picture three feet of hard-packed snow, a beautiful frozen lake, a mansion to live in, skiing and walking across the lake every morning, recording and coming back to catered French cuisine."

Upon completion of the record (produced by veteran Toronto producer Michael Phillip Wojewoda), the band was inundated with offers before signing with Seymour Stein's New York–based Sire Records, also home to Madonna. "We're anxious for *Gordon* to come out," said bassist Jim Creegan on the eve of its release. "It's a stage that we've gone through, and now we've got to put it out and move on. We've already written new songs, played them live and we're excited about them."

On the East Coast, grunge mania was taking over as Geffen, the L.A.-based label that had signed Nirvana and helped trigger the grunge movement, had scooped up locals Sloan for a two-record deal. Halifax, with its two universities and scores of local clubs, was a scene waiting to be discovered. Following the signing of Sloan by Geffen, Seattle indie label Sub Pop, which had released Nirvana's debut *Bleach* album in 1990, soon follow suit by signing Moncton's Eric's Trip and Halifax all-girl band Jale, thus triggering a minor East Coast music explosion.

"The whole business is very cartoon and parody-able," said Sloan vocalist/bassist Chris Murphy to writer Karen Bliss. "Since February, our music is not only considered good but also commercial — since Nirvana. I'm starting to take myself seriously, which is dangerous."

The band's EP *Peppermint* sparked all the fuss and Geffen took three tracks off the recording — "Underwhelmed," "Markus Said," and "Sugartime" — to add to the full CD release titled *Smeared*, which was also independently recorded but mixed and mastered by Geffen in L.A. "It's a crude recording, lovely and independent sounding," said Murphy. "I like to keep a pop sensibility. With all the noise, it's important to keep something hummable. I don't want pure ugliness. I want sweetness or beauty somewhere in there."

December's issue marked the finale of Danny Bonaduce's column. Conny had returned to *ME* as an accountant and had gotten into a dispute with Danny over how fast he expected to get paid. Conny concluded the conversation by telling Bonaduce his services were no longer required! I tried to call Danny back at his home in Philadelphia, but he wouldn't respond to my messages, so maybe he wanted his deal terminated.

27

AND IN

THE END

So where did it all go wrong? To this day, I still replay in my mind the string of events that led to the demise of *Music Express*. It all happened so fast and so unexpectedly.

I suppose the writing was on the wall when Bruce Jesse's employment at Musicland/Sam Goody was terminated. He had quarterbacked the deal and had been the go-to guy in the ongoing relationship between our two companies. Only after the fact would I learn I had been dealing with the wrong guy!

The villain of the piece turned out to be VP of marketing Gary Ross. It was he who fired Jesse and it was his decision to end our agreement and instead implement their own book in conjunction with one of his Minneapolis golfing buddies.

From that initial meeting in New York, I was confident I had secured *Music Express's* future as North America's number one music magazine. Yet in all my euphoria, I should have been reminded of a movie I had seen years before, *Oh Lucky Man*. The movie tells of a Northern English tea salesman (played by Malcolm McDowell) who encounters a series of escapades on his retail rounds. The movie's message being: when things are at their lowest, something positive happens — yet when things are at their highest, something negative pulls the rug out.

Los Angeles–based Wherehouse Entertainment and Dallas-based Sound Warehouse had been operating as our sole U.S. distribution outlets. We eventually secured a third distributor when a small Nashville-based chain called Cats joined us after a thirty-minute meeting. But by September 1992, our U.S. distribution system was too patchy and we were starting to get pressured by our printer Metroland over our mounting print bill, which we struggled to pay. The final blow came in January 1993 when Bruce Jesse called to say an internal conflict had resulted in Wherehouse losing their co-op funding. They could no longer support advertising in *Music Express*. To quote the great hockey player Tiger Williams, "We were done like dinner."

The blow of losing Wherehouse was just too much to take and it looked like we were toast. But then Allan Gregg had a better idea. Despite the fact his wife had been stricken with terminal breast cancer, Allan still found to time to pledge support for a revamped *Music Express,* with him taking over as publisher and me retaining my role as editor and advertising manager.

As *Music Express* had incurred considerable losses, Allan told me I had to bankrupt the magazine for him to pump fresh revenue into a new operation. This meant the *Music Express* name was dead and we titled the new project *Soundcan*.

The arrival of Allan Gregg as Publisher could have sparked the renaissance of *Music Express/Soundcan* as a solid Canadian operation — but it didn't! Allan was head of the influential Decima Research, which boasted all sorts of advertising agency contacts, and his role as manager of The Tragically Hip meant he was well connected and well respected by the music industry. Yet throughout 1993, the whole operation fell apart.

First off, he fired Conny Kunz, whom he had hired to design the book. Unfortunately for him, he fired her while she was still designing an issue. She refused to finish the job, and it was only when I gave her some of my ad commission funds that she agreed to release the book in time for our deadline.

Allan decided to again rename the magazine, this time *Impact,* and hired a new designer, Paul Sych, whose claim to fame was his work on designing new fonts. This meant that each page layout looked like a Rorschach inkblot test. Gregg then fired Robert Kunz as circulation manager, even though Robert was doing a terrific job working with our Canadian distributors. His replacement, Ian Marchant from Virgin Records, had no clue about distributing magazines, but it was pretty clear Gregg had other plans for Marchant.

Considering both Conny and Robert Kunz had got the boot, you didn't have to be Einstein to figure out who was next on his chop list! First he sent a memo telling Mary Dickie she was the new editor-in-chief and that I should concentrate on ad sales. Then one Monday morning I arrived at the office to find a terse memo on my desk declaring that Ian Marchant was the new publisher! Of course, I wasn't consulted on any of these decisions in advance.

My only consolation was that I was selling all the ad space and Gregg couldn't possibly interfere with that ... but he did. Over the years I had developed great relationships with the people at Bacardi, who annually committed to several ad pages per issue. I also had a good relationship with Maxell tapes, via ad manager Ted Vance, who always bought a full-page ad in each issue. Yet when their contracts came up for renewal, Gregg and ad assistant Kathy Bortoluzzi conveniently attended these meetings behind my back and told my clients I was no longer involved with their account. I knew I was a dead man walking. I could see *Impact* was doomed.

The end for me came on Friday, January 21. I was supposed to travel to Montreal on the Sunday to attend a series of meetings, yet Allan's accountant was being evasive about giving me the funds for the trip. The explanation for his odd behaviour was revealed when Gregg arrived for his customary Friday afternoon meeting — only this time to tell me I was no longer employed by *Impact* magazine.

I was momentarily stunned, but at the same time almost relieved — it wasn't like this came as a shock. Allan agreed to pay me until the end of February and he allowed me to take all the gold and platinum albums that had been issue to me and *Music Express* magazine. Kerry dropped by to offer his commiserations — but no one else did! So I called up Conny and Robert, gave them the news which they had been fully anticipating, and the three of us went to the pub and got drunk!

At the end of the day, Allan fancied himself as a music magazine publisher and felt he could do it without my involvement. He quickly realized that his political ties meant nothing when it came to creating a viable product and selling enough ad space to support that product. I knew how to do it and he didn't. I knew *Impact* was doomed!

28

PHOENIX RISING

So what happened to me when I walked out the door at 219 Dufferin Street for the final time?

Well, after a couple of days of mourning I phoned Tony Tsavdaris, who had just returned from the MIDEM conference in the South of France with Jeff Burns, and offered my services working press and promotions for his fledgling Strawberry Records (no relation to the U.S. operation). As I had been on salary at *Imapct*, I could claim unemployment insurance for about six months, so I offered to work free for that time with an understanding Tony would make me an offer of employment if things panned out. Tony could hardly refuse that offer. In March 1994, I got to see how the other side lived by working for Strawberry Records. To show I was serious, I brought along my first signing for the label, the Wild Strawberries.

Tony's office was an interesting setup. It was situated above Tony's East strip club, which he operated with his two brothers. One perk was you could call down to the kitchen at lunch and have an order delivered up to you by Ms. Nude Nova Scotia or someone else on the roster that week — although they were usually clothed at the time.

Working with Tony and Jeff, whose indie label was distributed by A&M, I was involved in new releases by Paul Dean, Virginia Storey, Slik Toxik, The Blushing Brides, and Rhymes with Orange. Strawberry Records nearly pulled off signing Moist, but the band ended up elsewhere.

What happened next probably deserves a book of its own. After spending about nine months recharging my batteries, I found myself wanting to re-launch a music magazine. I had been monitoring what was happening at *Impact*, and it came as no surprise to me that Alan Gregg pulled the plug on that endeavour when he realized that it wasn't easy running a music magazine.

With *Impact* in its death throes, I sensed there was still a need in Canada for a rock music magazine. Remembering that Q-107 Radio had developed a national radio-syndication network, I envisioned a print magazine that could operate as a companion to their network.

I contacted Danny Kingsbury, who was general manager at the station Q-107, with my proposal and I encountered a positive reception. It didn't hurt that Kingsbury and the entire Q-107 team had been familiar with *Music Express* and they could see the benefit of a companion print vehicle for their radio programming. Kingsbury set me up with one of the station's salesmen, a Welsh geezer called Chris Parfitt. We met at a pub at the intersection of Sheppard and Yonge and quickly agreed on how our new magazine, which I titled *Access,* would work with the station.

Tony Tsavdaris, sensing *Access* would be a great way to promote his roster, loaned me the funds to print our first issue. I had little trouble rounding up some of my old advertisers (Maxell, Bacardi, Molson) and in May 1995, the debut issue of *Access* was launched, with a cover feature and photo of Pink Floyd. Just as *Access* hit the record shops, *Impact* finally pulled the plug on their ill-fated publication.

Access served as Canada's rock magazine, but compared to *Music Express*, it rated as a bad sequel to a good movie, despite the efforts of editor Sean Plummer. From its inception in 1995 until its final death in 2010, *Access* unsuccessfully fought against drastic changes within the industry. Record stores, our primary source of distribution, were disappearing. Major record companies were amalgamating (we are now down to just three multi-national companies: Warner Canada, Universal, and Sony/BMG), and independent labels were being driven out of business by a lack of retail distribution.

Worse still, the 2008 economic recession meant that all of our key corporate advertisers began cutting back or disappearing. It was at this time that I started to warm to Doug Wong's prompting to write a book about my experiences operating *Music Express*.

The problem was that in my departure from *Music Express*, I had lost all my files, even the very first issue of *Alberta Music Express*. This problem was solved when Martin Melhuish suggested that I call Brock Silversides, who is the curator of the University of Toronto's library. He mentioned that he had just donated all his back issues of *Music Express* to the library.

Silversides, whose brother Lee worked for both A&M and Island Records, granted me instant access to the magazines, and I was like a kid in a candy store when I found myself surrounded by stacks of back issues. With this material, I could go right back to the first issues and chronologically map out the history of *Music Express* while acquiring quotes for this book.

I was enjoying writing this book so much that I was quite prepared to kick *Access* into touch. With the advent of the Internet and social media, the music industry as I knew it was dying, and magazine publications in particular were a doomed entity. When my former printers, Web Offset, decided *Access*'s fate for me by pulling the plug on my company, I became totally focused on finishing this book.

However, I did need to generate an income in the meantime, so in December 2010 I found myself working as a security officer for G4S, scrounging up what spare time I could muster to finish off the book.

What I did find, to my amazement, in updating information for my book is that the majority of all the bands I wrote about were still operational and were very receptive in recalling stories and anecdotes for the book.

Which brings me to August 28, 2012. I was working at the CNE — one of G4S's annual assignments — patrolling the midway concert stage and beer garden, making sure no miscreants wandered away from the cordoned-off area with their bottles of beer. I noticed that Trooper was performing at the band shell, so I used my night off to check out my old mates.

Trooper were amazing that night. Some fifteen thousand fans congregated in front of the band shell, older fans at the back and younger fans in the middle. The biggest surprise though was the kids at the front, rocking to "Raise a Little Hell" and "Here for a Good Time" and asking each other, who are these guys?

I met up with the band at their merchandise tent after the gig and was greeted like a long-lost brother by lead vocalist Ra McGuire and guitarist Brian Smith. Then Smith said something to me that totally struck a nerve. He said, "Hey Keith, whatever happened to that *Music Express* magazine of yours? We could sure use it now, we're not getting any press from the media, radio is only playing our old stuff, any thoughts on re-launching it?"

Ding! That imaginary light bulb flashed above my head. As I headed back to Scarborough on the Go Train that night I had an epiphany! What was stopping me from re-launching *Music Express*? Certainly, it wouldn't be a print magazine; the whole world had gone digital. But *Music Express* as a digital magazine — why not?

Hardly able to contain myself, I phoned up Chad Maker at Agency 71. His company deals in graphic design for the entertainment industry and had been designing *Access* during its ill-fated final stages and, right at the end, had created a digital version of that magazine.

Maker's reaction couldn't have been more positive. Early September I met with Maker, his partner Kirk Comrie, and designer Darryl Spreen, and they all loved the idea. Instantly we were brainstorming the contents of our new endeavour and enthusing about current digital technology and how we could insert video clips into the story and even create our own audio and video pages.

As it turned out, I couldn't have picked a more appropriate time to launch *The Music Express*. Rush was touring their *Clockwork Angels* release, Glass Tiger were opening for Roxette, Platinum Blonde were readying their comeback CD, even Triumph made the debut issue, as I interviewed bassist Mike Levine on the release of their *Concert in Sweden* DVD.

Plus I was able to feature a "Where Are They Now?" feature on Alias members Freddy Curci and Steve DeMarchi (complete with videos), run a sample first chapter of this book, and, linking up again with my Calgary photographers Charles Hope and Ian Mark, I was able to reprint some vintage photos from the *Alberta Music Express* days.

That debut issue of *The Music Express* (www.themusicexpress.ca) was launched at 11:00 a.m. on October 11, 2012, and as I write this chapter, *The Music Express* is still going strong and has been embraced by all the bands and artists that remembered the original magazine, plus the new breed of artists who only launched during the current digital age.

In summarizing a golden age of Canadian contemporary music through this book, I also became excited about future developments within the industry and the great achievements we could execute through modern technology. There is nothing more fulfilling than writing a story one day and seeing it posted online the following day accompanied by videos, photographs, and the ability to have readers download actual song tracks from the feature.

Hey, sounds like a strong premise for a possible *Music Express* sequel: *Keep Rockin'*.

ACKNOWLEDGEMENTS

It's safe to say that without the constant badgering by Calgarian Doug Wong, this opus would never have been completed. He convinced me that, yes, there was consumer interest in a Canadian book about the Canadian music scene. And, yes, people are interested in knowing about what it was like to tour with Bryan Adams, how Loverboy dealt with that Network U.S. payola scandal, and how Rush became such global stars. Another key figure is University of Toronto Library curator Brock Silversides, whose extensive collection of back issues of *Music/Rock Express* allowed me to forge the chronology for this book. I am also indebted to Martin Melhuish, who directed me to Brock's attention in the first place.

Going back to that crazy period in the mid-seventies, when the idea of launching *Alberta Music Express* first germinated, I have to thank the Calgary Confederacy of Lou Blair, Bryan Tucker, David Horodezky, Greg Thomas, Tommy Tompkins, Ron Sakamoto, the irrepressible Ken Graydon, and, of course, Mr. Wong for their initial encouragement. Kelly's Joe Thompson, who set up the magazine's first distribution system in Western Canada, Vancouver's Tom Harrison, photographer Dee Lippingwell, and Calgary's Sue Markowski ,who were there at the beginning. Also, my own photographers' Ian Mark and Charles Hope, who took some amazing photos that kick-started the mag. Charles continues to work for the mag and served as photo editor for this book. Bruce Allen and Sam Feldman were also there at the beginning, and although my relationship with Bruce has been up and down, I am sure he appreciates the support *Music Express* has given his artists.

When I moved to Toronto Terry Magee, Cam Carpenter, Larry Macrae, Anya Wilson, and David Farrell were strong initial supporters, and I soon developed a strong editorial and photographic team, which included Kerry Doole, Roman Mitz, the late Greg Quill, Dimo Safari, Phil Regendanz, Lenny Stoute, Tarin Elbert, Diane Collins, Drew Masters, Otis Richmond, Mary Dickie, and Perry Stern. Not to forget our office staff, which included Marian Bendeth, Ruth Woods, Julia Owen, Dean Haynes, Nancy Mayer, Janine Barker, Ken Tizzard, David Hazan, Harvey Wolfe, my sister Janice, Kim Woodward, and a slew of creative designers led by Darwyn Cooke.

I have to thank all the record companies based in Toronto, Vancouver, and Montreal, both majors and independents, who supplied me with editorial opportunities while suffering my constant haranguing for advertising dollars. Out of that scenario, I developed special relationships with the likes of Heaven's Gareth Brown; EMI's Paul Church and label president Deane Cameron; The Diamond Club's Randy Charlton; MCA's Randy Lennox and Steve Tennant; Anthem's Ray Danniels and Tom Berry; Attic's Al Mair, Neil Dixon, and Jake Gold; Aquarius Records' Keith Brown; MuchMusic's late-but-great John Martin; Kay and Michael White; Wolfgang Dios; and the ever present Keith "Kid Rock" Correa to name just a few. A special thank you to Musicland's Bruce Jesse, who gave *Music Express* such a wonderful shot at expanding into the States, and was there for us with Wherehouse Entertainment when our deal with Musicland went pear-shaped. I also need to thank Allan Gregg; although he saw things differently at the end, he was still a major supporter of our initial expansion.

Artist-wise, this book could not have been attempted without the gracious support of every band or artist featured on these pages. However, I do have to single out some special people who have become great friends as well as talent artists. I consider Alan Frew to be a special friend, eager to help out when raising awareness for our Joe Philion fundraiser, and who sacrificed his knee for our soccer team. The Payola$' Paul Hyde, Loverboy's Mike Reno, Trooper's Ra McGuire and Brian Smith, the lovely Lee Aaron, my Streetheart mates Kenny Shields and Jeff Neill, Jerry Doucette, Nick Gilder, Bryan Adams, Tom Cochrane, Bill Henderson, Platinum Blonde's Mark Holmes, Triumph's Rik Emmett, Goddo's Greg Godovitz, Helix's

Brian Vollmer, Coney Hatch's Andy Curran and Carl Dixon, Ian Thomas, The Stampeders' Rich Dodson, Kim Mitchell, April Wine's Myles Goodwyn, Brian Greenway and David Henman, Corey Hart, Alias's Steve DeMarchi and Freddy Curci, and Matt Minglewood have all been especially supportive over the years and are all still rocking.

On the international side of things, I would like to acknowledge a special friendship I forged with Sanctuary Music chief, Rod Smallwood, and Steve, Bruce, Adrian, Dave, Nicko, and Janick from Iron Maiden. Awesome musicians, great friends, and pretty decent football players who are still rocking the planet!

On a personal level I need to give a shout out to my three kids; Julie-Anne, Ryan, and Kyle, who didn't always get the attention they deserved; my siblings Bob, Gordon and Janice who used to bitch about getting albums and CDs as Christmas presents because they knew I got them for free; my two exes, Carole and Dawn; and more importantly, my long-suffering spouse Karen, who made the big mistake of being a devout *Music Express* reader growing up in Sydney, Nova Scotia.

I would like to thank my literary agent, Arnold Gosewich, for having enough faith in the book to shop it around and to find a publisher in Dundurn Press. I'd also like to thank Allister Thompson for championing my book at Dundurn, and my editor Michael Melgaard, who took my Stephen King–like tome and shaped it into something readable. Also at Dundurn, I'd like to thank my publicist, Karen McMullin; Courtney Horner, for designing the book; and publisher and president Kirk Howard.

I would be remiss in not thanking Agency 71's Chad Maker, Kirk Comrie, and former employee Darryl Spreen for embracing the concept of an online *Music Express* magazine (themusicexpress.ca) and turning it into a reality which is growing by leaps and bounds daily. My Calgary crew, photographer Charles Hope and writers Brian Stanko and Keith McTaggart; my Toronto scribes, Kerry Doole, Karen Bliss, and Roman Mitz; and my partner in crime, Ted Van Boort and his partner Karen Uildersma for being both an ace photographer and a creative genius.

And last, but by no means least, to Conny Kunz, The Dragon Lady. This book is as much about her as it is about me. Conny provided the initial inspiration to convince me we could make *Music Express* work. Aside from being the financial driving-force, she designed the book, ran the business, and freed me up to go globe-trotting around the planet. It has been a crazy trip with plenty of heartache and disappointment along the way, but considering that two people from Calgary took on the North American music industry and strove to make *Music Express* into such an influential force, it is to our credit that we created a legacy, one that is captured within the pages of this book.

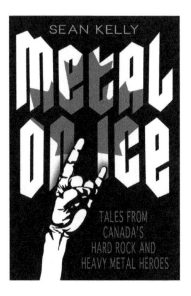

Metal on Ice
Tales from Canada's Hard Rock and Heavy Metal Heroes
By Sean Kelly

Canada has produced many successful proponents of the genre known as heavy metal, which grew out of the hard rock of the 1970s, exploded commercially in the 1980s, and then petered out in the 1990s as grunge took over, only to rise to prominence once again in the new millennium.

The road to Canadian musical glory is not lined with the palm trees and top-down convertibles of the Sunset Strip. It is a road slick with black ice, obscured by blizzards, and littered with moose and deer that could cause peril for a cube van thundering down a Canadian highway.

Drawing on interviews with original artists such as Helix, Anvil, Coney Hatch, Killer Dwarfs, Harem Scarem, and Honeymoon Suite, as well as prominent journalists, VJs, and industry insiders, we relive their experiences, motivations, and lifestyles as they strove for that most alluring of brass rings — the coveted record deal. It's a new perspective on the dreams of musicians shooting for an American ideal of success and discovering a uniquely Canadian voice in the process.

Available at your favourite bookseller

DUNDURN

Visit us at
Dundurn.com | @dundurnpress
Facebook.com/dundurnpress | Pinterest.com/dundurnpress